10649578

The New Legions

American Strategy and the
Responsibility of Power

The New Legions

American Strategy and the Responsibility of Power

Edward B. Atkeson
Major General, US Army (Retired)

ROWMAN & LITTLEFIELD PUBLISHERS, INC.
Lanham • Boulder • New York • Toronto • Plymouth, UK

Published by Rowman & Littlefield Publishers, Inc.
A wholly owned subsidiary of The Rowman & Littlefield Publishing Group, Inc.
4501 Forbes Boulevard, Suite 200, Lanham, Maryland 20706
http://www.rowmanlittlefield.com

Estover Road, Plymouth PL6 7PY, United Kingdom

Copyright © 2012 by Major General Edward B. Atkeson

All rights reserved. No part of this book may be reproduced in any form or by
any electronic or mechanical means, including information storage and retrieval
systems, without written permission from the publisher, except by a reviewer who
may quote passages in a review.

British Library Cataloguing in Publication Information Available

Library of Congress Cataloging-in-Publication Data

Atkeson, Edward B.
 The new legions : American strategy and the responsibility of power / Edward B.
Atkeson.
   p. cm.
 Includes index.
 ISBN 978-1-4422-1377-7 (cloth : alk. paper) — ISBN 978-1-4422-1379-1
(ebook)
 1. United States—Military policy. 2. United States—Armed Forces—
Organization. 3. United States—Armed Forces—Recruiting, enlistment, etc.
4. Immigrants—Employment—United States. 5. National security—United
States—Planning. 6. United States—Armed Forces—Stability operations. I. Title.
II. Title: American strategy and the responsibility of power.
 UA23.A778 2012
 355'.033573—dc23   2011032805

∞™ The paper used in this publication meets the minimum requirements of
American National Standard for Information Sciences—Permanence of Paper
for Printed Library Materials, ANSI/NISO Z39.48-1992.

Printed in the United States of America

Contents

Preface

Strategy and the Responsibility of Power

Early in September 2009 Admiral Mike Mullen, chairman of the Joint Chiefs of Staff, advised Congress that the success of the war in Afghanistan would likely require more combat forces than were then deployed in the country. Furthermore, he remarked that the conflict would require "much more time" than he had earlier indicated to reach a satisfactory conclusion.

An additional group of about four thousand trainers was scheduled to arrive in Afghanistan in two months' time. That would bring the American troop level deployed in the country to sixty-eight thousand, more than double the number at the beginning of the year. Whether the additional troops would be approved or not, the situation was clearly beyond the burden anticipated in previous planning cycles, and possibly beyond the political tolerance of the American people.

Shortly thereafter, on Monday, October 26, 2009, the *Washington Post* carried two articles on its op-ed page, both by especially well-known and skillful writers: David Ignatius and Fareed Zakaria. Both addressed an event of the previous day in Baghdad, Iraq. Ignatius described it as "A Morning from Hell." Zakaria quoted the American commander, General Stanley McChrystal, saying, "The number of additional troops needed misses the point entirely. The key takeaway is the urgent need for a significant change to our strategy and the way we think and operate."[1] The inspiration for both articles was the explosion of two massive car bombs—one at the Iraqi Justice Ministry, the other at the Baghdad provincial administration—which together killed and wounded more than six hundred people. This was Baghdad, almost seven years after the American invasion.

The most unfortunate aspect of the development was the apparent inability of the national leadership to formulate a military strategy appropriate for dealing with the challenges. "More of the same," when the situation is not altered by the last incremental change, should not, in and of itself, be considered the most useful strategic concept.

More troops? All right, but not heavily American, and not simply more NATO or indigenous units. The potential threat force is too large and too elastic to be strongly influenced (much less defeated) by the constructs we have been fielding for the last ten years. No, the answer may be more troops, but they need to be more *closely identified with their own personal interests, better recruited, better trained, better equipped for operations in their native environment, and effectively under American control and direction.* In effect, an indigenous American legion in Afghanistan.

How can this be? Isn't that an army of mercenaries? How could we recruit enough troopers? Could we develop a suitable model for broad application?

This book builds on observations, judgments, and questions of current practices to develop a very different approach to strategy for dealing with such problems and to shift the primary burdens and sacrifice from the shoulders of American soldiers and Marines to the youth of the countries most directly involved. There is no intention to divert fault or blame from one country to another, but to foster relationships between the United States and the people of stricken countries in which the United States has an interest, and in which there is a need of special encouragement and means for defense and stability to deal with perceived dangers and disturbances.

The subtitle of this book, "American Strategy and the Responsibility of Power," reflects the importance of strategy and the sense that the United States, as the most powerful country in the world, has inherited a special measure of accountability for insurance of global peace, health, and welfare, unmatched by any other state or combination of states. While some powers, in combination with others within particular regions, racial areas, or interests, may arrange groupings for specific purposes, the United States must stand ready to assist a broad range of nations in need of particular assistance, either when they are threatened with internal strife, or attack by a foreign power. Such is the *responsibility of power,* the spur for both the conception of military assistance in novel forms and the fulfillment of selected strategies.

The United States is not an aggressive power, but recognizes how such problems beset less well-developed societies and the dangers that such circumstances pose for neighbors, communities, regions, and the world at large. Therein lie the responsibilities of our country for curtailing local aggressions without necessarily assuming all of the burdens inherent in every conflict on every continent around the world. This book lays out for the reader possibilities for enhancing peace in the world without incurring virtual unilateral burdens, as has been our pattern in the last thirty-six years (since the fall of Saigon). All that the reader must offer is a disinclination to jump to conclusions without a fair hearing of the strategy proposed for a major change in most of our plans for future military (especially land) warfare.

The following text presents the case for a very different conceptual region of exploration (read strategy) for consideration by the United States for protection of its interests in the depths of the twenty-first century. The proposal applies not only to the Middle East but also to sections of Latin America, Africa, Southeast Europe, and Southeast Asia, essentially the full abroad—wherever the US government may anticipate a necessity to resort to force of arms to protect its interests.

1

A Troublesome War

One of President George W. Bush's most fervent supporters of the invasion of Iraq a short way into the twenty-first century, and a loquacious recorder of the ensuing strife and disappointment over the expanding battle, was Mr. Douglas Feith, former undersecretary of defense for policy. In his timely book, *War and Decision: Inside the Pentagon at the Dawn of the War on Terrorism*, Feith admitted that the choice of the "target set" to which the administration would assign blame for the September 11, 2001, terrorist disasters in New York, Pennsylvania, and Washington, DC, "was no easy matter."[1] In the colloquial, the question was "Who should we say are the bad guys?"

Feith reported having suggested virtually everything and everybody, from Al Qaeda to non-Islamist terrorist groups "like the Irish Republican Army or the Colombian *Fuerzas Armadas Revolucionarias*." And what about the "usual suspects": Iran, Iraq, and North Korea? Available intelligence did not seem to support any of these. There had to be a war for revenge against somebody, so he and his accomplices settled upon a "War on Terror," not otherwise defined.[2]

It is apparent from Feith's book that the planners figured that targets could be chosen and picked up as they went along. But whatever the target—or targets—the planners had to contemplate the arrest of many natives of whatever countries they would ultimately decide to overrun. Thus, they thought it necessary to address the problem of prisons and prisoners.

Since it was clear that the United States was dealing with a conspiratorial—possibly sub-national—group, it would likely need a prison system exceeding those normally accommodating prisoners of war. In Vietnam the United States had been able to turn prisoners over to the South Vietnamese government, but it would not have that convenience in the Middle East, at least at first, because it had no local allies. Besides, terrorists, the planners figured, are not simple soldiers doing their duty. They are "bad guys." Feith touched on the Guantanamo prison issue in a fraction of a page discussing the necessary size of the facility, but, notably, the word "torture" is not to be found, even in the index to the book.

The initial strategy was to strike Afghanistan with Special Forces, and then to crank up and throw the majority of available conventional forces at Iraq, expelling Saddam Hussein from office. Not everything seemed to make sense, but in Feith's view the plan had merit because it was "neither abstract nor remote." It would have to do, since "it was not possible to define the enemy with precision in any short, clear formulation."[3]

Clearly, proof of guilt was never the issue. Action was the watchword. Since we had already staged one war with Iraq, driving its forces out of Kuwait, and since Saddam's abominable government had survived, we assumed the worst. The plan was to attack Afghanistan, known to be involved in terrorism and poppy husbandry for the narcotics trade, but our main target would be Baghdad. We even invented new terminology (like "shock and awe") to convince the American people that we were the aroused and righteous. We could restore order in the East the way our hero sheriffs had done in the 1800s in our own West. But it was never quite clear how much we had to invent in order to sufficiently inflate our chests (and to head off impeachment of our leadership).[4]

The *New York Times*'s editor/observer, Carol Giacomo, looked back years later: "In those days" (2001–2003), she wrote, "Americans were reeling from the shock of 9/11 and completely focused on hunting Al Qaeda in Afghanistan. In Washington, though, talk quickly shifted to the next target—Iraq."[5]

As early as 2002 the White House had begun its campaign to build a public case against Saddam Hussein and his forces. The vice president had kicked the matter off with a speech at a national convention of the Veterans of Foreign Wars, accusing the Iraqi regime of building its capabilities for the manufacture of chemical and biological weapons and referring to mass destruction—clearly implying nuclear as well as chemical and biological devices. The plan to develop some rationale to underpin the administration's thirst for war was off and running. The next year would be the rat-hole-rush, cranking up the departments of state and defense, the CIA, and just about every other public agency in Washington, to prepare for war. Fact, evidence, and accuracy had little to do with the drive to marshal the nation and whatever allies could be persuaded to join the crusade.

In September, President Bush invited eighteen senior members of Congress to address the question of how "America and the civilized world" should deal with the threat posed by the regime of Saddam Hussein in Iraq. The initiative was a jolt to a number of the attendees. It had been a year since the terrorist attacks on the World Trade Center and other targets, but it was clear that the administration was prepared to link those with other outstanding issues, especially with the Saddam Hussein regime in Baghdad.[6]

"The issue isn't going away," the president told congressional leaders. "You can't let it linger." House Majority Leader Dick Armey and Senate Majority Leader Tom Daschle were taken aback, but the president asked that they say nothing about the matter until they had been fully briefed. The questions that hung in the air were "Why war? Why now?" Several senior administration officials, including the CIA chief, George Tenet, Secretary of State Colin Powell, and Vice Admiral Thomas R. Wilson, director of the Defense Intelligence Agency, had all said publicly that Saddam Hussein's military ambitions had been effectively constrained by his defeat in Kuwait ten years earlier. Regarding nuclear weapons, most experts were of the opinion that either Iraq's more serious programs were running behind, or the programs might not even exist. Nevertheless, war it was to be, and the principal motive was to be the removal of all weapons of mass destruction (WMD).

When the first aerial strikes were made, all seemed to be going well. The White House anticipated that one of the first blows might even settle the matter, with Saddam himself among the first to die. But he wasn't. Nor were there any reports of discovery of depots with WMD as the troops swept forward. The best they could do in the early days was to pull down the dictator's statue, to the cheers of the local crowd.

Unfortunately, the same sort of crowd that jumped on the statue would raid the stores, the museums, the palaces, and, most worrisome, the arms depots. American soldiers and Marines performed creditably, but as the campaign progressed, the "victories" became less clear, and less indicative of what might be expected in the future. Months—and years—would pass without the anticipated victory parade of thousands of returning troops down Fifth Avenue, in New York, as the campaign "Desert Storm" had been celebrated in 1991, with General Schwarzkopf leading the march.

All sorts of previously unknown organizations began to appear on intelligence officers' briefing charts: Abu Talha (Sunni, active around Mosul), the Anger Brigades (Shiite, commanded by Dhia al-Mahdi), Ansar al-Islam (Shiite, operational in Kurdish areas), Ansar al-Sunnah (an offshoot of Ansar al-Islam), Holy Warriors of Anbar (Sunni, based around Tikrit), Mahdi Army (Shiite, 6,000–8,000 members, active around Mosul, loyal to the cleric al-Sadar), the Muslim Clerics Association (known as a "vociferous" Sunni religious group), and so on.[7]

These disparate groups, juxtaposed with the large US military presence in Iraq, resulted in the provocation of the populace rather than reassurance. Both the commander of the US Central Command, General John Abizaid, and his force commander in Iraq, General George W. Casey, expressed concern for the problem. There could develop greater resistance on the part of certain Iraqi groups than had been supposed. As a consequence, the commanders refocused their attention on training and equipping Iraqi groups, much to the displeasure of figures on the civilian side in the Pentagon. The officers were relieved by Pentagon order in June 2004, and General Abizaid, the field commander, was ushered into retirement.

General David Petraeus followed General Abizaid in command of US forces in Iraq. He refocused the effort on counterinsurgency tactics, and pressed the indigenous government to do the same. Senior members of the US Army General Staff in Washington requested that the older commanders be retained in their posts, but President Bush dictated that the shifts take place as directed.[8]

Later, well into the war, Charles A. Duelfer, the top weapons inspector at the CIA, would report that his group had concluded in the fall of 2004 that Iraq had essentially dismantled its deadliest weapons program years before the US invasion. He would depict the United States as "a lumbering superpower whose top policymakers, particularly in the White House and the Defense Department, lacked any basic understanding of Iraq's history, motives and leaders." He reported that he had passed on entreaties from Iraqi officials to Washington, but never received an answer. He was to learn later that the Iraqis he had identified would be arrested, jailed, and have their homes raided.[9]

Unfortunately, no one in a responsible position in Washington had been heard talking about the novel form of war we had undertaken. Everyone knew we had a superb set of land, sea, and air forces for dealing with conventional or nuclear war in Europe, but this was not in Europe, nor was it even a conventional war after the first three weeks of heavy bombardment and armored maneuver. Thereafter, according to authors Williamson Murray and Major General Robert H. Scales Jr. (US Army, retired), it would become, for the most part, a replay of "the British Army in Palestine in the 1930s and Northern Ireland in the '70s and '80s, or for that matter, the Roman Army in the first-century Judea."[10]

With such a vague strategy it was not possible to forecast the total cost of the conflict with any expectation of accuracy. In June 2003, at the outset of the effort, the Department of Defense guessed that the cost might run somewhere between 60 and 95 billion dollars (a cautious thirty-five-billion-dollar spread). There was no official estimate as to how long the task might last, but little expectancy of more than a few months. Well within this time, the president addressed the crew of the aircraft carrier *Abraham Lincoln*, on May 1, as it approached the American eastern seaboard, returning from Middle Eastern deployment. A large "Mission Accomplished" sign, snugly tied to the bridge, caught everyone's eye, but the words would prove to be little more than an embarrassment—one of many to come.[11]

Two days after Christmas, 2009, the *Washington Post* published an editorial, "The Worst Ideas of the Decade," reporting the responses to the newspaper's query on the matter. "By far the most popular target was the war in Iraq." Also mentioned were "the doctrine of preemptive war, 'shock and awe,'" and the May 2003 "Mission Accomplished" banner.[12]

In 2004, a ten-man study team at the Cato Institute in Washington, DC, wrote that

> the [American] military occupation of Iraq was counterproductive to winning the war on terrorism, enormously costly, militarily and economically unnecessary, and politically unsustainable. Meanwhile, the presence of U.S. troops did little to advance liberal democracy in Iraq and much to inhibit such political development. Notwithstanding the optimistic predictions of the Bush administration and its ideological allies, the facts were irrefutable: Iraq was many years away from becoming a stable unified democracy, and there was little that the United States could do to speed the alteration of this state of affairs.[13]

What the Cato analysts did not know at the time was that in early 2004 Defense Secretary Donald H. Rumsfeld had already signed off on a presidential authorization for secret military strikes against Al Qaeda and other militants in Syria, Pakistan, and *anywhere else in the world*. Under this authority, a Navy SEAL team raided a suspected militants' compound in the Bajaur region of Pakistan. CIA officials watched that entire operation, real-time, in Washington, 7,000 miles away, by means of a video camera mounted on a remotely piloted aircraft.[14]

The following year would become known as the era of "the Revolt of the Generals." Major Generals Charles Swannack and John Batiste, who together had commanded two premiere units in the 2003 offensive—the 82nd Airborne and the 1st Infantry Divisions—joined other senior officers in retirement, sacrificing their careers, to vent their disdain for the secretary of defense, Donald Rumsfeld. "Rumsfeld," they said, was "not a competent wartime leader," but one who "made dismal strategic decisions . . . that resulted in the unnecessary deaths of American servicemen and women, our allies and the good people of Iraq." Rumsfeld, they said, "dismissed honest dissent" and "did not tell the American people the truth for fear of losing support for the war."[15]

Perhaps the dissident officer with the greatest public impact was Lieutenant General William E. Odom, former director of the National Security Agency. In his address to the US Senate Foreign Relations Committee, he said the United States had not adopted a new strategy with its "surge" of troops to Iraq. Instead, he said, it was simply a new tactic which did not merit a change of mind regarding the ultimate outcome of the war. He argued that "the surge is prolonging instability, not creating the conditions for unity as the president claims." He offered the following points:

- "[T]oday there is credible evidence that the political situation is far more fragmented . . . Prime Minister Maliki of Iraq has initiated military action and then dragged in US forces to help his own troops destroy his Shiite competitors. This is a political setback, not a political solution. . . . Also disturbing is Turkey's military incursion to destroy Kurdish PKK groups in the border region. That confronted the US government with a choice: either to support its NATO ally, or to make good on its commitment to Kurdish leaders to insure their security. It chose the former, and that made it clear to the Kurds that the United States would sacrifice their security to its larger interests in Turkey."
- "As an aside, it gives me pause to learn that our vice president and some members of the Senate are aligned with al Qaeda on spreading the war to Iran."
- "[C]onsider the implications of the proliferating deals with the Sunni strong men. They are far from unified among themselves. Some remain with al Qaeda. Many who break and join our forces are beholden to no one. Thus the decline in violence reflects a dispersion of power to dozens of local strong men who distrust the government and occasionally fight among themselves. Thus the basic military situation is far worse because of the proliferation of armed groups under local military chiefs who follow a proliferating number of political bosses."
- "[What] we are witnessing is more accurately described as the road to the Balkanization of Iraq, that is, political fragmentation."
- "I challenge you to press the administration's witnesses this week to explain this absurdity. Ask them to name a single historical case where power has been aggregated successfully from local strong men to a central government, except through bloody violence leading to a single winner, most often a dictator. . . . It took England 800 years to subdue clan rule on what is now the English-Scottish border. And it is [now] the source of violence in Bosnia and Kosovo."
- "How can our leaders celebrate this diffusion of power as effective state building? More accurately described, it has placed the United States astride several civil wars. And it allows all sides to consolidate, rearm, and refill their financial coffers at US expense."
- "*The only sensible strategy is to withdraw rapidly but in good order.* Only that step can break the paralysis now gripping US strategy in the region."[16]

A bit earlier (three years into the campaign, with the advantage of some hindsight) the Congressional Budget Office (CBO) reflected much higher figures for the cost of the war than had been heard up to that point: between $493 and $697 billion, not quite ten times the government's original guess. A team of analysts in 2008 more than doubled those figures, with a low of $1.8 *trillion* and a high of $4 *trillion*.[17] It is little wonder that the United States would soon suffer an acute economic recession. The federal government appeared to have plummeted into debt at a higher velocity than the banks holding second and third mortgages on homes for which the owners were unable to pay. And by September 2008, the "royal houses" of real estate, Fannie Mae and Freddie Mac, had to be taken over by the federal government.

American troop casualties in "the War on Terror" by early 2011 would exceed 46,600.[18] Total casualties from the conflict (US, UK, and Iraq-as-an-ally) were estimated at one hundred thousand. Bob Herbert, of the *Washington Post*, reported that studies showed that "a third or more of G.I.'s returning from the combat zones of Iraq and Afghanistan—more than 300,000 men and women—have endured mental health difficulties."[19] Reporter Lizette Alvarez added that 128 soldiers had committed suicide in just the last year.[20]

For his part, the president, apparently without regret, confessed that he suffered only from "hopeless idealism" regarding Iraq and Afghanistan.[21] The president may have had no regrets, but not everyone was able to limit his pain to such narrow expense. Over two million Iraqis fled their country, and another two million had been displaced within it. The "surge" (reinforcement of American forces) apparently reduced the violence in Iraq, creating a "breathing space" for political reconciliation, but there was still considerable concern that an American force withdrawal would result in a resurgence of interfaith conflict. In the view of Fareed Zakaria, the canny *Newsweek* editor, "only genuine [Iraqi] political power-sharing will create a government and an army that are seen as national and not sectarian."[22]

Other observers were no less skeptical. Colonel Craig Trebilcock, an American military lawyer with extensive experience in Iraq, pointed out that Iraqi leaders had very different interests and techniques than their Western counterparts for attaining their objectives. Further, their objectives varied widely from ours. Trebilcock cited, for example, the following "seven pillars" of Iraqi community:

1. Iraqi society is based upon strict patriarchal hierarchy under which a sheikh has absolute power over his tribe.
2. The primary concern of Iraqi officials is not democracy or the political evolution of a successful Iraqi nation-state.
3. If Iraqis do not value something, they will not fight for it.
4. In a society that is evolving from a difficult Bedouin desert existence, where water and other base staples of life have historically been in

short supply, the Iraqis have learned that the group that controls the resources of the province or nation lives, and those which do not, die.

5. Individual Iraqis are warm and generous people. As groups grow, however, whether family units, tribes, or entire sects, individual generosity to those not within the group wanes.

6. Trading and bartering for personal or tribal gain is part of the Iraqi/Bedouin culture.

7. Iraqis do not share Western concepts on the use, passage, or value of time. They believe that if a matter is truly important, Allah will control the outcome, and the personal efforts of individuals are merely tangential to that outcome.[23]

These factors notwithstanding, another major weakness in Iraqi behavior is reported to be simple theft—especially of oil. For example, the vital Sunni refinery on the Tigris River in north-central Iraq yielded up to one-third of its products to black market operations. As Richard Oppel reported in the *New York Times*, "Tankers are hijacked, drivers are bribed, papers and meters are manipulated—and some of the earnings go to the insurgents who are still killing more than 100 Iraqis a week." The matter immediately raised the question of whether the government in Baghdad ever really had control of the industry. American and other military officers reported that detainee surveys and other intelligence on insurgency indicated that "money, far more than jihadist ideology, was the critical motivation for a majority of Sunni insurgents in some provinces."[24]

One senior American officer said that about three-quarters of Iraqi detainees were not committed to jihadist ideology. In his view, it was the corruption of money that drove most of the criminals to illegal acts. In Mosul, far to the north, for instance, besides oil profits, men were encouraged to engage in illegal activities around soda and cement factories, kidnapping for ransom, and extortion in connection with local contracts.[25] Especially important to Americans assigned to Iraq, in almost any capacity, was a readiness to understand such tendencies among an impoverished populace—not necessarily to condone it, but to develop an awareness of the pressures upon the people to fall into such behavior.

Meanwhile, back in the United States, a small group of especially talented officers at the Army's University of Foreign Military and Cultural Studies at Ft. Leavenworth, Kansas, had been nibbling away at the ignorance of fellow officers coming into some of the more senior positions in Washington and overseas in the troop deployment areas. Throughout 2007 and 2008 the Leavenworth officers played "a cadre of devils," questioning much of the ambient lore about the Middle East. While some misunderstandings and hostilities toward the group arose, the members saw themselves as "in-house skeptics," noting that such groups might create instant antibodies. In their eyes, the mission was more important than the discomfort which might be experienced by some of their auditors.[26] The purpose was clearly to challenge some of the questionable lore which had emerged from various experiences in the Middle East.

But other parts of the criticism of our national effort, especially in Iraq, were even more disturbing. Dr. Anthony H. Cordesman of the Center for Strategic and International Studies (CSIS) in Washington, DC, pointed out that the situation in Iraq was made worse by the parallel effort in Afghanistan. There, in the spring, the war was "left in near limbo by the Administration." That allowed "the overall NATO/ISAF/UN/Afghan Compact[27] and GWOT (Global War on Terrorism)" to progress without any sense for the overall effectiveness of the effort against the Taliban, Islamist extremists, and Al Qaeda in Pakistan.[28]

Dr. Cordesman would write,

> This follows nearly seven years of war in which the Administration has left it up to Congressional agencies like CRS [Congressional Research Service], CBO [Congressional Budget Office], and GAO [Government Accountability Office] to guesstimate the cost of the fighting, and where the Department of Defense and Department of State had neither costed nor justified their overall wartime budget requests in realistic detail. Furthermore, for the sixth consecutive year, there was no out-year funding in the Future Year Defense Plan (FYDP) for any of the wars the US was fighting. . . . This combination of no plan, no program, and no budget for the Iraq War, Afghan War, [or General War on Terrorism] made it almost impossible to understand what the Administration was doing in any detail, and provided an open invitation to exaggerate the past and future costs of the war and the burden it placed on federal spending and the economy.[29]

"In short," Dr. Cordesman wrote, "it is hard to see how the Administration could do a worse job of explaining and justifying its strategy, plans, programs and budgets for war."[30] But that was not the worst of the "management" of the war. Particularly disturbing was the question of the handling of prisoners, with the likely mistreatment of friendly soldiers and civilians by the enemy in return for real or imagined misdeeds by our forces and agencies in the United States and abroad. According to the prominent writer Jane Mayer, in the planning period before the invasion of Iraq, in 2002, Defense Secretary Donald Rumsfeld issued a declaration that the US military no longer needed to follow the Geneva Convention in handling enemy Al Qaeda and Taliban prisoners. To toughen the regulations, White House lawyers turned to language that effectively changed the definition of torture. In its place they suggested terms like "enhanced," "robust," and "special" interrogations.[31]

These "enhanced," "robust," and "special" techniques appear to be based upon processes developed by Chinese interrogators during the Korean War. Charts describing the most effective concepts were flown to Guantanamo,

Cuba, in December 2002, where it had been determined US laws pertaining to torture would be least effective.

The Chinese motive had been primarily to obtain "confessions" from US military prisoners for propaganda purposes. Now they would be used to obtain intelligence. The "variables" ranged from complete solitary confinement to semi-starvation, exposure to heat and cold, and threats of death. Other techniques included "exploitation of wounds, filthy, infested surroundings and forcing prisoners to stand for exceedingly long periods."

Dr. Robert Jay Lifton, a psychiatrist who had written a book of his experiences in treating returned prisoners, expressed regret that his work had become a text for US government abuse. "It saddens me," he said, that his work on Chinese "thought reform" would be turned 180 degrees by the Guantanamo interrogators.[32]

Columnist William Safire sharply criticized the whole idea, writing, "We don't torture." Some locutions begin as bland bureaucratic euphemisms to conceal great crimes. As their meanings become clear, these collocations gained an aura of horror. "In this young century," he wrote, "the word in the news . . . is *waterboarding*. If the word *torture*, rooted in Latin for 'twist,' means anything (and it means the deliberate infliction of physical or mental pain to punish or coerce), then *waterboarding* is a means of torture."[33]

As early as 2003, Bruce C. Swartz, a Justice Department (Criminal Division) deputy in charge of international issues, repeatedly argued at White House conferences against harsh interrogation tactics. He warned that the abuse of Guantanamo inmates would do "grave damage" to the country's reputation and to its law enforcement record. A year later, the concerns of FBI agents about the interrogations first came to light. As time passed, Swartz was joined by a handful of other top Justice and FBI officials who warned that "almost certainly" such techniques would taint any legal proceedings against the detainees.[34]

The president's legal team, led by John Yoo and Jay Bybee, ruled out "electric shocks to genitalia," but not to other parts of the body. The staffers advised their chief that he could argue that torture was legal because he authorized it. The only way that it could be negated, they claimed, would be through impeachment, and that seemed unlikely in wartime.[35]

Yoo and Bybee underwent five years' investigation by the Justice Department for suspected professional misjudgment in drafting the justification for the Bush administration's use of brutal interrogation tactics for terrorism suspects. The department found them guilty of "flawed legal reasoning," but not of professional misconduct.[36]

A year later Donald Rumsfeld, the secretary of defense, secretly authorized new "extreme interrogation rules" and issued an oral order extending offensive interrogation techniques developed at the prison in Guantanamo Bay, Cuba, to the prisons in Iraq. Further, he directed the replacement of many trained military policemen at the infamous Abu Graib prison in Iraq with military intelligence personnel who would likely be more highly motivated to squeeze the prisoners for more detailed information. He also approved the use of ferocious dogs to intimidate the prisoners.[37]

A number of uniformed officers, trained in legal and appropriate interrogation techniques, attempted to have the brutal practices eliminated. Colonel Stuart Herrington, an expert in counterintelligence and interrogation, alerted his leaders that US Special Forces soldiers working with the CIA were abusing prisoners in ways he believed to be illegal. Also, Air Force Colonel Steve Kleinman, an experienced intelligence officer, indicated his view when he referred to Abu Graib as "the repository for our mistakes."[38]

But it would be another year before CBS's *60 Minutes* aired the first pictures of American soldiers tormenting detainees in Abu Graib. To his credit, Senator Richard Durbin, a Democrat from Illinois, forced his way into a secure room to see and report photos of American soldiers grinning and giving "thumbs-up" signs as naked and hooded Iraqi prisoners were forced to perform simulated sex acts, wear leashes, pile onto human pyramids, cower in front of vicious-looking dogs, and, in one iconic image, stand hooded with arms outstretched and electrical wires attached. The pictures included one of the battered corpse of Manadel al-Jamadi, with American soldiers giddily cavorting over it. The details of al-Jamadi's death remain a CIA secret.[39]

How much truthful information might have been gained from these frightful cases of American mistreatment of prisoners is not immediately apparent, but in August 2008 a British court handed down an important judgment in a case against an Ethiopian who was a British resident before his arrest in Pakistan, in April 2002. The British government had turned him over to American authorities who confined him to the prison in Guantanamo Bay, Cuba. The British court disagreed with an American decision to refuse to turn over materials to the prisoner that might help prove his innocence. He was at last told, after many years in confinement and incommunicado, that he would face trial in an American military court. The US government informed the British Foreign Office that the prisoner was "in good health" when he arrived in Cuba four years earlier, but it was anybody's guess how well he might have been at the time when the exchange of messages took place—if, indeed, he were even alive.[40]

Three months later the Pentagon announced that "war crimes" charges against five detainees at the Guantanamo prison were being dismissed. The news came within a week of the abandonment of charges against six other men for a "2001 plan to bomb the U.S. Embassy in Sarajevo, Bosnia-Herzegovina."[41] One may surmise that the government came to realize how hollow the charges against the latter group—perhaps all of the men—sounded when placed in juxtaposition with the US-led NATO heavy bombardment of Serbian targets (including, by accident, the Chinese Embassy) at the same time.[42]

No less perplexing has been the case of Mr. Binyam Mohamed, an alleged assistant to another party involved in the construction of a "dirty" (radioactive) bomb over six years earlier. The charges were dropped for lack of evidence, other than a statement by the accused—in all probability obtained under torture in a Morocco prison where he had been sent for "questioning." The case had been especially disturbing to British officials inasmuch as they had originally arrested him and turned him over to American authorities, so the case would appear to involve their toleration of torture.[43]

Perhaps one of the worst reports of American terror was written by Jumah al Dossari, a five-and-a-half-year Guantanamo survivor. He had been turned over to American troops by Pakistanis in 2001, probably for the bounty paid. Initially held in Afghanistan, he picked up his first scar from a lit cigarette pressed into his wrist.[44]

He arrived in Guantanamo in January 2002, where he was incarcerated in Camp X-Ray in a cage, forced to sit in the same position day after day. Under interrogation, his head was smashed down on a table. At one point he was beaten so badly by several soldiers that he had to be moved to the hospital intensive care ward for three days. At other times he was shackled to the floor for hours. After he tried to kill himself, he was placed in solitary confinement with only a pair of shorts to wear, but no bed. The cell contained only a dirty plastic mat and a toilet. Since there was no water tap, he had to drink and wash in the toilet. An air conditioner was run full blast around the clock to ensure his discomfort.

In desperation, Dossari slashed his wrists and tried to hang himself from the wall, but was discovered by his "attorney" before he could die. His only treasure was an expression of sympathy by a young female guard who whispered to him, "I'm sorry, what happened to you. You're human, just like us." In 2007 he was shipped back to Riyadh, Saudi Arabia, where the government had arranged to meet him.

One of the officers most closely concerned about the mistreatment of prisoners at the Guantanamo stink hole has been a middle-grade naval officer, Lieutenant Commander William C. Kuebler. He was totally opposed to many of the regular practices. The Bush administration's war crimes system "is designed to get criminal convictions," he said, with "no real evidence." Military prosecutors "launder evidence derived from torture. You put the whole package together and it stinks," he told a reporter. Seven years after the lawyers began to arrive, sharp differences in legal interpretations of the treatment of military prisoners have emerged, especially over their rights to federal courts. A sizable number of the officers share a sense that "Guantanamo makes military justice seem like watered-down justice."[45]

Not only in the context of the prison system, but certainly related, is the view of an observer who pointed out that "individuals have been the first target of criticism: President George W. Bush, of course, but also Vice President Dick Cheney; Donald Rumsfeld, the former secretary of defense; General Tommy Franks, the former commander of US Central Command; Paul Wolfowitz, the former undersecretary of defense for policy; L. Paul Bremer, the former head of the Coalition Provisional Authority; and George Tenet, the former CIA director." All except two of these individuals had been out of office for some time: the Bush administration was already on its second defense secretary, third CIA director, third commanding general in Iraq, and fourth top diplomat there—but there was no indication that the changes had reversed the worsening situation.[46]

Late in 2008 the G. W. Bush administration came to realize that much of the house of horrors it had managed to create in the previous years was in danger of becoming exposed. The public was beginning to hear about what was going on. The *New York Times* reported that the attorney general, Michael Mukasey, rushed out new guidelines for the FBI that permitted agents:

- To use chillingly intrusive techniques to collect information on Americans even where there is no evidence of wrongdoing;
- To use informants to infiltrate lawful groups, engage in prolonged physical surveillance, and lie about their identity while questioning a subject's neighbors, relatives, co-workers, and friends; and
- To expand the use (of the above) techniques on people identified by racial, ethnic, and religious background.[47]

The White House stated that the government would do the following:

- Ignore a provision in the legislation that established the Department of Homeland Security. The law requires that the department's privacy officer account annually for any activity that could affect Americans' privacy, and stipulates that the report cannot be edited by any other officials at the department or the White House. (The Justice Department argues that it would be unconstitutional to stop other officials from changing the report.)
- Maintain the prison at Guantanamo Bay, Cuba, in spite of previous statements that it would be closed. Both the secretaries of state and defense had concurred on its closure, but the vice president objected. The move was deferred for action by the subsequent administration.[48]

Charles D. Stimson, a former deputy assistant secretary of defense for detainee affairs, ventured that perhaps the worst treatments could be reserved for no more than a couple dozen prisoners, yet to be captured. He apparently feared that the system had been compromised through too broad application of extreme techniques of interrogation. Public knowledge of the practices could lead to federal prosecutors refusing to bring charges for risk of dismissal or acquittal.[49]

Another case, probably involving torture, has been that of Ali al-Marri, a legal resident of the United States. Since December 2001 he has been held, first in Peoria, Illinois, and then in a Navy brig near Charleston, South Carolina. A three-judge panel of the United States Court of Appeals for the Fourth Circuit Court in Richmond, Virginia, ruled in 2007 that the president lacked the authority to hold Mr. Marri without charges. In July, however, a full federal court of appeals vacated that decision with a 5-to-4 decision that the president had the authority to hold him as an enemy combatant. The case appears to await a final decision at this writing. The principal issue will likely define the power of the president to hold persons for an indefinite period if they are combatants. Even US citizenship will be no defense. The concern of those opposing the action, of course, is that due process, habeas corpus, and other basic constitutional and statutory rights for anyone accused of terrorist ties may be destroyed.[50]

A retired American general, Antonio Taguba, who conducted the first investigation at the Abu Graib prison, declared in a later report on the maltreatment of detainees: "The only question that remains is . . . whether those who ordered the use of torture will be held to account."[51]

In early 2009 the nightmare was cracked by the top Bush administration official in charge of deciding whether Guantanamo Bay "detainees" should be brought to trial. "We tortured [Mohammed al-] Qahtani," said the convening authority of military commissions, Susan Crawford. "His treatment met the legal definition of torture. . . . That's why I did not refer the case" for prosecution. The event was notable not so much for the decision, but because it was the first senior Bush administration official responsible for reviewing practices at Guantanamo to publicly state that a detainee had been tortured.[52]

All the while, the war dragged on. Iraqi troops were reported to be taking on an expanding range of responsibilities, but not without misgivings. The Iraqi infantry was reported to have achieved a tolerable level of competency in the final days of August 2008, but other branches—especially artillery and armor—still needed to be organized, equipped, and trained. Typically, one young Iraqi officer complained that "We are too many years behind other countries. We will need the coalition [international] forces until 2015." That may be so. A fifth of the unit's vehicles were rotting trucks, another vehicle was a bomb-demolished Humvee, all of which, "for some complicated bureaucratic reason," were still classified as operational.[53] Further, Iraq's relations with some of its neighbors—especially Iran—remain strained.

The Iraqis cannot count on American deliveries of everything they need. A reporter noted that considering the normal corruption and logistical problems, the Iraqi Army was years away from the capability to protect the country on its own. Allegedly, when the army received new equipment, it would sit, unprotected, in plain sight because no one knew how to operate it, or no one had issued orders for its utilization.[54]

In 2006 the US Joint Chiefs of Staff had studied the war quite closely and come to the conclusion that a "surge" reinforcement of US forces in Iraq would probably turn out to be a mistake. In their collective judgment, the forces had already been stretched to the breaking point, and greater emphasis should be placed on training and building up the indigenous forces. But the civilian leadership in both the Pentagon and the White House disagreed.[55]

Optimists pointed out the immediate benefits in the wake of the "surge" of US forces, which included five Army brigades and an additional Marine battalion. The streets of a number of Iraqi cities appeared to quiet down following the troop arrivals. And on October 17, 2008, the US government announced agreement with Iraq on the establishment of "date goals," which would result in the removal of all US troops from the country by the end of 2011.[56] Nevertheless, knowledgeable observers expect a substantial American military presence to remain in Iraq at least through 2012. The detonation of three synchronized car bombs in Baghdad on November 9, 2008, killing 28 people and sending 49 others to hospitals, raised questions about the effectiveness of the "surge." Bombings in the capital in just the first week of November exceeded the rates in the previous two months by over 50 percent.[57] And in December, retiring President George W. Bush underwent an embarrassing, if brief, assault of thrown shoes, together with accusations of acting like a dog, from an irate Iraqi journalist during his final visit to the Iraqi capital. The shoe hurler would be sentenced to three years in prison, but at least he wasn't tortured. On the contrary, the *New York Times* reported public remarks that "[e]very Iraqi wanted to beat Bush" and that Muntadader (the shoe hurler) made the people "proud of [them]selves as Iraqis."[58]

In Afghanistan, the security situation has shown signs of deteriorating. In July 2008 there were reports of a higher tempo of fighting with an "increasingly complex enemy," made up not only of Taliban fighters, but "also powerful warlords who were once on the payroll of the Central Intelligence Agency." Two particular such figures, Gulbuddin Hekmatyar and Jalaluddin Haqqani, officials point out, are the most dangerous of the hostile leaders. Their rise to power has been greatly enhanced by the American preoccupation with Iraq. As long as the United States remains heavily engaged in Iraq, it is unlikely that much progress could be made with the more dangerous internationally poised Afghan threat.[59]

The US aircraft carrier *Abraham Lincoln* (the same which bore the president's "Mission Accomplished" boast years before) was directed to support US operations in Afghanistan in midsummer 2008, along with the 24th Marine Expeditionary Unit (some 2,200 troops).[60] One prominent writer, John L. Harper, set an extraordinarily high bar for the president: "There is but a single sustainable model of national success: freedom, democracy and free enterprise, and the United States must extend its benefits everywhere." He went on to charge that "the U.S. delusion is a climate of righteous indignation and rallying the general public behind America's unnecessary wars."[61]

Further, he remarked,

> At the heart of the Bush administration's delusion was the belief that the Middle East Gordian knot was somehow ripe for a cutting by U.S. military power: Iraq's reconstruction and transformation to democracy would be rapid and largely self-financing; Iran, fearing Iraq's fate, would abandon its nuclear ambitions; the Palestinians, seeing the light, would accept a deal like the one they had rejected at Camp David; terrorists everywhere would lose heart. To this could be added a seemingly willful denial of one of the basic lessons of Vietnam: not only was a large foreign military presence no substitute for legitimate and self-reliant local forces; it is one of the obstacles to the emergence of such forces in Iraq.[62]

Finally, Harper insisted, "The war [in Iraq] distracted attention and resources from the campaign against al-Qaeda and its allies in Afghanistan, and won new sympathizers and recruits for jihad against the West."[63] His view was supported in Washington in testimony by Mr. Peter Goss, director of Central Intelligence, to Congress in February 2005.[64] But not only did Iraq "distract attention," enemy agents operating out of neighboring—and assumed friendly—Pakistan became a very serious matter. These hostile elements, aimed at Afghan targets, came to regularly operate from the "Northwest Territory" on the Afghan side of the border. So troublesome did they become that President Bush issued license to American forces to invade Pakistan when they believed it to be necessary—without regard for authorization by the Pakistani government.[65]

The Islamabad government protested: "Unilateral action by the American forces does not help the war against terror because it only enrages public opinion. In this particular incident, nothing was gained by the action of the troops."[66] Admiral Mike Mullen, the US chairman of the Joint Chiefs of Staff, expressed doubt about the success of the campaign if it continued on its established course. Nevertheless, he testified before the Congressional House Armed Services Committee, expressing confidence in the United States' capability to eventually achieve its objectives.[67]

But that could take more time than anyone has yet suggested. Admiral Mullen himself predicted that 2009 would be "an even tougher year." A draft intelligence report noted by the *New York Times* identified three reasons for lack of progress in Afghanistan: "rampant corruption, a booming heroin trade, and increasingly sophisticated attacks from militants based across the border in Pakistan. Unless all three are addressed quickly, the war in Afghanistan could be lost."

The *Times* also noted that "the United States will also have to send more troops into Afghanistan and persuade its allies to send more. . . . Germany's commitment of another 1,000 troops was commendable, but marred by its refusal to deploy them in southern Afghanistan where the fighting is the heaviest." The paper continued its observation, "Washington must also come up with a better mixture of incentives and pressures to persuade Pakistan to shut down Taliban and al Qaeda havens."[68]

Whether that would happen or not, there was a growing group of observers who saw little opportunity for gain in any aspect of the undertaking. Brigadier Mark Carlton-Smith, Britain's top commander in Afghanistan, was quoted as saying flatly, "We're not going to win this war." And he was backed by his senior, British Ambassador Sir Sherard Cowper-Coles. The latter's view was simple enough: the current strategy was "doomed to fail."[69]

Finally, the *New York Times* challenged its readers: "Imagine if Mr. Bush had not invaded Iraq in 2003 and instead had put all this country's resources and attention into defeating Al Qaeda and the Taliban in Afghanistan. Even optimistic analysts said that things had gotten so bad that, even with the best strategy, it could take another five or ten years to stabilize Afghanistan."[70] We added many more troops—another 21,000 for Afghanistan and Pakistan in 2009—but followed pretty much the familiar approach of the preceding year: we sought to improve the Afghan government and its military, to cut the drug trade, and to improve the quality of equipment in local hands, but none of that was really new, nor did it constitute a strategic change. At best it was more of the same prescription our troops had been given over the previous half decade.[71] Fatalities in Afghanistan would approach one thousand. Total fatalities in the "War on Terror" were estimated at 4,429.[72]

Unfortunately, along with this operational pessimism, an increasing number of American soldiers appeared to perceive their role in events to be markedly less attractive than when they first volunteered or were called to active duty. In October 2008, Secretary of the Army Peter Geren called for a joint effort with the National Institute of Mental Health to study an alarming increase in soldier suicides (115 in 2007, and 93 in the first eight months of 2008). Further, for half of the cases reported, there was no apparent cause.[73]

In early 2009 *TIME* reported grimly on "The Dark Side of Recruiting." The article started with the observation that "the wars in Iraq and Afghanistan are now the longest-waged by an all-volunteer force in U.S. history." It went on to emphasize that "even as soldiers rotated back to the field for multiple and extended tours, the Army requires a constant supply of new recruits. But the patriotic fervor that led so many to sign up after 9/11 has been eight years past at this writing. That leaves recruiting with perhaps the toughest, if not the most dangerous, job in the Army. [In 2008] alone, the number of recruiters who killed themselves, [while not large] was triple the overall Army suicide rate. Like posttraumatic stress disorder and traumatic brain injury, recruiter suicides are a hidden cost of the nation's wars."[74]

The principal problem has been the internal pressure on military recruiters to fulfill their quota of at least two new recruits per month. The time required to fulfill that objective has worked out in some cases to be close to thirteen hours per day for each recruiter. A management attempt to relieve some of the pressure within the organization of recruiters with a picnic prompted one overworked soldier to joke that "within the recruiting command, even family fun is mandatory."

While the Army has taken a number of steps to rectify the problem, the adverse economic and labor situations in the United States and the raising of the maximum age limits for military recruits from 35 to 42 are expected to ease some of the pressure on recruiting. Still, with only three in ten young Americans meeting the mental, moral, and physical requirements to serve, recruiting may continue to be a problem—unless the US government accelerates its employment of "civilian contractors" to serve in the place of soldiers.[75]

As of March 2009, contractors made up 57 percent of the Pentagon's force in Afghanistan, and if the figure is averaged over the past two years, it becomes 65 percent. This development is not particular to the current situation, but represents a percentage growth of almost 300 percent since the Korean War. Analysts indicate that the military has lost some of its logistics and support capacity, especially since the end of the Cold War, and that there are additional skills necessary in the present conflicts—such as language and high-tech skills—which were not needed as acutely in earlier wars. The problem could become serious if it is not soon remedied in some way.[76]

Yes, it has been, and continues to be, a troublesome war. It has come to be referred to as "the long war." A number of scholars connected with the Foreign Policy Research Institute in Philadelphia made the following comments during a seminar on July 14, 2009:

- "What we now sometimes refer to as 'the Long War' . . . was seared into our collective national consciousness and animated our collective response. . . . [Its beginning] marked the second most violent day in U.S. history, exceeding Pearl Harbor and even D-Day in fatalities. Only Antietam's bloody wheat fields have witnessed more carnage in a single day."

- ". . . al Qaeda is a more diffuse organization. . . . [S]ix years later, Afghanistan remains a troubled land."
- "The early occupation of Iraq went well for six months, but then turned sour as political enemies vied for national and local control. The operational plan has been labeled 'perhaps the worst plan in American History.'"
- "The cost for what has been accomplished to date [March 2009] is completely disproportionate to the limited gains."[77]

The notable author Thomas L. Friedman took one step further. "It is crunch time on Afghanistan," he wrote, "so here's my vote: We need to be thinking about how to reduce our footprint and our goals there in a responsible way, not dig in deeper. We simply do not have the Afghan partners, the NATO allies, the domestic support, the financial resources or the national interests to justify an enlarged and prolonged nation-building effort in Afghanistan."[78]

In 2010, almost a year later, a prominent columnist would write, "The war in Afghanistan will consume more money this year alone than we spent on the Revolutionary War, the War of 1812, the Mexican-American War, and the Spanish-American War—combined." Throwing in Iraq brings the total cost to second place behind only the Second World War.[79] At this writing, the nation is spending more for the military, after adjusting for inflation, than it was at the peak of the Cold War, the Vietnam War, or the Korean War. And our battle fleet is larger than the next thirteen navies combined, according to Defense Secretary Robert Gates.[80]

Yes, it has been, and at this writing continues to be, a long war. In time, the United States must either develop a more effective strategy or get out of the game.

2

The Wider War as We Chose to Fight It

Awaiting the settlement of the wars in the Middle East has been a little like waiting for the damage reports on Hurricane Katrina after it struck the Louisiana coast at high tide. Everybody knew that much of the housing along the shore had been poorly designed and built in the wrong place. But, as the storm drew a bead on New Orleans and rose to category 5 strength (winds reaching 175 mph), not enough of those who should have known better sounded warnings of anticipated disastrous flooding from as many as fifty breaches in the river levees. Floods would cover 80 percent of the city, 1,836 people would ultimately be found dead, and another 705 would disappear forever.[1]

By 2006 we had already seen the deaths of many more American soldiers in the war, and over one hundred thousand citizens of Iraq. But the storms showed only marginal signs of abatement, as was expected in Iraq in another couple of years. Katrina went ahead to spread its damage over a half-dozen other cities in as many states. Similarly the war in Afghanistan and Pakistan went on with renewed energy, and only vague hopes for relief could be detected in Iraq. But there was no practical end in sight. "Far overreaching all previous wars in American history since the Revolution," one columnist wrote, "the U.S. seems almost paralyzed, mesmerized . . . and unable to generate the energy or the will to handle the myriad problems festering at home."[2]

This should not be surprising. *Esquire* did not publish its special edition identifying "the best and the brightest" by its "strategist" among the faculty of the US Naval War College, Dr. Thomas P. M. Barnett, until late 2002, and the guiding manifesto for the administration, Barnett's landmark article, "The Pentagon's New Map," until March 2003. It would be another year (2004) before the word would reach the larger public in book form (with the same title, but with a subtitle, "War and Peace in the Twenty-first Century").

According to one reviewer, the work "provides a cutting-edge approach to globalization that combines security, economic, political and cultural factors to do no less than predict and explain the nature of war and peace in the 21st century." Another reviewer commented that Barnett "may turn out to be one of the most important strategic thinkers of our time."[3]

In his introduction we find a new view of American global involvement, including his description of our "drift[ing] through the roaring nineties, blissfully unaware that globalization was speeding ahead with no one at the wheel. The Clinton administration," he wrote, "spent its time tending to the emerging financial and technological architecture of the global economy, pushing worldwide connectivity for all it was worth in those heady days, assuming that eventually it would reach the most disconnected societies."

"[T]he U.S. military," he went on, "engaged in more crisis-response activity around the world in the 1990s than in any previous decade of the Cold War, yet no national vision arose to explain our expanding role. Globalization seemed to be remaking the world, but meanwhile the U.S. military seemed to be doing nothing more than babysitting chronic security situations on the margin."[4]

In this regard, he may have oversold his argument. He was careful to limit his criticism of US forces to the 1990s, but in doing so he missed an important event. In 1989 the US forces had just completed one of their most successful operations in Panama. And perhaps he forgot about US air operations in isolated communities in Bosnia-Herzegovina in 1993 after 100,000 people had been killed, either in the deteriorating Yugoslavia or as a result of the fighting there. Twenty-five thousand US troops were moved into Hungary, Croatia, Macedonia, and Albania.

And maybe he forgot about the lingering East-West problems in Europe. NATO had extended its borders to Belarus and Ukraine. But it is not easy to argue, as Barnett has, that in the early 2000s we should no longer have spent money to deal with a high-tech war against a large, sophisticated military opponent, such as Russia. While our army was about the same size as Russia's, theirs was largely in Europe, while our center of gravity was thousands of miles away. Further, the Russians had more strategic missiles than we did: 756 intercontinental ballistic missiles to our 687. And more submarine-launched missiles: 504 to our 464. In many respects the balance was about even, but to maintain that balance we were obliged to seek higher technology systems.[5] We knew perfectly well what the balance was, and few militia leaders were dreaming about "a war that no longer existed," to use Barnett's words.[6] At best, he was reading into the future.

Barnett goes on to explain that he is proposing "a new grand strategy on a par with the Cold War" which will meet the American "scream" for action to clean out the "ozone hole" (his term for the less well-developed countries on earth). Barnett claims to foresee citizens of an American Union who understand the stakes and the "opportunity to make globalization truly global."[7]

Whether American leaders were aware of Barnett's argument or not, there was to be war in the Middle East, and the principal motive was the removal of all weapons of mass destruction (WMD).[8] Early in 2006, members of both parties in Congress supported the creation of a bipartisan Iraq Study Group to assess the situation in that unfortunate country. Senators James A. Baker III and Lee H. Hamilton co-chaired the effort. Eight other former senior members of the three branches of government formed the body, while some fifty experts constituted the working groups. Interviews were accomplished with well over a hundred American and Iraqi state officials, academics, and military officers. The study lasted over eight months.[9]

The report noted that "violence was increasing in scope and lethality, fed by Sunni Arab insurgency, Shiite militia and widespread criminality." It called for a diplomatic effort with every country that had an interest in avoiding a chaotic Iraq, including all of Iraq's neighbors and key states outside the region. It also called for the formation of a "support group to reinforce security and national reconciliation with Iraq, neither of which Iraq can accomplish on its own."[10]

Further, it called for an "internal approach," which it assigned primarily to the Iraqis. The government was expected to assume responsibility for internal security, while US forces would take over responsibility for combat operations. It was envisioned that the US mission would evolve into a supporting role, with the Iraqi Army gradually assuming primary responsibility for combat actions. In this manner US forces could gradually be removed from the country. The study expressed an expectation that all US combat brigades would be out of the country by the first quarter of 2008. Subject to unexpected developments in the security situation on the ground, it was anticipated that all combat brigades not necessary for force protection could be out of Iraq. At that time, US combat forces in Iraq could be deployed only in units embedded with Iraqi forces in rapid-reaction and special operations teams, and in training, equipping, advising, force protection, and search and rescue. Intelligence and support efforts would continue.[11]

Perhaps most notable in the report was the following comment: "If the Iraqi government does not make substantial progress toward the achievement of milestones on national reconstruction, security, and governance, the United States should reduce its political, military or economic support for the Iraqi government."[12] Clearly, the group did not wish to endorse the unlimited powers and war policy which the administration had adopted.

A year later, Iraq became notable as the "second most unstable country" in the world, just behind seven others competing for first place: "war-ravaged, poverty-stricken" Somalia, Zimbabwe, Ivory Coast, Congo, Afghanistan, Haiti, and North Korea, according to the Fund for Peace and *Foreign Policy* magazine. In spite of billions of dollars in foreign aid, and the presence of 150,000 US troops, Iraq collapsed and then continued to slide steadily from its previous high state of order under Saddam Hussein. According to Fund for Peace President Pauline Baker, "The report tells us that Iraq is sinking fast." And the fighting continued apace.

Some have come to refer to the conflict in epochal terms—essentially a return to infantry-focused events, just less intense than the grand sweeps of men fighting through the trenches and barbed wire of 1918. More than half of our battle deaths in the struggle were of infantrymen trying to find the enemy, either as scouts or in ambushes. With few exceptions, kill ratios of American soldiers and enemy fighters, once the battle was joined, were heavily in the Americans' favor (typically nine to one within fifty meters), but fighting in buildings, unfortunately, could run as close as parity.[13] And then, of course, there was always the problem of distinguishing the bodies of the fighters from those of innocent civilians. The outbreak of fighting in Basra and Baghdad did not involve many Western forces, but sorely tested the Iraqi government's ability to suppress flare-ups in city environments, and, ultimately, the American ability to make further troop withdrawals.[14]

But this was hardly news. In February 2008, the *New York Times* remarked in a lead editorial that "Nearly everything about President Bush's botched war of choice (which he initiated without visible Iraqi provocation) made it much harder to win Afghanistan's war of necessity." (Afghanistan had been the original site of preparation for the terrorist attack on the United States.)

Speaking just the previous day, Secretary of Defense Robert M. Gates had argued that the safety of Europe from terrorist attack by Islamic extremists was directly linked to NATO's success in stabilizing Afghanistan. Inaction in that arena, he remarked, could expose Europe to attacks of the same enormity as the 9/11 assault on the World Trade Center buildings in New York and the Pentagon in Washington, DC.

"The really hard question the alliance faces," he said, "is whether the whole of our effort is adding up to less than the sum of its parts." He argued that training for every soldier and civilian deploying to Afghanistan should meet the Alliance standards, and that a high-level European official should be appointed to coordinate all international assistance. He called especially for NATO cooperation and civilian reconstruction.[15]

It was a little difficult to tell whether the US was achieving "the sum of the parts" with its own troop deployments. Writing in the *Washington Post*, Charles Krauthammer suggested that certain prominent political opponents committed "a rank falsehood" in accusing Senator John McCain (the Republican candidate for the presidency in the forthcoming general election) of seeking "an endless war in Iraq." He had, apparently, made a statement indicating a desire to pursue the war indefinitely, but the context suggested that he may have meant only to reassure the leaders of the host government that we would not desert them if they would suppress terrorist elements in their midst. The problem with the debate in the United States government was that it had not clarified the real question on people's minds: How long should we be prepared to pursue the Iraqi War if a satisfactory conclusion continues to escape us?[16]

Of course, the longer the war lasted, the greater the expense in monetary terms as well as in human lives. In March 2008, the Congressional Joint Economic Committee summoned notable experts, including Nobel Prize–winning economist Joseph Stiglitz and Goldman Sachs International Corporation Vice Chairman Robert Hormats, to assist in determining the likely cost of the undertaking. "For a fraction of the cost of this war," said Mr. Stiglitz, who had written a book titled *The Three Trillion Dollar War*, "we could have put Social Security on a sound footing for the next half-century or more."[17]

Further, Mr. Hormats pointed out, "Normally, when America goes to war, nonessential spending programs are reduced to make room in the budget for the higher costs of the effort. Individual programs that benefit specific constituencies are sacrificed for the common good. . . . And taxes have never been cut during a major American war."[18]

"But they have been now," Mr. Stiglitz added. "Because the administration actually cut taxes as we went to war, when we were already running huge deficits, this war has effectively been entirely financed by deficits. The national debt has increased by some $2.5 trillion since the beginning of the war, and of this, almost $1 trillion is due directly to the war itself." Mr. Stiglitz went on, "Nearly 40 percent of the 700,000 U.S. troops from the First Gulf War, which lasted just one month, have become eligible for disability benefits. The current war is approaching five years in duration. Imagine, then, what a war—that will almost surely involve more than 2 million troops, and will almost surely last more than six or seven years—will cost."[19]

Mr. Stiglitz's forecast turned out to be more conservative than that of the CIA Director Michael V. Hayden. General Hayden had warned that the Afghanistan-Pakistan border had become a "clear and present danger" to the West, and would be the most likely origin of another terrorist attack on the United States.

"It is very clear to us," he said on NBC's *Meet the Press*, "that Al Qaeda has been able, for the past 18 months or so, to establish a safe haven along the Afghan-Pakistan border area that they have not enjoyed before." He added that terrorist groups in that region were particularly trying to recruit people with Western backgrounds. "They are bringing operatives into that region for training—operatives that . . . wouldn't attract your attention if they were going through the customs line at Dulles with you when you're coming back from overseas," Hayden said.[20]

In an address to the University Continuing Education Association in New Orleans, Ambassador Chas W. Freeman Jr. provided an additional perspective.

> In current dollars we are spending about 28 percent more on our military each year than we did during the Korean and Vietnam Wars, and over one-third more than at the height of the Reagan defense build-up against the late, unlamented Soviet Union. We are spending considerably more on military power than the rest of the world put together—three and a half times as much as the highest estimate for China, Russia, Cuba, Iran, and North Korea combined; and at least 12,000 times as much as Al Qaeda and all other terrorist groups with global reach. It is not clear what enemies justify all this money. Whoever they are, if military expenditures are the key to national security, we've got them where we want them. . . .
>
> It used to be thought that the purpose of war was to secure a more perfect peace. That is an objective that invokes diplomacy to translate military triumph into new arrangements acceptable to both victor and vanquished. It implies war planning focused on the question: "and then what?" and the conduct of war in accordance with a strategy that unites political, economic, informational, and intelligence measures with military actions and a well-crafted plan for war termination. In Iraq a brilliant general had belatedly come up with a credible campaign plan but his plan was still unconnected to a strategy. Our plan to end the fighting was apparently to hang around until the Iraqis decide to make peace with each other. That might take a while. In the strategy-free zone that is contemporary Washington, no one wants to second-guess a celebrity general, but any reading of David Petraeus' manual on counter-insurgency must lead to the conclusion that, in Iraq, "victory" remains undefined and missing in action.[21]

Of course, one must keep in mind the fact that the United States was fighting two wars (Iraq and Afghanistan) while it postured itself in anticipation of others: Iran, Pakistan, and Syria, for example. The NATO Alliance is committed exclusively to Afghanistan, but even there the allies showed a reluctance to furnish adequate troops to deal with the problems. While the United States, Great Britain, and Canada readily committed combat units to the task, others, especially Germany, Italy, and Spain, preferred to deploy smaller detachments to relatively safe areas.[22]

Some observers suggested that it was not surprising that central European nations that suffered extraordinary punishment in past conflicts shied away from minor threats to their interests at considerable distances. As one reporter wrote, "In the post–cold war world, individual members can't be expected to automatically take part in missions outside the alliance's traditional European sphere."[23]

American and British forces played the major part in the recovery of Western Europe in World War II and furnished the critical central defense systems in the Cold War, so it was not surprising that they would again play the leading roles in the current situation. Further, the terrorist attacks on New York and Washington in 2001 were key ingredients in our government's disposition toward matters in the Middle East, and one may add other factors, including the security of Israel and other friendly countries—especially those with significant oil resources. Other NATO countries may sympathize with these points, but not so far that they would attach the same level of importance to the problem as has the United States. The result, rather unfortunately, is a two- or three-tiered system, with some powers—especially the United States—playing a disproportionate part.

History is important, but it is not the only influence. The unbalanced deployment of NATO troops in the Middle East, with Americans on the heavy side, is believed by many to be largely due to the attitude of our political leadership. One writer, retired US Army Colonel Douglas MacGregor, described his view of American military power as driven by ideology rather than strategy, adding that "when ideology masquerades as strategy, disaster is inevitable."[24]

In recent months similar views have begun to be heard in England. Great Britain, America's closest ally, has been rather less fulsomely blamed for its supporting role in the wars. The Conservatives, under the leadership of Prime Minister Tony Blair, were able to maintain control of Parliament for four critical years, until 2007, upholding American policy in Iraq and Afghanistan all the while. The Liberal Democrats, who opposed the war, did not attain power until later in the conflict when the names of Iraqi cities, like Basra and Fallujah, had become household names and the American manipulation of the evidence of Iraq's weapons of mass destruction had become a public scandal. The London *Economist* wrote that "Iraq turned out to be as catastrophic as it was controversial," concluding that "nothing else Mr. Blair or the new prime minister, Mr. Gordon Brown, was likely to do would be as momentous."[25]

Further, the *Economist* article reinforced the MacGregor thesis, describing the Bush doctrine as "scorched." It pointed out that (1) Iraq's "weapons of mass destruction failed to materialize, and (2) the links between al-Qaeda and Saddam Hussein's regime proved tenuous at best." Then it questioned whether attack was the best form of defense and pointed out that America's travails in Iraq may have emboldened the Iranians. Finally it challenged the idea of a "bandwagon effect" which might bring additional allied forces into the fray. Instead, it argued, the allies have tried to further distance themselves from the "debacle" in Iraq, where the hostile "jihadists have gotten a foothold." And it went on to say that the war has damaged America's confidence in its own power.[26]

The Cato Institute in Washington, DC, released a report on the war in February 2008. Key observations in the document included the judgment that many foreign policy experts and analysts had misread lessons from the Iraq invasion. In the eyes of the authors, there was a widespread view in the United States that the enterprise could have been successful if more troops, a better counter-insurgency doctrine, or greater interdepartmental cooperation could have been attained. But was the operation fundamentally flawed? The Cato study rejected the thesis that, but for US governmental mistakes, Iraq was ours to make over. On the contrary, the document argued that military power affords us an ability to reshape states, but it does not afford us the power to run them. In sum, America has the muscle to conquer other countries, but administration is a different matter.

The best way to promote American security, the study concluded, was through restraint—"a wise and masterly inactivity in the face of foreign disorder." In this context, it argues that "we should resurrect the notion that the best way to spread democracy is to model it. Our ideology sells itself, especially when it is not introduced at gunpoint or during a lecture to the natives instructing them on how they ought to run their country." The final words of the authors were that "learning the right lessons from our experience in Iraq should convince Americans that preserving our power sometimes requires restraining it."[27]

Substantially reinforcing the "think tank" arguments were the words of many of the officers holding the reins of troop control. April 2006 was an important midpoint in which a "revolt of the generals" blossomed prominently across the country in the national news media. With few exceptions, the focus was clearly on Secretary of Defense Donald Rumsfeld and his immediate staff. Other targets were the Bush administration and its supporters in Congress.

Patrick Buchanan was an early participant in the storm, with a story of six retired Army and Marine generals denouncing the Pentagon's war planning and calling for the resignation or other discharge of Secretary Rumsfeld. Notably, most of the officers had held major commands in preparation for the campaign. Buchanan summarized the "unmistakable" message to President Bush: "Get rid of Rumsfeld or you will lose the war."[28]

In his article, Buchanan also quoted *Washington Post* columnist David Ignatius: "Rumsfeld should resign because the administration is losing the war on the home front. As bad as things are in Baghdad, America won't be defeated there militarily. But it may be forced into a hasty and chaotic retreat by mounting domestic opposition to its policy. Much of the American public has simply stopped believing the administration's argument about Iraq, and Rumsfeld is a symbol of that credibility gap. He is a spent force."

Buchanan focused sharply on the president's dilemma: "If [the president] stands by Rumsfeld, he will have taken his stand against the generals whose credibility today is higher than his own. But if he bows to the Generals' Revolt and dismisses Rumsfeld, the generals will have . . . dethroned civilian leadership and forced the commander in chief to fire the architect of a war upon which not only Bush's place in history depends, but the US position in the Middle East and the world. The commander in chief will have been emasculated by retired generals. The stakes could scarcely be higher. Whatever one thinks of the Iraq war, dismissal of Rumsfeld in response to a clamor created by ex-generals would mark Bush as a weak if not fatally compromised president. He will have capitulated to a generals' coup. Will he then have to clear Rumsfeld's successor with them? Bush will begin to look like Czar Nicholas in 1916."[29]

Another writer for the *Washington Post*, Max Hastings, took a slightly different track. He recalled Winston Churchill's wartime chief of staff, General Hastings "Pug" Ismay, who had tired of taking lunch at his old army club in London because at every mouthful he had to swallow a view of how his master should run the war. In self-defense Ismay resorted to lunching at White's, a venerable aristocratic restaurant where few members had noticed that a conflict was taking place.

Unfortunately, Secretary Rumsfeld had already done considerable damage to the Army by effectively silencing the chief of staff. In response to congressional questions before the invasion about how many troops would be required to subdue all of the various Iraqi forces and reserves, General Eric Shinseki responded, "Hundreds of thousands of troops," and implied that the campaign might last much longer than the period for which the plans were being prepared. The general was not fired for his response, but he was no longer allowed to take an active part in the planning process.

Thus, the war stretched into its fifth year, having been pursued in almost as many years by nothing less than the "hundreds of thousands" of troops of General Shinseki's estimate. One may note only that the deputy secretary of defense, Paul Wolfowitz, who "corrected" him so promptly, was, in time, not only relieved of his duties in the Pentagon, but also fired from his next position as president of the World Bank. Press reports of his departure indicated he was forced out of the bank by the executive board for ethics violations.[30] They read, in part, "reviled by much of the staff as an arrogant intellectual who cared more about his ideas and image than about the institution or its customers."[31]

Not terribly surprising under an administration that would treat the Army's highest-ranking officer with such cavalier abandon was the disclosure of a secret authorization of "harsh" interrogations of prisoners—not only in the combat area, but virtually anywhere around the world. A "sweeping legal brief," written in 2003 by a high-ranking official in the Justice Department, provided license for the arrest of suspects wherever they might be. An instructor at Yale Law School described the document as "a monument to executive supremacy and imperial presidency."

The eighty-one-page opinion authorized harsh interrogation methods by military prison officials, reasoning that US federal laws prohibiting personal assault were not applicable to military interrogators dealing with Al Qaeda detainees because of White House authority during wartime. It also argued that many American and international laws did not apply to interrogations held overseas—hence, one may assume, a government inclination to gather prisoners in Guantanamo Bay, Cuba, rather than the United States.[32] Clearly, the American leadership wished to avoid the protective cover provided to Nazi prisoners in the United States in World War II.

Three years into the war the US Army Strategic Studies Institute published a summary of its assessment of how badly the war was going. Professors David C. Hendrickson and Robert W. Tucker cooperated in an effort to bring their views to the Army at large and to the students and faculty of the Army War College in particular. They summarized their findings as follows:

- "Though the war plan to topple Saddam was brilliant, planning for the peace had been woefully insufficient.
- The United States did not have a sufficient number of troops to restore order in Iraq after the US invasion and also failed to develop a plan to stop the widespread looting that occurred in the immediate aftermath of the fall of Baghdad.
- The administration erred in disbanding the Iraqi Army, which might have played a valuable role in restoring security to the country.
- The United States erred further in its harsh decrees proscribing members of the Ba'ath party from participation in Iraq's public life—a decision, like that of disbanding the army, which needlessly antagonized the Sunnis and pushed many of them into the insurgency.
- The Bush administration also needlessly antagonized the international community—including both the United Nations and European allies—making it much more difficult to obtain help for the occupation and reconstruction of the country.
- The Bush administration was too slow in making funds available for reconstruction and created a labyrinthine bureaucracy for the awarding of contracts."[33]

Interestingly, the authors found that in their opinion, the great national mistake was not a squandered "opportunity to reconstruct the Iraqi state through mind-numbing incompetence," but the enterprise itself. They quote an unidentified senior diplomat from the region, who commented,

"When you commit a sin as cardinal as that, you are bound to get a lot of things wrong," and, "When you drive down a street in the wrong direction, no matter which way you turn you will be entering all the other streets in the wrong way."[34]

Such criticism, however, appears to have made little impression on the White House. As the war passed its fifth anniversary and began a new phase of sectarian violence, the president reaffirmed his zeal for "victory" and argued that his policies "merited the sacrifice" which they entailed.[35]

Vice President Dick Cheney matched the president's determination with his bone-chilling response to an ABC News reporter's question regarding the fact that two-thirds of Americans believe the war isn't worth the fighting. "You don't care what the American people think?" the reporter asked. "You can't be blown off course by polls," the vice president replied.[36]

It would hardly seem likely to be the result of opinion polls, but some information began to emerge that even the long-term organizational structure of the Army was beginning to have problems. About half of the young West Point classes of 2000 and 2001 were resigning, rather than staying on to serve multiple tours in the Middle East.[37] Gun battles over the same short stretches of sand, year in and year out, were taking their toll. Not surprisingly, without a national draft, an increasing need for additional enlistments has lowered the standard for volunteers. In April 2008, the Defense Department announced that both the Army and Marine Corps had been obliged to accept 25 percent more recruits with records of legal problems ranging from felony convictions and serious misdemeanors to drug crimes and traffic offenses. "Conduct waivers" for Army recruits rose from 8,129 in fiscal year 2006 to 10,258 in fiscal year 2007. For Marine Corps recruits, the figures were substantially higher: from 16,969 in 2006 to 17,413 in 2007.[38]

The former presidential national security advisor, Zbigniew Brzezinski, indicated that there was a "smart way out of a foolish war." He wrote, "The case for U.S. disengagement is compelling in its own right, but it must be matched by a comprehensive political and diplomatic effort to mitigate the destabilizing consequences of a war that the outgoing Bush administration started deliberately, justified demagogically and waged badly."

"The war has inflamed anti-American passions," Brzezinski went on, "in the Middle East and South Asia." He especially deplored a prolonged US military occupation. In his view, the longer US forces remain in the country, the more difficult it would be for an indigenous government to develop its own capability to assume the leadership. Further, as long as American forces remain, the ability of Iraq's neighbors to develop cooperative attitudes toward the United States will be postponed. Brzezinski advocated that the US arrange a regional conference in 2009 promoting stability and economic development throughout the region. Such a move, he argued, would help to mitigate the risks of further destabilization connected to

American disengagement. He suggested that Iraqi's neighbors, who were themselves vulnerable to religious and political strife, would very likely appreciate such an initiative.[39]

Concurrent *Iraq Arabic News* appeared to support Mr. Brzezinski's remarks. Aswat al-Iraq reported that some 32,000 prisoners were held by US and Iraqi authorities, but only recent changes in the amnesty law had permitted courts to consider release of persons requesting review and favorable action on their cases. As of March 16, 2008, barely 1 percent of the cases had been considered and granted favorable action.[40]

Brzezinski concluded his testimony with an assertion: "The only sensible strategy [for us in Iraq] is to withdraw rapidly, but in good order."[41] His conclusion was remarkably close to the expressed wish of the Congressional Iraq Study Group of 2006—if just two years later. Nevertheless, the conflict rolls inexorably on.

And it shows little more than momentary doubt about its future. There was quite a surprise in March 2008, when the top American commander in the Middle East, Admiral William Fallon, resigned. He did so shortly before the appearance of his subordinate, General David Petraeus, the field forces commander, before Congress, testifying in favor of slowing the rate of troop withdrawals from the country. The admiral explained his move as one intended to counter "ongoing misperceptions about differences between his ideas and US policy." Further, he said, he wished to "allow the secretary of defense and our military leaders to move beyond this distraction and focus on the achievement of our strategic objectives."[42]

For his part, General Petraeus cited the arrival of two 200-ton electric generators to be delivered across Anbar Province to the Qadas power plant north of Baghdad as a notable mini-step forward. The delivery, he reflected, is real news. Then he added that the saying "nothing in Iraq is easy" could be a perfect metaphor for the country in its current condition.[43]

A cease-fire was (more or less) in effect when the equipment was delivered. But that did not last for long. Reports of the generators and of suspended conflict in Baghdad in mid-April were brushed from the front pages of the newspapers by reports of the Iraqi president, al-Maliki, making a surprise trip southward to Basra to lead a counterattack against the activist Shiite militia. It was the largest Iraqi operation since the fall of the Saddam Hussein regime, involving some 30,000 soldiers and policemen. US forces, anxious to see how the government forces might perform, held back. Unfortunately, the government forces were no match for the Mahdi Army. The indigenous troops outflanked the president's forces, demanding their withdrawal. Eventually, the government force was able to restore order, but the damage had been done.[44]

"There can be no reconciliation between the Sunni and Shi'ia sects as long as Muqtada [the Shia leader] is alive," a reporter reflected as she left the country. "For all the success of the [American] surge, it has not exorcized Iraq's sectarian demons. Behind the painted walls, the murderous rage I saw in 2006 and '07 continues to fester."[45]

The pattern of hostility between Baghdad and the geographical extremities of the country goes back well earlier. Save for the current weakness of the central government, the incident in 2008, featuring central government troops versus the Shia street toughs in Basra, was reminiscent of events in 1991 when Saddam released his elite Republican Guard against the rebellion in the south after the first Gulf War. At the time, his officers had deceptively negotiated an arrangement with General H. Norman Schwarzkopf, the allied commander, to keep possession of their helicopters, nominally "to transport wounded soldiers and other tasks" in Kuwait and southern Iraq. With American clearance, the Republican Guard adapted the fleet as helicopter gun ships, and used them to put down Shia rebels resisting their campaign of suppression. The American administration had encouraged the uprising; now it had granted permission to the Iraqis to use their aircraft as they saw fit. General Schwarzkopf said he had been "suckered" by the enemy.[46]

But there was no effort to "un-sucker" the general or otherwise intervene in the struggle. Saddam's troops "plunged into their new task with a brutality that was exceptional, even by the harsh standards of the Baathist regime. In the holy cities of Najaf and Karbala thousands of clerics were arrested and hundreds were arrested and summarily executed. Any turbaned or bearded man who took to the street ran the risk of being arrested and shot. People were tied to tanks and used as human shields, while women and children were indiscriminately shot."[47]

Dr. Anthony Cordesman, of the Center for Strategic and International Studies, appeared to draw similar observations and conclusions about the later (five years on and counting) American campaign. In anticipation of US congressional hearings in the Capitol Building with Ambassador Crocker and General Petraeus the following day, Cordesman posted a most thoughtful analysis of the Iraqi situation up to April 7, 2008, on the Internet. In spite of his reputation as skeptic regarding the war, he offered what he regarded as a "best hope" for dealing with the problem. "The U.S. position," he wrote, "is now distinctly more tenuous than before the intra-Shi'ite fighting, but the U.S. presence is still the best hope for the future. Given the Sadr/Mahdi Army distrust of the Maliki government and the Iraqi Army, the U.S. also offers the best chance of providing stabilizing military presence in Baghdad and central Iraq."[48]

It must be borne in mind that the Iranians have been invaded by Iraq in recent memory, and there are bound to be a number of scores to settle on Tehran's mind, dating back to the last century. With Saddam and his Baathist doctrine in the trash bin of history, the Shia Iranians and their Iraqi co-believers are likely to find that they have more in common and greater freedom of choice than they have had in the past. The new government in Baghdad must bring itself to understand the temptations of the peoples on both sides of the Shatt al-Arab for a closer relationship, even the possibility of a merger, which could result in the commissioning of the most powerful state in the region, right on its doorstep.

Perhaps the most important question now is how much stabilization is necessary to engender confidence that some American forces can withdraw without provoking full-scale civil war or unduly tempting an Iranian invasion. Yes, invasion. If the United States can be taken to war in Iraq on as slim a rationale as President Bush and his neo-conservative henchmen offered the American people in 2003, perhaps Tehran could be similarly enticed by a fading American presence to its west. The Iranians have the memory of the 1980 attack by Saddam Hussein, and now they have the reality of a presidentially concocted Sunni assault on their Iraqi Shia cousins in the Basra area to feed their thirst for revenge. All they have to do is wait for most of the Americans to leave.

But wait they must. Well into 2009, US General Ray Odierno, commander of all US forces in Iraq, indicated that four-fifths of his combat troops would be withdrawn by June 30, 2009. This might amount to an exodus of 50,000–70,000, leaving as many as 64,000–84,000 (largely administrative) troops in place. If the Americans further delay their departure, Tehran would almost certainly wait.[49]

There is no scripted schedule which a troop withdrawal must follow. While a delay in the US departure may strengthen the Baghdad leadership, Tehran would lose a bit. But it could gain much by withholding its assault until the Americans finally go home. The Americans have been in the region long enough to be both politically and psychologically fatigued. Meanwhile, of course, aid may be provided by Tehran to its Iraqi Shia co-religionists to ensure that they are ready to strike once the last US troops depart.

Good news? Yes, there was some. Perhaps most important for our own self-respect were reports of efforts to back away from policies favoring the torture of prisoners. A star example was the resort to a simple act of kindness in the handling of a tough captive who had information of high value. Abu Jandal, who had been a closer associate of Osama bin Laden than US intelligence had ever had access to before, became much more cooperative when he was handled civilly. The treatment included provision of sugarless cookies to avoid inflaming his known diabetes. According to the press report, after that he no longer thought of Americans as the great evils of the earth, but rather as human beings, and he became a cooperative source of high-value information.[50]

3

What Have We Overlooked?

In October 2007, the German publication *Der Spiegel* reported that "more than 30,000 foreign troops are enlisted in the US Army, many of them serving in Iraq. Their reward for risking their lives for their adopted country is US citizenship." It went on to say, "Since September 11, 2001, the United States has granted citizenship to 32,500 foreign soldiers." Further, "In July 2002, US President George W. Bush issued an executive order to expand existing legislation to offer a fast track to citizenship to foreigners who agree to fight for the US Armed Forces. About 8,000 non-Americans have joined the US military every year since then." The foreign recruits (as of October 2007) represent 5 percent of all recruits.[1]

At about the same time, David J. Katz, a former US Special Forces officer, and later the director of security and intelligence at Luster National Corporation, published an intriguing article, "Iraq Needs a National Guard." He made a well-reasoned case for an indigenous part-time guard, led and equipped by the US Army's Green Berets. While not identifying any particular date for initiation of the scheme, he suggested that it would be a "standard and immediate component of any and all U.S. Phase IV [post-conflict] operations." In his view, it would "plug the gap in conventional force structure where insurgents typically operate, matching their tactical disadvantages and revaluing their social benefits."[2]

Wikipedia, the online encyclopedia, specifically notes that "many members of the U.S. Marine Corps are of Latin American nationality and not U.S. citizens. The U.S. Army made extensive use of foreign soldiers, particularly Irish and German, during the nineteenth century; German Jewish troops were common in the U.S. Army during World War II. However, as a rule, many, if not most, non-American troops in the United States Armed

Forces are there seeking the expedited United States citizenship that came with completion of a term of service, and they could be seen as aspiring Americans rather than outright foreigners."[3]

It is healthy that such a discussion should be explored now, even if, for other reasons, major decisions have to be postponed. The United States has had considerable experience in post-hostilities occupation and constabulary work from various conflicts, stretching from the US Civil War to World War II, but the development of forces based upon indigenous teams clearly loyal to the interests of the United States has not been its specialty. That is not to say that the Katz model for a national guard is not useful, but rather that it would be highly preferable to ensure that any scheme for investment in indigenous units include consideration of the important dimension of loyalty. The Middle East is not a region noted for internal cohesiveness, domestic harmony, or tolerance for differences of political or religious belief. The Katz model for an independent national guard does not appear to give much attention to this aspect of the issue any more than the ongoing program of US support for the Iraqi Army does.

Among democratic nations, an indigenous, non-sectarian army is a most basic instrument for the defense of the country and the protection of the population. But in the case of Iraq, one must take into consideration the realities of sharp differences among Sunni, Shia, Kurdish, and other religious groups. These are not simple differences between political parties, but fundamentally different belief systems that delineate the lives and practices of the groups. American or other Western forces working with Middle Eastern counterparts must take these factors into consideration.

Appropriately enough, the Iraqi military command chain runs upward through the Defense Ministry to the highest political authority. American interests in Iraq have been ensured through advisory officials and political connections operating comprehensively at all governmental levels. Nominally, in the wake of the 2003 US-Iraqi conflict, the troops on both sides came to operate roughly as allies in the field. But the Iraqi Armed Forces are not a formal ally of the United States, and avoid any such identity. The US goal, since the defeat of the Saddam Hussein regime, has been the creation of indigenous forces, generally along the lines of those of any government badly in need of local support in the face of a broad internal national disturbance.

As for the problem of augmentation of American forces, the Pentagon has turned to the recruitment of skilled immigrants living in the United States with temporary visas, offering them the chance of becoming US citizens in as little as six months. Immigrants who are permanent residents, with documents commonly known as green cards, have long been eligible to enlist. But the new effort, for the first time since the Vietnam War, opens the armed forces to temporary immigrants if they have lived in the United States for at least two years.

It is expected that the temporary immigrants will have more education, foreign language skills, and professional expertise than many Americans who enlist, helping to fill shortages in technical affairs, such as language interpretation, medical care, and intelligence analysis. As Lieutenant General Benjamin Freakley, the director of US Army recruiting, has said, "The American Army finds itself in a lot of different countries where cultural awareness is critical. There will be some very talented folks in this group." The program is expected to produce some 1,000 volunteers in the first year for all services, and perhaps eventually expand to as many as 14,000 per year.[4]

In February 2009 the US government enlarged its programs for foreign military enlistees. At the same time it broadened its recruiting categories to include a number of temporary immigrants. The new arrangement, known as "Military Accessions Vital to the National Interest," was aimed at reducing shortages of personnel with medical and foreign language skills. Initially targeted to reach a thousand enlistees in the first year, the program is expected to make subsequent arrangements for other skill areas and thousands of additional enrollees. While it has been necessary to reject many applicants for various reasons of unsuitability, expectations remain optimistic for the longer term.[5]

As Katz has pointed out, there will be a continuing need for American military expertise for some time following the current cooperative operations and projected US withdrawals, and perhaps considerably beyond that. The question is, if the United States wishes to ensure the security of a foreign state, yet avoid the continuance of a large military presence, how might that best be accomplished?

In 2008 the United States Institute for Peace launched a "Task Force for Responsible Withdrawal from Iraq," suggesting some twenty-five initiatives in favor of the withdrawal of Americans on "a short time line." The task force argued that with a new administration in the White House, it was time to "come to our senses, stop digging and climb out of the hole." Further, "no adjustment at the tactical and operational level will get us to where we need to be. Only strategic change can get us on the road to recovery." From this perspective, only total troop withdrawal could:

- draw Sunni and Shia alike into the political process;
- reduce the appeal of Al Qaeda in Mesopotamia;
- restore the credibility of the Iraqi government; and
- unblock international cooperation.

The task force also pointed out the following:

- Very few Iraqis think that the United States is doing a good job in their country.

- Iraqis believe that the US invasion is the root of violent differences among them. The departure of occupying forces is the key to national reconciliation.
- Stability must be achieved by the Iraqis themselves.
- There is no endpoint to restricting the access of the "Sons of Iraq" formations to heavy weapons. This is the "lever of control over native forces typical of a colonial power."[6]

Two thoughtful senior fellows associated with Washington think tanks, Drs. Max Boot and Michael O'Hanlon, have argued that "now is the time to consider a new chapter in the annals of American immigration." They suggest that the United States could form a foreign legion "by inviting foreign individuals to join the US Armed Forces in exchange for a promise of citizenship after a four year tour of duty."[7] In this manner the United States could attract some of the region's most enterprising and talented individuals. Their plan would provide a new path toward assimilation for undocumented immigrants who are already in the United States, but lack the green card necessary for either a quiet private life or enlistment in the armed forces. Notably, the Department of State operates an annual random selection of 50,000 green card applicants, but the number of applicants is so large that the chances of any single individual receiving a card are quite modest.[8]

A principal interest of the US government under these circumstances, of course, would be a solution to the pressing problem facing the Army and Marine Corps: the fact that these services need to grow to meet current commitments, yet cannot easily do so (absent a draft) given the current recruiting environment. The government machinery must ensure that applicants accepted for enrollment in the Armed Forces are granted green cards at appropriate times in their service.

Boot and O'Hanlon went on to point out that foreign military recruits would address one of America's key deficiencies in the battle against Islamist extremists, "our lack of knowledge of the languages and mores in the lands where terrorists reside. Newly arrived Americans can help us avoid trampling on local sensitivities and thereby creating more enemies than we eliminate."[9]

They also argued that while the US services have met most of their recruiting goals, much of the credit must go to the relaxation of age and aptitude scores, which has allowed many individuals with criminal records to enter the service. The enlistment targets, they say, have also been met largely by substantially increasing the numbers of recruiters and the amount of advertising dollars.

Further, they pointed out, "with most soldiers and Marines already on a third or even fourth deployment since September 11, 2001, it is doubtful that the all-volunteer force can withstand such a commitment at its current size." Even if it could, they argue, it is unfair to ask "so much of so few for so long."[10] Thus, they aver, we have in hand exactly the circumstances for transitioning to a greater reliance on foreign volunteers. While it may take some time to convert a few selected US Army and Marine Corps elements to "foreign" status, it should not be difficult to replace small groups of Americans, departing upon completion of their tours, with small "packages" of foreign recruit groups, perhaps on a temporary basis, until, over time, the desired mix of federal and foreign constituency units is attained, trained, and tested.

While certainly not an exact reproduction of other such organizations in history, the Boot and O'Hanlon proposal suggests the adoption of many of the same provisions, especially where ultimate citizenship is an important objective. Throughout the centuries, foreign legions have relied primarily upon promising participants to provide the next corps of noncommissioned officers, and in some cases, even commissioned officers. While first-term personnel are usually individuals from selected foreign lands, once the initial training cohort is absorbed and trained (as might occur in a few years), it can be assumed that a number of specially skilled troopers with the capacity for training further inductees will be identified. In many cases processes of this nature have proved very satisfactory. The objective, of course, is to develop a corps of trained men and women of foreign birth who are motivated—or motivatable—to support the major public beliefs and principles of the United States, while reducing the enormous financial and human burdens of maintaining exclusively American national forces in foreign lands or regions.

Just as the major points of the foregoing paragraphs were being made, the news of an additional challenge to American—and global—security burst forth. The *New York Times* ran a front-page report on August 9, 2009, headlined "Climate Change Seen as Threat to U.S. Security." It included the following statement: "The changing global climate will pose profound strategic challenges to the United States in coming decades, raising the prospect of military intervention to deal with the effects of violent storms, drought, mass migration and pandemics, military and intelligence."

Further, the report pointed out, "such climate-induced crises could topple governments, feed terrorist movements or destabilize entire regions." It detailed the results of war games and intelligence studies of the future, pointing out that "vulnerable regions, particularly sub-Saharan Africa, the Middle East and South and Southeast Asia, will face the prospect of food shortages, water crises and catastrophic flooding driven by climate change that could demand an American humanitarian relief or military response."

In Congress, key leaders have sought to bring the matter to the attention of their peers. Senator John Kennedy of Massachusetts commented that the continuing conflict in southern Sudan, which has killed and displaced tens of thousands of people, was a result of drought and the expansions of the deserts in the north. He commented, "That is going to be repeated many times over and on a much larger scale."[11]

The point here is to counsel that the United States should press ahead with a full investigation and thorough review of all of the concepts behind "foreign legions," both historical and modern. Such organizations have existed in lands and ages all around the world for different reasons, and under different operational conditions, dating back to the forces extant in ancient Rome. In modern times these have included the British Gurkhas (with their frightful "kukris," or curved knives, even on latter-day battlefields), the Royal Dutch East Indies Army, the Rhodesian Light Infantry, and the French and Spanish Foreign Legions—all suggesting potential models of value. All merit investigation.

Perhaps surprising to some, the legendary French Foreign Legion stands out. Most remarkable in this notable (and highly modern) force is an internal structure of loyalty, which has been built up over the years. This is a loyalty not to the soldier's home country, not to France, but to the Legion. That is where successful enlistees learn the essence of their trade, with the Legion. Their dedication to the organization is second to none.

As early as the second year of the second American attack on Iraqi forces (2005), it became clear to many in the United States and abroad that the latter campaign might not be on a winning course any more than the first, but for a different reason. In commenting on Boot and O'Hanlon, an online article titled "America Needs a Foreign Legion" argues that an unsuccessful campaign in Iraq would likely result in a national attitude of "great reluctance to send US expeditionary forces to foreign lands."[12] It likens the probable popular reaction to that following the fall of Saigon in South Vietnam.

A slight turn toward isolationism, the article continues, might, on the whole, be a good thing, but there will be occasions when intervention will be appropriate, most desirably with international support. The issue brings to mind the terrible ethnic slaughter in Rwanda in 1994, when American forces suffered an embarrassing loss of Special Forces troopers and an inability to stabilize the situation. In that case, as in so many others, the American forces were not specifically trained or familiarized with the hostile forces.

A substitute for a conventional American invasion, it has been argued, could be an intervention by an American-led foreign legion, including a number of former members of the communities actually invaded. Such a force, in this view, if armed and trained to American standards, led by US officers, and supported by US intelligence and logistical systems, could be highly successful. A strong implication is that such a force could count within its ranks a significant number of warriors familiar with the operational area, the language spoken, and possibly even a number of the personalities—both friendly and unfriendly. Such a force, under American control, could clearly expect to achieve a number of objectives normally beyond the reach of regular US units.

The force would be led by American officers and noncommissioned officers. Below them might be a number of US citizen volunteers, as indeed, we may note, is the practice in other foreign legions (almost half of French Legionnaires are native French speakers), but, more importantly, there would be many volunteers desperately seeking citizenship. Successful inductees, one may reasonably argue, should be enabled to earn legal grounds for citizenship after some number of years' service, with opportunities for retirement with a pension after another appropriate number of years. With an estimated twelve million immigrants currently living in the United States illegally, the times would appear ripe for legislative action to establish the program.

While, clearly, observers have different views of the details, most find common ground regarding training. Some argue that the training could be more strenuous than that required of current American soldiers in view of the greater perceived reward for service—*citizenship*. The previously mentioned online article characterizes the toughness of the training as an effort to "break the man to build the soldier."[13] Such inducement is not applicable to most American recruits today because there is no draft or other mechanism to compel their service.

There may develop an argument over the toughness of various training programs. Certainly, Special Forces units would be likely winners among competitors today. Of course, legion recruits would be inducted for combat—not exactly the first matter on a recruiter's tongue when he or she is seeking enlistments for an all-volunteer Army, National Guard, or Reserve organization. A legion "diploma" would be a strong credential for men and women seeking a new life in a new homeland.

In sum, there is a need for an experiment with a new branch of our forces—similar in some respects to Special Forces, but designed for greater interaction within the societies in which they would be expected to operate. The organization would be capable of working closely with a broad range of individuals and indigenous security and military elements—perhaps in some cases going as far as to recruit additional men and women for membership within the legion's organization. With continuing requirements for specialized skills and knowledge, additional staff and combat capabilities would likely become a recurring condition. The time to explore the details involved and to form a test structure is clearly now.

Looking a little further into tomorrow's tomorrow, the United States might be wise to broaden the model suggested in the previous pages. For all intents and purposes the United States will remain in a senior position among Western nations in the future, and can expect that most friendly nations will expect it to take the lead in dealing with outbreaks of third-world hostilities whenever such affairs exceed the management powers of international agencies, especially the UN.

Back in 1995, Antonia Handler Chayes and George T. Raach, members of the US Commission on Roles and Missions of the Armed Forces, pointed out, "When the most serious threat was war with the Soviet Union, we could focus almost exclusively on deterring—and if necessary, fighting and winning—that conflict. Now, US security policy and strategies must be fundamentally reexamined in order to develop forces and methods of operations that can cope with multidimensional challenges that go far beyond conventional warfare."[14] Today the United States finds itself in the future they had in mind, and, indeed, its challenges go far beyond "conventional warfare." In addition to the Middle East, the United States has little difficulty finding potential areas of dispute in Latin America, Sub-Saharan Africa, the Balkan states, the Middle East, and Southeast Asia.

Finally, a point regarding the legitimacy of foreign legions, which are often confused with mercenary troops: Article 47 of the Geneva Convention of 1949 essentially exempts mercenaries from the Laws of War. But it defines mercenaries as conflict participants who are "promised compensation substantially in excess of that promised or paid to combatants of similar ranks and functions in the armed forces of that party." In the United States we have the highest-paid soldiers in the world, and we have never paid foreign participants more than we have our own troops. We need units with special geographic, cultural, and linguistic savvy. We don't need mercenaries.

Few challenge the proposition that the United States is the most powerful country in the world. While some suggest that the United States has bitten off more than it can chew in the Middle East, no responsible observer has expressed a view that it risks military defeat in the field. American ground forces have certainly suffered higher casualties than most public officials have apparently expected from operations in Iraq, Afghanistan, or Pakistan, either with its allies or standing alone. Moreover, there is no one visible school of thought in the US leadership voicing an opinion that "victory," however defined, is likely within the next few months or years. Moreover, in public discussions, the number of additional troops required in the three countries, beginning in 2010, appears to have been used as a substitute for a professional explanation of the intended approach to the conflict(s).

A reexamination of the common meaning of the term "strategy" appears to be in order. *Webster's New International Dictionary* describes strategy as "the science and art of employing the armed strength of a belligerent to secure the objects of war." Further, in a more restricted application, it offers the following: "strategy is the science and art of military command, exercised to meet the enemy in combat under advantageous conditions." While one may certainly consider the number of additional troops an important factor, especially for political purposes, there are clearly many other matters which also influence the outcome of battle.

In this respect, the range and killing power of weaponry and the facility with which it may be applied under various circumstances are certainly important. No less important are troop morale, training, and the qualities of leadership at all levels of command. Further, the dispositions of supporting populations, on both sides, are important, and may certainly be considered manipulable by political leaders. Hence, while numbers of combatants are important, history is replete with details of how successful leaders with moderately sized forces have defeated larger formations. For example, the superiority of Israeli forces to those of its Arab neighbors has been demonstrated repeatedly since the foundation of the Jewish state.

Early in the American Civil War the Army of the Confederacy demonstrated capabilities superior to those of the North, in spite of the North's substantial numerical and positional advantage. The South had a force barely two-thirds that of its opponent at the First Battle of Bull Run, but won the day, hands down. And a year later, in the Union Peninsular Campaign, the Confederate forces, with their backs to their capital, drove off five Union corps with a manpower disadvantage of seventy-four thousand gray coats facing ninety thousand blue coats on the Union side.[15] It was not until later, after President Lincoln came to recognize General Ulysses S. Grant's skills, that the war turned clearly in the Union's favor.

Clearly, if our leadership is looking for a new strategy, it must direct its questions considerably beyond "How many additional troops will be required?" More troops applying old doctrine would not seem to be a formula for success. And certainly, no more reassuring is a report of the vice chief of staff of the Army, General Peter W. Chiarelli, that in the first ten and a half months in 2009, 140 American soldiers on active duty took their own lives, while 71 others no longer on active duty did the same, rather than face the contingencies of military life in a nation at war.

"This is horrible," the general said. "Every single loss is devastating." The report added that the Army had not been able to identify causal links among the suicides, except that soldiers are more likely to kill themselves when they are away from their stations where help is readily available. Substance abuse (drugs and alcohol), which can be related to mental health problems and suicide, is on the rise in the US Army, the general added, saying that the US Army is short some eight hundred behavioral health specialists. "I have been pounding the system," he said, "to determine what we need after eight years of war."[16]

Nevertheless, as a great power, the United States has found itself in leading positions in many locales around the world, with other powers often looking to the United States for support and leadership, especially where the government is close to losing or has lost control and the lives of citizens have become seriously endangered. The following chapters identify many areas where such problems have come to the fore, and where help is urgently needed.

4

The Legion: Whence the Concept?

The legion has been a distinctive military organization for centuries, probably best known for its formulative era within the Roman Empire. At that time it consisted of some four to six thousand troops, usually with small detachments of cavalry and more heavily armed infantry in accompaniment. The legions were numbered and occasionally bore the names of the territories in which they served, such as III Cyrenaica in North Africa, or XVI Gallica in France. Or they might be named for emperors: VII Augusta or VII Claudia. Early on, under Emperor Augustus (27 BC to AD 14), the units were made up entirely of Roman citizens, but as time progressed, the legions became more dependent upon local enlistees aspiring to Roman citizenship. Citizenship for oneself and one's family was of almost incalculable value.[1]

Roman military organization and weaponry were far better developed than those of almost any potential challenger in the then-known world. Further, Roman military engineering was virtually unchallenged. Roads, walls, bridges, theaters, and even ships were all within the range of possible construction by a legion. One admiring writer observed that Roman legions "mined silver and gold, dug canals and manufactured standard weapons and shoes," and not on a modest scale. Such flexibility and range of skills proved virtually unbeatable in the raw terrain in which the legions served. Hadrian's Wall in Britain, which stretched seventy miles, from Newcastle to Carlisle, was constructed over a surprisingly short period, from AD 122 to 124. It was composed largely of solid rock, and could provide either a defensive barrier or a forward line from which forces could be launched on offensive operations. Standardization, spirit, and soldierly qualities were all in abundance in the legions. All of these stood out in every camp, which was shaped to the standard square, surrounded by a ditch and walls, and provided with gates and streets. All these would be centered on the holiest of the holy, the standard "eagle" of the legion, together with a treasure chest into which each soldier made a deposit on payday. Above all else, the soldier would fight to defend the legion's (and his personal) life savings in the treasure box.[2]

The legions, of course, were not the only forces available along Rome's thousands of miles of conquest. Auxiliaries loaned additional strength to the empire, but typically were of lower caste, with fewer Romans enrolled, less robust equipment, and half the pay of the legionnaires. The most important prize a non-Roman legionnaire might win upon retirement would be a formal expression of appreciation from the emperor, together with Roman citizenship. With this system the empire attained and maintained substantial security along four thousand miles of frontier, enfolding some seventy million people. In 1776 Edward Gibbon would publish his first volume of *The History of the Decline and Fall of the Roman Empire*, recalling the formation of the Roman legions (some 4,500 to 6,000 troops). He wrote, "[The Romans] sought the friendship of the barbarians and endeavored to convince them that Roman power was actuated only by the love of order and justice. The terror of the Roman arms added weight and dignity to the moderation of emperors. This military strength was clearly on display during the time of Hadrian and the elder Antoninus."[3]

Centuries later, and under the auspices of a different Rome, other legions would be formed in Europe, of mixed citizenship and origin, but the concept gradually faded as time passed. Catholicism had its battles, but it couldn't win them with only Swiss Guards. The mercenary Swiss would have their day later, but in the eleventh and twelfth centuries the pope was obliged to call upon a broader slice of the military power of central Europe for serious work for salvation in the Middle East. The Turks had taken the Holy Land, and a broad international effort was needed to save Jerusalem and other important sites of the New Testament.

In 1095 Pope Urban II called for an international campaign to drive the "unbelievers" from Palestine and to save the Holy Sepulcher, which was rumored to have been put to the torch. Participation by European Christians, the pope promised, would serve as full penance for any wrongs committed. Further, the homes of the volunteers would be protected while the men were absent on the great mission. Estimates of participation stretched from 60,000 to 100,000 military-capable men. High-ranking noblemen led their troops. The undertaking was largely successful, but resulted in widespread butchery of thousands of Muslims and Jews.

There would be a succession of nine Crusades, stretching on into the thirteenth century, including one by "children." The fifth Crusade was launched by a visionary French peasant boy—a sort of male Joan of Arc—

from Marseilles, in hopes that the youngsters might succeed where their elders had failed. The entire undertaking was a disaster, with groups diverted into terrible situations by unscrupulous ship captains and others. The children were sold into slavery or perished from hunger or disease. War with the Turks continued long after the Holy See dropped all effort of sponsorship, but the great energy had been exhausted. Nevertheless, the experience had considerable impact on the development of Europe. Many of the participating princes became more interested in secular matters affecting the extent of their powers than in pleasing the Vatican. Further, the experience of international cooperation in distant wars did much to increase Western knowledge of the East—but not necessarily for the better. Still, the sense of international military mission, conducted along the lines of international legions, had been placed firmly on the record books.

In 1756, Great Britain, smarting from General Braddock's defeat in the New World the previous year at Ft. Duquesne (later Pittsburgh, Pennsylvania), sought to balance the scales with the formation of a volunteer "Royal American" regiment made up of American, Swiss, German, and British volunteers. The four battalions of the regiment were assembled on Governors Island, New York. A Swiss citizen, Henri Bouquet, long noted for his ideas on military tactics and troop management, and a few others were given commissions and placed in command of important elements of the force. Bouquet assumed command of the first battalion, and he introduced new tactics more suitable to the terrain than the old European styles. The regiment would earn fame for victories at Louisbourg and Quebec, which finally wrested Canada from France in 1759. At Quebec the regiment earned the motto *Celer et Audax* (Swift and Bold).[4]

Throughout the eighteenth and nineteenth centuries Polish formations could be found in Italy, Turkey, and Hungary, fighting for a measure of independence, and in 1848 the prominent Polish poet Adam (Bernard) Mickiewicz organized a two-hundred-man unit, with papal blessings, to fight for Italy against Austria. It fought alongside others in Lombardy and on the barricades of Genoa against the royalists in defense of the Republic.[5] Twelve years later, Giuseppe Garibaldi, one of the greatest generals of the time, brought French, Polish, Swiss, and German troops together in an International Legion to bring about the liberation and unification of Italy. The legion was later reinforced with Hungarian, British, and other elements, increasing the strength by some 2,500 men.[6]

Perhaps the greatest British success with foreign troops occurred on the other side of the world. Early in the nineteenth century the British noted the outstanding tenacity of Nepalese (Gurkha) troops in defense of their own territory and encouraged them to volunteer for military service with the semi-official East India Company. The company was independently responsible for large areas of India under British territorial control.

Over the years the Gurkhas (with their murderous "kukri"—curved knives) ran up an extraordinary series of victories over various contestants on the Indian subcontinent, particularly in battles in 1826, 1846, 1848, 1857, and 1917. In one campaign the 2nd Gurkha Rifles lost 327 men of a total of 490 while holding on to a house of strategic value. The regiment was awarded the honor of adopting their distinctive rifle green uniforms with scarlet edges and traditional British insignia.[7]

In the words of Field Marshal Lord William Joseph Slim, First Viscount, "The Almighty created in the Gurkha an ideal infantryman, indeed an ideal Rifleman, brave, tough, patient, adaptable, skilled in field-craft, intensely proud of his military record and unswerving loyalty. Add to this his honesty in word and deed, his parade perfection, and his unquenchable cheerfulness, then service with Gurkhas is for any soldier an immense satisfaction."[8]

Gurkha regiments served abroad with distinction in both world wars. (They were at the Dardanelles in 1915, as well as in France for most of the war.) Following World War II, six Gurkha regiments joined the independent Indian army, while four others joined the British Army and were posted to Malaya. Again, they were noted for heroic accomplishments during the Malayan Emergency, as they had been in Burma in the Second Great War. In 1962 they formed their own artillery battalion, and ten years later, during the upheavals of the Chinese Cultural Revolution, they were transferred to Hong Kong to secure the island. Other elements were stationed in Brunei and the United Kingdom, in the latter case, to mount the Queen's Guard.[9]

In 1974, when the Turks invaded Cyprus, the 10th Gurkha Rifles were dispatched to the island to protect British interests, and remained there with peacekeeping duties. Twenty years later, when Hong Kong was returned to China, the Gurkha headquarters was transferred to England, to administer a much smaller Gurkha Brigade: just 3,400 troops and officers. Since then, Gurkha detachments have been deployed to the Falkland Islands, Afghanistan, Kosovo, Bosnia, and East Timor.[10]

In August 2009 the British actress Joanna Lumly was met in Lahure, Nepal, with one of the most extravagant welcomes she had ever experienced. She was mobbed at the airport and lauded by the speaker of the Nepal parliament as a daughter of the nation. What had she done? She had persuaded the British government to allow United Kingdom residency to Nepali Gurkhas who had served in the British Army, but had retired before 1997 (when the law regarding Gurkha service had been written, with little consideration for those who had served and fought in earlier days); as Lumley had argued, "If someone is willing to die for a country, he should be allowed to live in it."[11]

The issue was not a small one. In 2008 the retired Gurkhas' income was estimated to amount to 17 percent of Nepal's national income. Now, with retirement in England an option, government accountants in the old country, while recognizing the justice of the new law, have to worry more about the domestic balance sheets. But justice has been done.[12]

In 1830, the Netherlands government formed the Royal Dutch East Indies Army, as part of the colonization of the islands which would later come to be known as Indonesia, with largely native troops, informally known as the "Dutch Foreign Legion." But European volunteers were not overlooked. As with the French Legion, German, Belgian, and Swiss volunteers were welcome, along with native South Moluccan, Timorese, and Manadonese.

The Dutch organization faithfully defended the home nation's interests in local campaigns against indigenous groups until 1904, when the territory was deemed to have been pacified. In 1940 the Germans invaded and occupied the European homeland, but the insular territories remained under Dutch control and the protection of the KNIL (Royal Netherlands East Indies Army) until after the Japanese invasion and occupation in 1942.[13]

The KNIL was a respected force with many volunteers from Europe. But not all instances of foreign military recruitment work out well, such as when the circumstances anticipated are not honestly conveyed by the recruiter to the enlistees, or when the duties required are not fully understood by the recruits. Then serious trouble is highly probable. Racism can also undo much good will.

For example, in 1827, the emperor of Brazil, Dom Pedro I, sought to recruit a few thousand Irishmen, accompanied by families, to reinforce his troops fighting with Argentina for control of Cisplatina (later to become Uruguay). His agent, one Colonel William Cotter, did not bother to inform the Irishmen what was expected of them, particularly that they would join a few thousand Germans for training in Rio de Janeiro and go from there straight into battle. Cotter promised only free passage, free land, six shillings per day, and military training as local militia.[14]

The first ship was wrecked off Tenerife, in the Canary Islands, with the loss of half of the passengers. The replacement ship had to make an emergency stop at another island to save the people from starvation. It was almost a year before it arrived in Brazil. Once there, the volunteers encountered black slaves who accused them of being nothing more than white slaves for the emperor. Numerous fights broke out.

As it happened, the Germans had been similarly deceived. Soon, the great majority of the Irish and Germans were in revolt. Whole blocks of Rio de Janeiro were razed. The emperor was able to rally a few Brazilian troops and most of the slaves to stem the uprising by the rebels. Some marines from visiting British and French ships also came to the rescue. Losses were heavy on both sides, but after a few days order was restored. The Germans were sent to outlying provinces in southern Brazil. About half of the original 2,400 Irish recruited were able to get back to Ireland—at the emperor's expense. Others went to North America; one family sailed directly to Portland, Maine. Others made it to Canada, but found themselves penniless upon arrival.

The result of the rebellion was the destruction of two of the emperor's best units and the surrender of his claim to Uruguay, which would become an independent buffer state between Brazil and Argentina. This was no "foreign legion" story, only one of misled people launched on a false cause.[15]

The Swiss Guards are still, at this writing, in evidence as the principal gatekeepers to the Vatican. They have a longer history and a better reputation than those who sought employment in Brazil, however frequently they, too, have been termed "mercenaries." Formed in the fifteenth century as protectors of the French court, the "Hundred Guard," as they were officially known, underwent expansion to regimental status in 1567. A separate element, the Papal Swiss Guard, had been established in 1506.

The term "mercenary" is often misunderstood, implying in some cases an illegal or improper practice. This is an error. According to the "Additional Protocol I" to the Geneva Convention of August 1949, "A mercenary is a person who is not a national or party to the conflict, and is motivated to take part in the hostilities essentially by the desire for private gain, and, in fact, is promised by, or on behalf of a party to the conflict, *material compensation substantially in excess of that promised or paid to combatants of similar ranks and functions in the armed forces of that Party.*"[16]

In the case of US forces, and in a few others, the pay of the regular forces is so much higher than that of most others that the "compensation substantially in excess of that paid to combatants of similar ranks and functions in the armed forces of that party" simply does not arise. The point becomes clearer as we note how civilian personnel have been used as additional manpower in the current conflicts in the Middle East.

With "everlasting peace" declared between France and the Vatican in 1516, the various detachments did not anticipate trouble with incompatible loyalties, however much one element might exceed another in size or duty. Francis I of France took advantage of the situation to employ some 120,000 Swiss troops in various conflicts not involving the Vatican.[17]

The most famous episode in the history of the Swiss Guard was its defense of the Tuileries Palace in 1792, during the French Revolution. More than a third of the 9,000 Swiss were killed in battle or massacred after surrendering. Another two hundred would die of their wounds or in the subsequent mob massacres.[18] The Revolution marked the end of the government's regular practice of hiring foreign units, but Napoleon ignored the rule and employed four Swiss regiments for operations in both Spain and Russia. The Swiss were discharged when the Tuileries was stormed in July 1830, but two years later many of the men were individually recruited to serve in the newly raised French Foreign Legion for service in Algeria. (See chapter 5 for details of the French Foreign Legion.)

The Swiss record for foreign service is especially remarkable. For over two hundred years they served the House of Savoy and the Kingdom of Sardinia, and for seventeen years the court of Frederick I of Prussia. Twice (in the eighteenth and nineteenth centuries) they served the Kingdom of Saxony, and through most of the eighteenth century Swiss Guardsmen served the Kingdom of Naples and the Netherlands. For a brief time (1748–1767, during the reign of Empress Maria Theresa) some three or four hundred Swiss served at the Winter Palace in Vienna. To the present day, the oldest courtyard in the palace is referred to as the "Swiss Court" (Schweizerhof).[19]

In 1860 Giuseppe Garibaldi, of Italy, took advantage of the readiness of the Swiss and others to adopt foreign uniforms with his call for an International Legion for the liberation of Italy, as well as their own homelands. The organization would include some 2,500 Frenchmen, Poles, Germans, Hungarians, British, and others.[20]

One of the remarkable developments early in the twentieth century was the assignment of three American regiments to French command, essentially paralleling the legion concept. In 1918 the US Army subordinated three black national guard regiments to French command to reinforce the French position. The American 93rd Division was reported to have acquitted itself well, earning the first French award of the Croix de Guerre. It was especially notable for its capture of enemy artillery, machine guns, and an important section of railroad. One member of the force displayed extraordinary valor, winning the US Medal of Honor, while others won the Distinguished Service Cross (next in order after the MH) and a number of other French awards. The American force suffered the loss of 3,500 men in action, and 591 still lie in graves on French soil.[21]

In more modern times, recruits for the Swiss Guard in the Vatican have been single males with high school diplomas who have completed Swiss basic military training. The term of service may range from as few as two years to as many as twenty-five. The recruits pledge their readiness to give their lives for the protection of the reigning pope and the Sacred College of Cardinals when in session. The troopers are trained in the use of small arms currently in use by the Swiss Army, as well as an array of ceremonial weapons. The use of modern arms, as well as ceremonial equipment, is taken seriously in view of the attempted assassination of Pope John Paul II in 1981 and the murder of the commander of the Guard in 1998 by a member of the Guard itself. The murderer subsequently committed suicide.[22]

In the Middle East, one of the most famous foreign legions was that developed to ensure peace in the land to the east of the Jordan River, the largely barren territory that was home to transient tribes, but of no particular interest to the British or French governments. In 1920 the British high commissioner in Jerusalem authorized a British officer to form a "Trans-

Jordan Mobile Force" for patrol of key points in the region with troops from a native "legion." Later, when the friendly Arabian Amir Abdullah arrived in the capital, he brought an additional few hundred men to help protect the public roads in the region. Not long thereafter, the British formally recognized Abdullah's authority and increased their contribution to the "Arab Legion." The force would grow to include an RAF squadron and an armored car company.[23]

Tribal unrest flared up in 1926, and the Trans-Jordan Frontier Force was tasked with protecting the area's borders. The joint detachments were considered official units of the Crown on the British side, but they were really unequal to the job. Hostile elements in the region continued to exploit vulnerable targets.

A British officer, John Bagot Glubb, who had been assigned to the region early on, gradually rose in rank and stature until he gained an appointment with heft. He took command of all friendly forces. He knew the territory, spoke the language, and was of sufficient rank to demand respect from all other groups in the land. He knew the native Bedouins particularly well, and favored them with promotions and key assignments. His influence expanded as he brought the force strength up to some 1,600 men.[24]

In 1940, after the fall of France, the British General Wavell visited Trans-Jordan and was so impressed that he doubled the size of the mechanized force, under the title of "the Mechanized Regiment of the Arab Legion," even though the "Legion" was not much larger than a big battalion.

In April 1941 the pro-Nazi Arab leader, Rashid Ali, seized power in Iraq, laid siege to the RAF base at Habbaniyah, and threatened to invade Trans-Jordan. General Pasha quickly directed a preemptive strike toward Baghdad. Modest as the Allied force was, it approached the Iraqi capital within two weeks. By mid-May the British-led Jordanian Legion had control of the key fortress in the area and moved on to cross the Euphrates River, threatening Baghdad. But an armistice was declared, and attention turned to Syria. The officers of the British general staff were so impressed by the performance of the Arab Legion that they resolved to substantially reinforce the organization. Had the Free French not expressed objection to British operations in Syria, the Legion might have overrun the country and its capital.

Following the Allied invasion of Normandy in June 1944 the Mechanized Regiment might have been deployed to the Balkans, should the Allies have landed there. It was reequipped with heavier artillery for the operation, but as matters developed, the Germans were withdrawing from Greece, and the Arab Legion stood down. On May 25, 1946, Trans-Jordan became an independent state with King Abdullah I on the throne. The Legion took part in the celebration parade in the capital, and a contingent would be in London the following month for similar festivities. The common judgment was that the Legion had acquitted itself well under Glubb's leadership.

However, as time went on, the king was obliged to dismiss Glubb as an internal political act and to transform the Legion into an element of the official Army of Jordan.[25] Nevertheless, to this day, the Jordanian Army looks to Great Britain and its armed forces as good parents and friends in time of need. A high proportion of Jordanian officers are graduates of the British cadet school at Sandhurst, and "the old school tie" fits snugly.

In 1948 the Legion fought alongside other Arab forces in the first Arab-Israeli War. But the British government shied from responsibility and ordered all British officers to return to the east bank of the Jordan River. The embarrassment was keen as the officers were ordered by London to leave their units just as the troops were getting into battle. The remarkable spirit of the officers was made clear when they sneaked back to join their troops in the action, reportedly "to a man." Nevertheless, Glubb Pasha had lost utility in the Arabs' eyes, leading to his dismissal.

The "legions" of Czechoslovakia, and those identified with them in two World Wars, stand somewhat apart from those sharing most of the attention in this review. While in several instances the Czechs accepted recruits from other countries, or sources, such instances were more often the exception than the norm. As a relatively small European country, Czechoslovakia tended to be a provider rather than an employer of volunteers.

In 1914 a number of Czechs and Slovaks living in France formed an element of the French Foreign Legion, called "Nazdar," and they would later distinguish themselves in battle at Arras. About a thousand others in Russia formed a "Czech Fellowship," and assumed scouting and patrolling duties with the czarist forces. Their performance was of sufficient value to swing international respect favorably for the Czechoslovak National Council, led by Professor T. G. Masaryk in France.

In 1916 a Czechoslovakian legion was formed in Russia as part of a Finnish division, and it grew rapidly to about 50,000, to form an army corps. But as the number of volunteers grew, and as the communists gained power, many Czechs sought transfers to the Western Front in France to escape control of the expanding Red Army.[26]

At the same time, German operations in the east were gaining ground, and Lenin sought peace with Berlin to facilitate his destruction of the czarist forces. Masaryk, on the other hand, sought to bring the eastern Czechs to the west, via the trans-Siberian railway and then Vladivostok. With American aid and a deal with the communists which required leaving most of their weapons in Russia, the troops were finally withdrawn and shipped practically around the world to become part of the Allied forces in France.

Meanwhile, the third front, in Italy, also brought Czech units into action. In September 1918 six volunteer infantry and an artillery regiment were committed in the Dos Alto Mountains and around Lake Garda in the northern part of Italy.[27]

Some quarter-century earlier, Spain had formed a foreign legion which accepted both Spanish and foreign recruits. The multinational acceptance policy tended to restrain the number of foreign volunteers who could be accommodated. Historically, three-quarters of the Spanish Foreign Legion had been composed of Spanish citizens. The organization had been established in January 1920. Originally stationed in Morocco, early operations were aimed at the native Riff and their leader, Abd el-Krim. Operations were rough, cruel, and brave. It was reported that when Dictaroe General Primo de Rivera visited Morocco in 1925, he was appalled to find one battalion of the legion awaiting inspection with human heads stuck on their bayonets.[28]

That same year the Spanish legionnaires cooperated with French troops of similar backgrounds to destroy the native Riff in northern Africa. The Spanish attacked the enemy from the north while the French attacked from the south. Abd el-Krim was forced to surrender in the face of a well-timed and -directed operation. That settled, the legion was transferred to the homeland in 1934 and was used to subdue an insurrection by miners in the Asturian (northern) part of the country. After the outbreak of the Civil War in 1936, the troops were again back in home territory. It was clear that the "nationalists" couldn't win the war without the legion. General Francisco Franco, who would grasp the reins of power, made sure that they would get legion support.

Rather less well known than the European legions was the American Abraham Lincoln Brigade (of approximately battalion size), which joined others in Spain shortly before World War II on the side of the legitimate government—albeit a leftist and partially communistic one. The Spanish rightist revolutionaries, aided by Nazi Germany and Fascist Italy, were amply equipped and supplied to defeat the leftists in battles from 1936 to 1939. Germany was particularly generous in airlifting units of the Spanish Legion from North Africa to Spain and committing both fighter and bomber units along the combat frontiers. In addition, the Germans committed heavy anti-aircraft units wherever the legitimate Spanish government posed an air counterthreat. Italy was no less supportive of the rightist, counter-government forces, sending some 70,000 troops to work with the troops under General Francisco Franco.[29]

After the Fascist victory in the civil war, the Spanish Legion was back in Africa under Madrid's control, providing a balancing force to Moroccan banditry in the region. However, in April 1956 Spain agreed to withdraw from Morocco with the exception of Spanish Sahara and two or three small territories. Unfortunately, while the agreements might have quelled much of the conflict in the area, groups of Moroccan irregulars persisted in attacking key Spanish settlements. The region continued to be troublesome to both the Moroccan and Spanish governments.

The legion played an important part in the security of Spanish interests, especially in 1961 with the formation of an elite Spanish Foreign Legion Parachute Battalion. Some quarter of a million unarmed Moroccans took part in a "March of Conquest" in 1975 to recover part of the territory in question, but they stopped short of forcing confrontations with the legion. The following year the legion was pulled out. Since joining NATO, Spain has ceased accepting foreign recruits for its prized organization, and the name for the force has been changed to simply "the Spanish Legion." Its primary function in recent years has become that of an international force employed in conjunction with those of Western allies. In that capacity the legion has become a valuable element in disputes in Bosnia, Croatia, Angola, Haiti, El Salvador, and Guatemala. The current strength of the organization is estimated at about 10,000 troops.[30]

Sympathy in the United States for the Spanish leftists in the mid-1930s jelled into an active campaign to enlist volunteers to join the battles. Some 2,800 from all over the country signed up. Notably, the group included men and women with a wide range of religious beliefs, races, and capabilities. American communist organizations covered the costs of most of those who could not afford the transatlantic fare. The Americans would join another 37,900 international volunteers supporting the Republican cause.[31]

The first black man to lead an integrated American military force, Oliver Law, who took command of the legion for a time, would perish in battle against the Fascists. Those who followed him were obliged to disguise themselves as tourists because it was illegal for an American to fight in a foreign war. Such was not the case for the German and Italian supporters of the rightists, and there was no practical limit to their aid. Support from the Soviet Union was modest. In the spring of 1938 the Spanish prime minister, Juan Negrin, decided to withdraw all foreign soldiers from the war, and the government's fate was sealed. The Fascist government under General Franco took control of the country in 1939. Ernest Hemingway, a leftist sympathizer, would remark, "No men ever entered the earth more honorably than those who died in Spain."[32]

Almost three-quarters of a century later, a far more liberal government in Madrid would offer Spanish citizenship to all foreign survivors of the anti-Fascist ranks from any country. One of the honorees in 2009 was an American, Matti A. Mattson, ninety-two years of age, who had snuck into Spain in 1937, hiding in a shipment of wines from France. He would serve as an ambulance driver for the Republican side as one of 2,800 volunteers from the United States.[33]

Perhaps the most prominent American experience with a foreign legion was the institution of the Philippine Scouts in 1900. For the most part, its members were Filipino citizens enrolled in the US Army, but receiving less generous pay. They served under the command of American officers and a few Filipino graduates of the US Military Academy at West Point. In a notable exception to the classic pattern of foreign legions, the Scouts were limited by law to service in the Philippines. With the cessation of internal hostilities in 1919, the Philippine Scouts were grouped into three infantry and three field artillery regiments, and a single cavalry regiment. At the outbreak of World War II, the Scouts numbered about 11,000 men on active duty. They fought well, and after the final surrender of the Philippines in April 1942, many of those who could escaped to continue the fight as guerrillas.[34]

Another valuable American battle experience with foreign nationals developed in Southeast Asia, with the employment of captured enemy guerrilla fighters in the Vietnam War. Rather than incidentally exploiting prisoners, the "Kit Carson" program was designed to turn the loyalties of selected captive enemy volunteers, assigning them, in many cases, back to control of the units which first captured them. The US Ninth Infantry Division was particularly active in the undertaking, essentially adding a Vietnamese "Tiger Scout" (alternative term) to each infantry squad. A postwar analysis of the program held that "their guerilla skills, their local knowledge, familiarity with the local language, and their ability to communicate with the Vietnamese people made them invaluable." The "Scouts" suffered from an inability to speak English, but their performance was frequently credited in reports. In sum, they were "useful in softening these barriers," though they were not decisive.[35]

Thus we find that the concept of the foreign legion has been a broadly practiced, time-honored model for the organization, command, and control of military forces composed of troops from one or more foreign countries, under the leadership of a more powerful host state. While frequently focusing on a specific geographic area or region, and upon the interests of a central power, they have broadened the base for the undertaking of vital tasks and taken advantage, not only of the increased numbers of troops, but also of the skills which properly trained local peoples can bring to such an undertaking. In the first chapter we noted the difficulties involved in Middle Eastern combat in which the United States has unnecessarily deployed hundreds of thousands of American troops, civil affairs officials, and support personnel unfamiliar with the territory, languages, and peoples, where the battle may be fought in the homes of the populace. Many of those deployed from the United States have proven to be considerably less efficient than local counterparts might have been, had they been previously enlisted, trained, and oriented in the manner in which most international legionnaires are regularly trained.

The key, of course, is the regular enrollment of interested and capable foreign volunteers for the arduous training and regular service required for membership in a highly skilled and loyal force, with broad understanding of the purpose, capabilities, and advantages of service (such as American citizenship and settlement, if desired, in the United States) after a specified period of time. The following chapter offers a glimpse into the lives and challenges of volunteers for a renowned organization which can trace its history back to 1831.

First, however, we must clarify the legal status of the foreign legions and mercenary soldiers in the context of the laws of war. The employment of soldiers of one country by another is governed by the Additional Protocol of the Geneva Convention (APGC 77) of 12 August 1949 relating to the "Protection of Victims of International Armed Conflicts." Paragraph 2, article 47, "Mercenaries," reads, as stated previously, "A mercenary is any person who . . . is promised, by or on behalf of a Party to the conflict, material compensation substantially in excess of that promised to combatants of similar ranks and functions in the armed forces of that Party."[36] The employment of foreign troops at wages of US troops has not been a prominent development in US history. Compensation of cooperating forces of other countries has often been made by separate governmental agreements, but almost without exception on a scale clearly below the normal compensation provided to US troops. Accordingly, almost all foreign troops under American control are in no way associated with mercenary practices.

That is not to say that the United States has never contracted with any persons for the performance of military duties at rates higher than those paid to American soldiers. On the contrary, in the pursuit of its political and security objectives in the Middle East in the current century, the US government is known to have contracted with at least one civil firm for persons to fulfill just such duties. The company recently known as "Blackwater Worldwide" and "Blackwater USA," currently "Xe Worldwide," is believed to train more than 40,000 men and women per year for military services. At least 90 percent of the company's revenue comes from US government contracts, of which two-thirds is from no-bid contracts.[37] But this is not the kind of legion we would wish to suggest for a central role in fostering international peace in the name of the people of the United States. It may provide certain important services in bringing peace abroad, but its functions are not sufficiently defined to merit its substitution for full military unit deployment.

In April 2009 Blackwater Worldwide lost its contract with the US Department of State for protecting American diplomats. In some circles, Blackwater had come to represent American violence and impunity. An incident in downtown Baghdad in 2007, in which an apparently unprovoked shooting resulted in the deaths of seventeen civilians, appeared to be the key cause of the cancellation of Blackwater's employment contract. The firm was quickly replaced by another organization, Triple Canopy, which assumed virtually all of the tasks connected with State Department security in Iraq. A sizable number of Blackwater's field employment team were quickly hired on by the Triple Canopy to fulfill the protective requirements.[38]

Two reporters for the *New York Times* did their best to report the extent of questionable behavior of the former Blackwater company. In early September 2010 they wrote that the company had created a web of more than thirty "shell" firms, in part to obtain millions of dollars in government contracts after the parent firm fell under suspicion of unethical practices with the federal government.[39] Since 2001, Blackwater is believed to have received up to six hundred million dollars in questionable contracts. In addition, the US Congress has shown an increased level of concern with an associated company, Paravant, which has employees known to have killed two Afghans in connection with a contract. Some contractors appear to have adopted postures not very different from those of mercenary troops in earlier centuries.

But this is not the sort of "army" that the United States would want to field in its wars, either now or in the future. In July 2009 two West Point professors offered their views in an article, "Contractors on the Battlefield and Our Professional Military Ethic." They pointed out that

> [o]ver the last eight years of fighting in the Central Command area of responsibility, contract employees have played a vital role in supporting our vital interests. Many aspects of a sustained campaign simply cannot be accomplished without them. . . .
>
> There seems to be little debate that some support functions—food services, logistics, maintenance support and training—can and should be contracted out. The use of contract linguists, very often native speakers, also logically seems necessary because of the time it takes to develop such a high level of fluency. The private security contractors who especially come into question [are] those who must carry weapons to fulfill the requirements of their contract. . . . The all-volunteer force competes with private contractors for high quality recruits. The military's ability to retain its trained and experienced soldiers is clearly influenced by them, working side by side with contractors—usually for far less money. . . . By their very nature, however, the two differ in their outlook and ethical approach to their mission. The military's professional culture is firmly grounded in selfless service to the nation. Although individual contractors and many companies' cultures express patriotism, a contracting firm's work ethic is primarily rooted in profit. When military service members and contractors serve together in the far reaches of the world, these differing cultures often clash, resulting in "cultural" tensions that can challenge the professional military ethic. . . . Most contractors cannot and will not involuntarily work in a 24/7 context unless so stipulated in their contract.[40]

Another exceptional case is that of US State Department foreign national employees, nonmilitary personnel, employed to defend five specific compounds being vacated by departing American military soldiers, or to provide "quick reaction forces" to rescue civilians in trouble. The last US combat brigade reportedly departed Iraq the third week of August 2010. Remaining troops, reportedly 56,000, are expected to return to the United States, but no specific dates have been disclosed. Further, the remaining guards are expected to be equipped with sixty mine-resistant vehicles and to expand their fleet of armored cars to 1,320 and their aircraft to 29.[41]

Contract technicians do not compose the kind of legion we would wish to suggest for a central role in fostering international peace in the name of the people of the United States. They may provide certain important services for the overall effort to bring peace abroad, but their functions are not sufficiently broad to merit their substitution for full military unit deployment.

In following chapters the reader will be acquainted with areas of the world where the organization and deployment of local military units with carefully selected and thoroughly trained natives may be developed under the supervision of American officers for the stabilization and benefit of all countries involved.

5

The Survivor: The French Foreign Legion

Up to this point we have examined the nature of the conflicts we face, our manner of dealing with them over the last decade or so, and the experiences of a number of other powers throughout history—especially those which have found utility in the formation of foreign legions. Of the existing countries we have noted, one in particular stands out: France. The French Foreign Legion is undoubtedly the best known, worldwide, of those still in operation. While many of the legions of which we have taken note provide a degree of insight on America's security challenges in coming years, none appear to have had the breadth of experience and the modern capabilities of the French organization.

All of these legions stem from conditions peculiar or pertinent to their day, but it can be valuable to review the past when the path ahead is unclear. History tends to suggest likely trails if the analyst is sensitive enough to recognize the lessons of experience. The United States' problem today is to shape and equip itself to deal with the trials still on its "to do" list. What must be done first?

Clearly, the first chore is to define the country's problems so we may focus on the best way, or ways, to solve them. As many have noted in the Middle East, religious influences may range from mild to virtually dominating in some countries. Again, the concentration of critical territories falls well within the borders suggested by Dr. Thomas Barnett's *New Pentagon Map*.

As we have seen, the search and maintenance of empire was often the premiere driver of competitive nations in the first twenty centuries following the foundation of Christianity. To some degree, it still has relevance today. We simply tend to think of the problems in different ways. But, as in the past, international competition continues to focus on economic,

61

political, and cultural factors. Religious factors may range from slightly influential to virtually dominating in some eastern countries.

As may be readily noted, with the exception of border and immigration troubles, few of the problems in the United States are "here" (within the country). Most of them follow the World War I marching song, "Over There!" The big difference appears to be that "over there" is quite different today than it was in 1917. Islamic teachings have come to cut a wide swath over one hundred thousand miles across, mostly in Africa and Asia. And it was not difficult for President George W. Bush to rationalize attacks on Iraq, Afghanistan, and parts of Pakistan in return for terrorist-style aircraft crashes on buildings in our homeland. Nor is the United States entirely inexperienced in the seizure of foreign lands which we believed we could manage better than the natives. Panama, Cuba, and the Philippines have all flown the Stars and Stripes without full explanation to the inhabitants.

Rudyard Kipling clearly had his fellow countrymen in mind when he wrote his unforgettable "Recessional" in 1897. But in our extended position, so far in the twenty-first century, we would do well to keep a marker in the books as we pursue our expansive policies.

> God of our fathers, known of old
> Lord of our far-flung battle line,
> Beneath whose awful hand we hold
> Dominion over palm and pine . . .
> Far-called our navies melt away
> On dune and headline sinks the fire:
> Lo, all our pomp of yesterday
> Is one with Nineveh and Tyre![1]

We know what happened in those empires. Many of our military problems today stem from a lack of national comprehension of our situation. The answer to the question of how far we ought to go to achieve "success" continues to escape us. We may still be shocked by the tenacity of some of our foes (and the peculiar misbehavior of some of our highest-ranking military officers and their staffs), but, for the most part, nationwide, we still expect a higher level of satisfaction from our ventures in the Middle East than simple force withdrawal in 2011 and 2012. In any event, there is no guarantee that our enemies will adjust their planning strictly according to our announced troop withdrawal charts. Their operations may be influenced by other factors quite beyond our calculations.

As for the rest of the more troublesome regions, we have at least the guidance offered in Thomas Barnett's definition of the "functioning core" (where things run more or less rationally). He also highlights the "nonintegrating gap," where most of the problems of international security lie. While the 2001 aircraft crashes into the Twin Towers in New York and the Pentagon in Washington, DC, grabbed the nation's attention, most of the subsequent action was "over there." A big difference appears to be that "over there" is somewhat more distant now than it was in 1917, and solutions do not seem to jell as quickly as they have in the past. The battles may be smaller, but we are less satisfied with a decade of conflict in the Middle East than we were in the two World Wars in shorter periods.

International competition today continues to be driven by many of the same factors as of old: economic, political, cultural, and religious gain. And conflict over territory is as common now as it has been in ages past, and not necessarily between neighboring states. Terrorist attacks have been executed across a wide stretch of targets, from southern Africa and the eastern Mediterranean to cities in a score of European countries. Certainly, the current enemy actions in the Middle East have been more tactical and somewhat vaguer (less specific) than those of the Axis powers in 1941, the North Koreans in 1950, or even the North Vietnamese in 1965.

A principal difference today is that there is substantial interest and extensive international machinery (the UN, World Bank, NATO, etc.), all of which tend to dampen nascent drives for unilateral gain. Further, there is the existence of a global leading democratic superpower—the United States of America. While the United States does not aspire to become "the policeman of the world"—witness its fleeting determination to prevail in Vietnam—it still has unique interests and capabilities which tend to urge it into a leading position in the face of international disputes, particularly those involving radical changes in established governments, racial or religious disharmony, or sharp economic shifts threatening American or other Western interests. Hence, again we must note the cogency of the subtitle of this book: "The Responsibility of Power."

As far as we can tell, the United States faces no government like that in Berlin, Tokyo, or Hanoi that has been calling the shots. For the most part, enemy operations (bombs and terrorist shootings) rely on the skills of self-appointed malcontents in Afghanistan, Pakistan, Iraq, or some other troubled area. We do not feel we are doing as well as we were in earlier years against more conventional foes, leaving our national expectations unmet. Under current circumstances, we cannot see the end very clearly, and we do not anticipate participation in a grand peace conference at a measurable point in the enemy's fallen "capital." Settlements nowadays are more likely to be made off-line, or still more simply by the disappearance of the enemy.

In this context, it is not unusual for the United States to intervene in foreign disputes, especially armed conflicts, including in areas of the world in which it has little more than a modest interest or understanding. And this may be undertaken, not for conquest or empire, but often simply as revenge for a hostile act, or in an effort to prevent current events from spreading, or to alleviate the suffering of an underdog. Most campaigns may be considered successful if they stem from foreign aggression and can be concluded with dispatch. Unfortunately, America's wars in the twenty-first century have not clearly met either condition. Nor does the record offer great promise for improvement in the near future.

On October 12, 2009, the *Washington Post* reported that the United States had suffered 4,352 fatalities in Iraq. Three months later it posted the news that another 942 soldiers had been killed in Afghanistan. Our committed troop levels at the time were running at about 183,000.[2]

Looking back, we have to note that the Korean War was a draw, while Vietnam was a loss. Panama ("Just Cause") was a great success, while our Battle of Mogadishu ("Blackhawk Down," 1993) was a disaster. Our current wars in the Middle East have passed the half-decade mark, with the commitment of hundreds of thousands of troops, and are still cloaked in considerable doubt about how much longer they may continue. The costs in American military dead, wounded, and missing have been measured in tens of thousands while the costs in dollars run into the trillions. Overall, considerable doubt remains about the resolvability of our Middle East venture.

As a matter of course, we have undertaken studies of why we have not done better in these conflicts, and multiple reasons have been identified—but not with sufficient confidence that we can be assured of success in the future. In particular, we have not developed confidence that we have discovered new ways of dealing with these sorts of conflicts which would allow us to reshape our military assets to facilitate early victories in the future. While it may be true that we have now developed thousands of officers and noncommissioned officers with experience in Iraq and Afghanistan, next time the battle may be somewhere else, and unless we return to the present battlefields within a few years, we are liable to find that the regionally experienced leaders are evaporating assets. They may simply retire or die. And the next battle may be in the Congo, or maybe Zamboanga. (We have been there before, but not in strength since 1914.)

Of course, there are other factors. An important one is the question of comparative military skills. Those we associate with special forces units (parachuting, survival, stealth, intelligence gathering, clandestine movement, killing, etc.) stand out. Of the units we have reviewed, none seem especially pertinent. For that we must examine one more: the French Foreign Legion. And, notably, this is one of few such organizations yet surviving, but with notable history and notoriety. It merits special investigation.

A prominent military historian has provided us with a nineteenth-century eyewitness description of the organization as "a solid troop; maneuverable, admirably practiced in shooting and marching, and entirely in the hands of its leaders. The men obey, not with submission, but with spirit and assiduity. One might say that the constant exercise of the will of the leader works on them like a hypnotic suggestion. One sees in the eyes of the soldiers that they are attentive to orders, proud to maneuver well, and conscious of their worth. It is superfluous to dwell upon the amount of work one must require of the instructors to obtain this result. They carry it out with zeal, even fanaticism, in the expectation of campaigning with the men that they prepared for this end."[3]

In the view of the author of the book in which the above quotation appeared (Douglas Porch), the words may have been undeserved, but they were presented in acknowledgment of the popularity of the concept. Porch also wrote, "The Legion forms an important part of France's military self-image, but not a central part. The Legion does not so much run against the current of history; it defies it."[4] Whatever he meant by that, one should note that a significant practice in the legion, not to be noted in other military organizations, is that of the "sacred" code of anonymity. For first-term recruits, no communication with home or loved ones may be permitted. On the other hand, any man who wishes to "disappear" may assume a different identity for as long as he pleases, provided he does as he is told.[5]

A more recent writer, Howard Simpson, leaves his readers with a rather different, and somewhat more sympathetic, impression. His volume lends greater focus to a particular branch of the Legion—the paratroopers. These are men between seventeen and forty years of age, routinely subjected to a three-week selection process. The induction procedure compares favorably with those used to ensure the selection of capable men by the US Armed Forces, involving IQ tests and physical, psychological, and security examinations. From there the legion aspirant is subjected to sixteen weeks' training "designed to turn him into a combat soldier." The process culminates in a five-day exercise or raid involving "a march of seventy-five miles or more, with heavy packs over rough country in freezing winter weather or hot summer conditions." This last test includes river and gorge crossings, night movements, and live-fire combat exercises.[6]

Thereafter the legionnaire receives his regimental assignment, which may be in one of the countries linked to France by a post-colonial defense agreement. This might be the Central African Republic of Chad or Lebanon, Somalia, Gabon, or Bosnia. A Bosnia assignment might find him as part of the international force, IFOR, in the former Yugoslavia, dealing with peacekeeping duties with NATO countries and Russia.[7] Other possibilities are Camp Raffalli on Corsica for airborne training or helicopter assault practice. Still others are French Guiana in South America, or French Polynesia in the South Pacific. Whatever it is, each man is fully tested in his profession by exercises or actual combat.

A recent review of the current French Foreign Legion notes that the popular vision of the organization, typified in the past by heroic drama—"Beau Geste" or "March and Die"—are no longer fitting. Its troops are more likely to be recruited on the Internet, and more likely to find themselves securing the sewers in Nice against terrorist bomb plots than chasing natives on camelback across the deserts of Africa.[8]

Economic necessity is the principal incentive for most legion recruits in the twenty-first century, and the native languages range from Asian (Chinese, Korean, or Japanese) to European (Spanish or Romanian). Typically, the young men represent some twenty-one different countries. Language training is clearly no less important than physical conditioning. After four months, recruits are expected to have learned some four hundred to six hundred French words—considered the minimum to hold one's own on a battlefield or at the mess table with one's contemporaries.[9]

John Robert Young writes that "the Legion has overcome a major teaching problem in communicating to a group of recruits who may, among them, speak ten or more different languages. The teacher uses a system of simple pictures, making his students repeat the French words for the images and objects until they get it right. Sometimes it is a slow process—but reportedly, it works."[10]

Legionnaires nowadays serve side-by-side with French police and army troops patrolling train stations and airports as part of counter-terrorism efforts. Assignments abroad, in addition to those noted, may be to Afghanistan or the Ivory Coast, among others. Notably, they all go abroad under the same set of regulations. And they all must surrender their civilian identity documents and assume false names.[11]

Their "code of honor" is pitched at a high level. To summarize typical points:

Each legionnaire is your brother;
You must respect traditions;
You are proud of being a legionnaire;
You are an elite soldier, your weapon is your most precious possession;
Your mission is sacred;
You act in combat without passion or hatred;
You respect vanquished enemies;
You never surrender your dead or wounded.[12]

In his sixth chapter Howard Simpson, one of the most recent assessors of legion airborne operations, describes "the elite of the elite," the commissioned and noncommissioned officers of the Commandos de Recherche et d'Action dans le Profondeur (with the unfortunate English acronym "CRAP"). They have qualified for free-fall jumping with last-minute manual parachute opening.[13] No one below the rank of corporal is permitted. Each parachute regiment of the legion has had one or more of such advanced teams since 1970, while the parachute regiments of the regular French Army have acquired them only since 1980. Even the Direction General de la Securite Exterieure (DGSE—the French equivalent of the United States' CIA) often turns to the legion for its serious clandestine parachute penetrations.

As the author points out, the commandos of the select legion parachute units tend to be more mature than those of the average legion unit. Many of them come from NATO countries— Italy, Spain, Great Britain, Germany, and the United States. The author notes that their operational interdependence as commandos appears to erase the barriers of rank without affecting efficiency. Their missions stretch from intelligence collection to the destruction of specific targets, the establishment of security within hostile communities or units, or the seizure or liberation of important figures.[14]

Americans are not present in the legion in large numbers. The author reported having been told that some ten to twenty Americans enlisted in the legion each year, but they were not in obvious abundance during his visit. Legion statistics reported that some two hundred enlisted in the legion during the four years of the First World War. One factor that may inhibit enlistment is the assignment restrictions of men with less than five years service. However, once the five years are done, a wife may be absorbed into the legion's "family," with assigned quarters, medical support, and an understanding community. All married commissioned and noncommissioned officers are assigned quarters as they are absorbed into the military community around the unit bases.[15]

Under the rubric "honneur et fidélité," one author, whose work most easily touches the heart of the legionnaires, has written that "the Legion reflects the natural character of France." But, more specifically, his paragraphs come closer to stinging the eyes when he relates such stories as that of the wife of a British consul in a remote corner of Africa who found solace in a stressful time with the proximity of a legion detachment. "It is a great relief," she is reported to have remarked, "to know that a Foreign Legion (detachment is) just down the road."[16]

Legion recruiting literature makes a broad appeal to potential enlistees. In mid-2008 it read, "Whatever your social or professional status might be, whether you are married or single, the French Foreign Legion offers you a chance to start a new life. . . . Join the 7,699 legionnaires and noncommissioned officers hailing from 136 different countries, including France. Build yourself an exceptional future in which 'honor' and 'fidelity' are fundamental values." It went on: "By joining the French Foreign Legion, one is sure to be part of the news that makes the headlines either in France on maneuvers, or on external operations in French territories abroad . . . (French Guyana, New Caledonia, Mayotte, la Reunion, the French West Indies)." And "Whether restoring or keeping the peace, or exercising crowd control, the Legion has been able to adapt to all situations in all theaters of conflict (the Gulf War of 1990–1991; Kampuchea and Somalia in 1992–1993; Bosnia, Kosovo, and Macedonia in 1993–2003; Central African Republic in 1996. . . .) Today, the legionnaires are engaged in Afghanistan, Kosovo, Chad, the Ivory Coast and anywhere else they might be needed by France."[17]

The seven articles of the code of honor in the legion are specific and demanding:

1. Legionnaire: You are a volunteer serving France with honor and fidelity.
2. Every legionnaire is your brother-in-arms whatever his nationality, his race or his religion might be. You will demonstrate this by the strict solidarity which must always unite members of the same family.

3. Respectful of traditions, devoted to your leaders, discipline and comrade-
   ship are your strengths, courage and loyalty are your virtues.
4. Proud of your status as a legionnaire, you display this in your uniform
   which is always impeccable, your behavior always dignified but modest,
   your living quarters always clean.
5. An elite soldier, you will train rigorously, you will maintain your weapon
   as your most precious possession, you are constantly concerned with your
   physical form.
6. A mission is sacred, you will carry it out until the end, at all costs.
7. In combat, you will act without passion and without hate, you will respect
   the vanquished enemy, you will never abandon your dead or wounded, nor
   surrender your arms.[18]

Significantly, the French Foreign Legion maintains close professional
connections with other Western forces around the world, especially with
the US Army. At this writing the French Legion has a professional officer,
Lieutenant Colonel Philippe Chabot, assigned to the faculty of the US Army
Infantry Center at Ft. Benning, Georgia. He is an officer of keen intellect and
deep understanding of both US and French military doctrine and objectives. The interchange of such high-quality officers between the two armies
greatly enhances the understanding between them, especially between special forces on the US side and the French Foreign Legion, deployed, as it is,
around the globe.[19]

French Legion historical experiences and current US operations may have
some similarities in the size and doctrine of opposing forces. Typical in
both cases has been the irregularity of most operations on both sides. The
maneuvers of large enemy forces, à la Verdun and Stalingrad, are clearly
out of fashion, or at least beyond the capabilities of most anti-Western
forces today. Counter-terror operations, on the other hand, have developed
as common experiences for both the United States and the forces of other
recognized governments.

Hence, we have seen the emergence of terrorism as a preferred tactic, or
strategy, of "red" (opposing) forces. Just as the United States has learned
that its own commercial aircraft can be converted to weapons of terror
(such as on 9/11), it has also learned that its own regular forces on foreign
territory require situational training for dealing with native troops in operational areas—both friendly and not-so-friendly. Henceforth, "terrorism"
will be a major topic for study and exploration by US tactical and strategic
military colleges of all land, sea, and air branches.

6

Where to Begin? And Then What?

Early in 2009, writing in *Foreign Affairs*, Bennett Ramberg delivered a cogent review of US precedents and commentary regarding the withdrawal of forces from active theaters of operations. The span of his investigation stretched from Vietnam in the 1960s to Iraq in 2009, as we approached yet another attempt to reduce our involvement in foreign hostilities in a new decade. He quoted President Lyndon Johnson bemoaning his dilemma between "running out of Southeast Asia" and promoting "trouble in every part of the globe—not just in Asia but in the Middle East, in Europe, in Africa and in Latin America." So concerned was Johnson that a retreat would open a path to World War III, Ramberg wrote, that the US would eventually sustain over 53,000 troop fatalities before it could write off the Vietnam War as not worth the candle. The United States held on until 1972 before withdrawing all American troops. The South Vietnamese government stood essentially alone for another two years before it crumbled.[1]

More cogent with respect to Iraq early in the twenty-first century, Ramberg suggested, was the case of US intervention in Lebanon several decades earlier. The land had been torn apart by an array of different domestic interests since 1975, with Syria a partial player. In 1982 Israeli forces invaded in an attempt to oust the Palestine Liberation Organization (PLO), adding yet another ingredient to a boiling kettle. The Reagan administration in Washington sought to settle the imbroglio with the cooperation of French and Italian forces. That just made things worse. Syrian agents assassinated Bashir Gemayel, the Lebanese president. With their principal Lebanese ally dead, the Israeli forces pressed on into Beirut and transported cooperating Lebanese militia men into the Sabra and Shatila refugee camps where PLO fighters were known to have taken refuge. The carnage was so sickening that

President Reagan ordered US troops to help the Lebanese government re-store stability. But, instead of a peacemaking force, the Americans had come to be regarded as just another militia without a clear mission.[2]

The utility of the American forces lessened as casualties continued to mount. Ultimately, the loss of a number of US aircraft and of 241 American troops in a truck bombing of a Marine barracks undermined American determination and prompted overwhelming popular pressure for with-drawal. On February 7, 1984, President Reagan ordered US forces out. As the deputy national security advisor, John Poindexter, ungraciously told reporters, "the immediate fighting in the streets of Beirut is a problem for the government of Lebanon and the Lebanese armed forces to control."[3]

The fighting would go on for another six years, and no real stability was gained until after the 2006 Israeli-Hezbollah war. Ramberg drew a paral-lel between the problems the United States faced in that war and those it would encounter in Iraq from 2003 forward. Then he cited the conclusion drawn by the Reagan administration at the time: "cutting losses is better than staying the course."

Ramberg summarized his observations in the following way: "When the mounting U.S. casualties started to appear needless, when the policymakers failed to identify vital national interests that an on-the-ground presence would protect, and when no clear strategy emerged—Washington called it quits." Further, he commented, "Despite much foreboding, the United States' exits in these examples better served its interests than soldiering on would have."[4]

Ramberg's other case was that of Western, especially US, intervention in Somalia on the eastern Horn of Africa in 1993. Some 350,000 inhabitants, including one-quarter of those under five years of age, had died from civil strife and famine. Another million and a half were in danger of following their kinsmen to the grave. Eight hundred thousand were without shelter. Warlords ruled the land. Only US intervention, providing food and 25,000 troops, along with half as many more from over two dozen other countries, could bring any stability. With a taste of success, another 4,000 troops from other countries, and a reduction in American military hands by 50 percent, it was presumed that peace might return to the Horn of Africa.

Hardly. Anarchy quickly returned. Local militias slaughtered twenty-four Pakistani peacekeepers distributing food to the population. The United States mounted a helicopter-borne attempt at retaliation, only to encounter frightful street-by-street resistance, including the dragging of dead American soldiers from downed helicopters through the alleyways. The events would come to be known by a published rendition of the con-flict, *Blackhawk Down.*[5] Our premiere battle helicopter had been brought down by kids with Kalashnikovs.

With these experiences in the background, Bennett Ramberg raises the imminent question of recent, turn-of-the-decade US policy toward Iraq. "It could have stuck to the agreed timetable and [left] in 2011 . . . or it could have withdrawn much sooner. . . . On the one hand, a modern adaptation of Nixon's 'peace with honor' formula would try to save the United States' reputation by prolonging its stay, spending more blood and treasure, and wagering that Iraqization would outperform Vietnamization. On the other hand, Washington could swallow its pride and follow the lessons of Vietnam, Cambodia, Lebanon, and Somalia: 'Where internal political dysfunction overwhelms external attempts at stabilization, getting out sooner rather than later is the United States' best chance to protect its interests.'"[6]

Not far from Ramberg's argument we find the opinion of a seasoned diplomat, Ambassador Ryan C. Crocker, US representative to Iraq until January 2009. Before his departure, he remarked publicly that the planned withdrawal of American troops ran "some very serious risks," from the resurgence of the insurgent group Al Qaeda in Iraq, to a collapse of faith in a nascent Iraqi state that still faces what he called "enormous challenges."

"A loss of confidence," he said, could create a "chilling effect" causing people to "pull back, dig the trenches, build the berms and get ready for what comes next." He denied having said that such events would happen— only that they could happen. He chose terms such as "still fragile" and "still reversible" to describe the country he was leaving.[7]

The announced presidential goal for American troop withdrawal has been nineteen months (from 1 January 2009), which would have placed the point of initiation of the action sometime in mid-summer 2010; but not long after assuming office, President Obama stretched the target to the end of 2011. Notably, many reporters have mentioned the possibility of retaining a number of troops for special purposes beyond the specifics supported by both the US and Iraqi governments.

Another prominent journalist in the Washington, DC, Center for Strategic and International Studies (CSIS) has pointed out that since World War II all but one insurgency, worldwide, have concluded in victory for the insurgents. He cited the French in Indo-China and Algeria, the United States in Vietnam, the Marxist-led FARC in Colombia, and the Hukbalahaps in the Philippines, who fought both the Americans and their own government, and later the Japanese. He also named Afghan tribal elements which fought the Russians for nine years—and won. Now, he points out, the Taliban groups have been fighting the United States and its allies for five years or more, and in his view an allied victory is less likely than at any time in the past.[8]

The facts in the matter are not reassuring. Whatever historical parallels may suggest, another major troublesome factor cannot be concealed: simple theft—especially of oil. The vital Sunni refinery on the Tigris River in north-central Iraq yields up to one-third of its products to black market operations. As Richard Oppel has reported in the *New York Times*, "Tankers are hijacked, drivers are bribed, papers and meters are manipulated—and some of the earnings go to insurgents who are killing more than 100 countrymen in a week."[9]

And perhaps an even greater "troublesome factor" identified by two Washington analysts is that

> some key political players, strengthened by Iraq's enormous recent progress, are less interested in moving their country forward than in using every tool at their disposal to put themselves in advantageous positions after the American withdrawal. Worse still, some—perhaps many—are doing so by exploiting the immaturity of the political process and the ambiguities in Iraq's constitution.
>
> [Further,] Iraq has several important challenges that could strain its political system over the next year. They include the return of up to four million displaced people to their homes; the release of thousands of people detained by coalition forces, some of them surely dangerous; and the continued search for permanent jobs for the largely Sunni Sons of Iraq, whose actions against the insurgents in Anbar Province were a key to the success of the "surge"; falling oil prices that will hamper the government's ability to pay its workers; and the more general tasks of increasing oil exports, employment and quality of life for the Iraqis.
>
> Perhaps the most vivid demonstration of the problems Iraq faces is the enormous tension brewing between the autonomous Kurdistan Regional Government, led by Massoud Barzani, and the central government led by Prime Minister Nuri Kamal al-Maliki. During the years of warfare between Sunni and Shiite Arabs, the Kurdish issue lay dormant. But now it has roared back to the forefront. Nearly everyone we spoke with, Kurds, Arabs, Americans and others—described the situation as explosive and the enmity between Mr. Barzani and Prime Minister Maliki as ferocious.
>
> The Kurdish difficulties do not revolve around suicide bombers, visions of seventh-century caliphates, disdain for the United States or pure sectarian hatred as in Sunni-Shiite civil war. They concern the cold, hard issues of land and oil and cash, as well as the distribution of power between Iraq's center and its regions and provinces.[10]

With respect to Afghanistan, Dr. Henry Kissinger weighed in with the view that the United States could not withdraw, nor could it sustain the strategy that it had pursued up to that point. He saw the stakes as very high. Victory for the Taliban in Afghanistan, in his view, "would [have given] a tremendous shot in the arm to jihadism globally." He argued that America had pursued traditional anti-insurgency to create a central government. But that approach, he wrote, could not succeed in Afghanistan. No foreign conqueror had ever succeeded in occupying Afghanistan. "The country is too large, the territory too forbidding, the ethnic composition too varied, the population too heavily armed." The economy has been sustained through the sale of narcotics. There is no significant democratic tradition. His prescription for Afghanistan was a military strategy concentrating on preventing the emergence of a coherent, contiguous state within the state controlled by the jihadists. In practice, he suggested, this would mean control of Kabul and the Pashtun area. The emergence of a jihadist base on both sides of the mountainous Afghan-Pakistan border, he warned, would be a permanent threat to hopes for a moderate evolution and to all of Afghanistan's neighbors.[11]

The Taliban has a relatively safe base in Pakistan just as the North Vietnamese did in the north and the west (Laos and Cambodia) during their war with the United States. While the Pakistani Army has some 120,000 troops based in its seven federally administered tribal areas (FATA) along the 400-mile Afghan border, the local Pashtun population is sympathetic to the Taliban and Al Qaeda. The US government estimated that 84 percent of all containerized cargo and 40 percent of all fuel for American coalition forces operating in Afghanistan passes through either Pakistan, via the Khyber Pass, or Kabul, through Baluchistan or Kandahar. Just how unstable is Pakistan?

William Dalrymple writes about Pakistan with a sharp pen, and with such powerful strokes that he leaves little oxygen for his readers. He writes of "the catastrophe that is rapidly overwhelming Western interests in the part of the world that always should have been the focus of America's response to September 11: the al Qaeda and Taliban heartlands on either side of the border of Afghanistan and Pakistan." And "the situation could hardly be more grim. The Taliban have reorganized," he argues, "advanced out of their borderland safe havens and are now massing at the gates of Kabul."[12]

> The Taliban already controls over 70 percent of the country, up from just over 50 percent in November 2007, where they collect taxes, enforce Sharia law, and dispense their usual rough justice. . . . In less than eight months, as if Ali Zardari's new government has effectively lost control of much of the North-West Frontier Province to the Taliban's Pakistani counterparts. . . . Afghanistan is once again staring down the abyss of state collapse, despite billions of dollars in aid, forty-five thousand Western troops, and the deaths of thousands of people. The Taliban have made a dramatic comeback. . . . The international community had an extended window of opportunity for several years to help the Afghan people—they failed to take advantage of it.[13]

Typical of the overall situation was a strike by the Taliban in December 2008 with a car bomb on a school in Shalbandi at which people were lined up to vote in an election for the National Assembly. More than thirty people were killed and some two dozen wounded. A government spokesman claimed that the attack was a result of local resistance to Taliban orders by the populace. However, the head of the Awami National Party, Afrasiab Khattak, commented that "disrupting elections is a general strategy for these elements."[14]

Less than a month later, fierce fighting broke out with a Taliban attack on a Pakistani paramilitary outpost in the Mohammand district, west of Shalbandi. The action took on a multi-dimension aspect as Afghan Taliban Sunni gangs sought out opposing Shia gangs in the Hangu District, forty to fifty miles inside Afghanistan.

Clearly, the message from the most knowledgeable observers is that Iraq is a possible escapee from Al Qaeda or other extremist Islamic control, but matters are more serious in northwestern Pakistan. Unless the Karachi government can establish control over its Afghan border provinces it cannot govern all of its territory.

If the United States wishes to withdraw a significant number of its forces from the area, it is apparent that either large numbers of UN, NATO, or other forces will be required to replace them, or some other formula must be developed. While the international contingents have been helpful, there is little evidence that reinforcements from other countries would be able to cope with the Islamic fundamentalist forces that have been noted so far, or even that other nations would be interested in filling in for departing American elements. The conditions appear to be ripe for another solution: gradual replacement of existing US and other forces by carefully recruited, well trained, American legionary forces, composed of indigenous volunteers under the command and control of American commissioned and noncommissioned officers. While infantry units may dominate the rolls initially, over time, the forces should be tailored for the specific challenges and circumstances of the type which we have noted in our study.

It seems likely that significant numbers of indigenous recruits might be raised primarily through appeal to youths interested in bettering conditions in their land, as well as by the payment of somewhat higher salaries than they might otherwise expect in pursuit of their regular trades. But before this happens, Afghanistan either has to straighten itself out or look for another strategy.

In April 2009 the *New York Times* reported that senior officers of the US Army in Afghanistan were seeking volunteer Afghan fighters in the country's Wardak Province to take up arms against the Taliban terrorist organization. The United States had found considerable receptivity among certain Iraqi groups in their country, and hoped that a similar program could be developed in the east. The Afghan national army was disinclined to venture far into the area, and it was hoped that men from local indigenous groups, Tajiks and Hazaras, could have greater success in Wardak Province than the government in Kabul.

But the signals have been mixed. The previous month one local Taliban leader had come forward with ten of his men to surrender to the government, but shortly thereafter he and his wife, his brother, his uncle, and his daughter were found murdered. Clearly Afghanistan is different from Iraq and is a patchwork of different (and apparently dynamic) loyalties. An American officer commented that he didn't think the Afghans "even know what side they are on."[15]

Let us look again at the legion model, especially for Afghanistan. First, locals signing up for the American Foreign Legion would not just learn a secret handshake. They would disappear. No one outside the US government would know where they went. If terrorists sought revenge through the infliction of punishment on other members of the family, the recruit would be unlikely to know it. He may know his kinsfolk's address and attempt to sneak out a message or two sometime in his first year of service (itself an expulsive offense), but he would be closely monitored and have no return address at which he could be reached. All suspicious mail would be funneled through the US staffed legion headquarters.

And the counter-motivation built into the system would be large: likely the offer of US citizenship after a period of service (five or six years). As we have noted, some 110,000 foreign persons receive green card documents for residency each year. It would be reasonable to grant a similar number of such documents to veterans of American-led foreign legions worldwide, especially under circumstances amounting to honorable service under combat conditions, wherever such recruits could earn credits by taking the place of American troops.

Notably, President Obama himself has pointed out the successful separation of many Iraqi insurgents from the hard-core elements of Al Qaeda in Mesopotamia, venturing that "there may be some comparable opportunities in Afghanistan and in the Pakistani [frontier] region."[18] Such moves would mesh well with an effort to enlist regional natives into US-led formations dedicated to the protection of peoples of all stripes. While certain ideological differences may suggest particular organizational and deployment practices, such as the assignment of enlistees of particular faiths to compatible units and districts, the central direction of all such forces should ensure that interfaith problems (e.g., Sunni vs. Shia Islamics) be minimized. It also suggests that it would be wise to seek out suitable, flexible religious figures (e.g., Islamic chaplains) to strengthen the bonds between the overall mission and the volunteers.

A number of Afghan and Pakistani experts have weighed in at high levels regarding American policy in the various conflict regions. One, Reuben Brigety, a specialist on Afghanistan at the Center for American Progress, has remarked, "It is clear that you have to have a political solution to Afghanistan, and I wouldn't rule anything off the table, including conversations with some aspects of the Taliban."[19] Such opinions can be insightful, and helpful at the strategic level, but they should not interfere with the more immediate problem of providing adequate military force in the theater as scheduled American troop withdrawals are undertaken. There must be a provision for adequate residual force under US control upon the initiation of US troop drawdown.

That is not to say that US soldiers, or units, should be replaced by legionnaires on a one-for-one basis, or even one for ten. The principle should be to seek a way to maintain necessary security over time. Natives born to the language, the culture, and the geography possess skills of military value useful to Western forces of the line—or even to all special forces. The objective is to recognize these native values and skills, and to integrate them into organizations to mix with the power inherent in US training, equipment, leadership, and communications practices.

Thus, the development of indigenous forces under American control has decided advantages, but the structure must not be put to too severe a test too early in its formulation. The legions will be relatively new organizations with which, in the beginning, neither American staffers nor Arab volunteers will have more than fleeting experience. There are many reasons to expect success with the concept, but bare-bones reliance upon such formations is probably too great a risk to take until both they and their American leadership have adjusted to their circumstances.

While there is every reason to expect success in the field, too early a hand-off of responsibility, from wholly US organizations to American-led, Arab-manned ones, could well prompt criticism similar to that of observers against the departure of Allied Forces from South Vietnam (including the cessation of bomber aircraft support). Over the past half-dozen years many American and Arab commissioned and noncommissioned officers have worked with one another as advisors and counselors, and it may be important to identify these personnel to work with the initial legion elements.

The presidential identification of 2011 as the terminal date for American troop deployments in the Middle East seemed a valid guide for planning at the time it was drafted, but it must be understood that American-led foreign legions will be quite different from both regular American and allied units, with both advantages and disadvantages. The principal advantage of an American legion force over existing American-advised, but indigenously manned, units is likely to prove to be expeditious responsiveness to orders from American sources. Also, we should expect a higher level of communications security in American legion units, where such matters would generally be handled by US personnel, than in American-advised units where the host nation provides all staff members except advisory personnel. By the same token, most interception of hostile communications would likely be handled by experienced native language speakers.

On the other hand, certain disadvantages may not prove trivial. One is likely to be the ability of local volunteers who are having second thoughts to desert under pressure. Home may be just around the corner. Further, the risks of disloyalty, even subversion, cannot be overlooked. Nevertheless, it would seem most likely that unit performance of American legion forces in the field would improve in most important respects as the volunteers gain experience and a greater sense of identity with US interests and their own long-term well-being. Some degree of surveillance, especially of newcomers, including restrictions on private mail and personal associations, must be maintained.

It should be borne in mind that the locations of current Middle Eastern conflicts in Iraq, Afghanistan, and the frontier districts in Pakistan set a complex patchwork quilt for whatever US, NATO, or other friendly forces may be deployed. The various lines of supply and communications are long, difficult, and dangerous. Connections with forward units are troublesome at best, and are likely to remain as vulnerable to interdiction by insurgent forces as ever. Further, the great expanse of potentially hostile territory covered by Iran minimizes many opportunities for inter-theater coordination.

In the case of Iraq, the problems have been alternatively overcome by co-operative arrangements at the national level, between deployed American forces (often with selected Iraqi units) on the one hand, and the regular, indigenous Iraqi national forces (Sunni, Shiite, or Kurdish) on the other. It is in Afghanistan and northwestern Pakistan that the problems have loomed rather larger. Afghanistan is a land-locked country with complicated relations among its various tribes and with its neighbors. It suffers from long, dangerous internal lines of communications between its own inhabited areas and along the western border. However, it would not be surprising if a mix of Afghan-American and Pakistani-American legion units could come to provide a higher level of security than either of the Islamic states has recently been able to accomplish on its own.

As time progresses, and as larger legions come into being in Iraq and Afghanistan, it may be beneficial to develop a multilateral "partnership" with US/Iraqi and US/Afghan legions working with remaining US and indigenous national units on both sides of the border. This could foster a common sense of mission and organizational cooperation. Each participant would remain under his or her designated commander and staff, but the fullest effectiveness of the combined forces could be attained with the creation of an overall international staff, on the model of NATO, with a single overall (rotating) commander, international headquarters, and staff.

Also, it may become possible to reduce residual US direct support detachments with the development of legion elements capable of quadrilateral service, including support to US, Iraqi, Afghan, and international (legion) elements throughout the Middle East. As the various forces develop (or reduce, in the case of US force commitment) standardization will become increasingly important, and could likely be most efficiently handled as a special function of legions.

At some distance behind these matters (optimists might even wish for earlier consideration) should be the matter of Iran. While Iran may or may not be close to nuclear weapons development, it may come to pose a distinct threat to its neighbors, most specifically to Israel, and to other Western interests in the region. For the visible future Iran does not appear to offer any opportunities for US-local national military cooperation. The best that can be said is that in the Middle East things can change—and sometimes rather quickly.

On the other hand, the population of the United States includes a surprising number of people of Iranian extraction. According to the Iranian Study Group of the Massachusetts Institute of Technology, the number currently approaches 400,000, due largely to the internal strife connected with the expulsion of the Shah in 1979. The country underwent an explosive revolution, causing thousands of upper-class citizens to flee the land, seeking refuge in the West, especially in the United States. Other large groups are to be found in Europe and other Middle Eastern countries. Of those in the United States, a majority of adults have college degrees; in part this is because their initial purpose in coming to this country was to secure a Western education. While the number of US Iranian residents without green cards does not seem likely to be large, it would not be surprising if an Iranian legion with as many as three or four battalions could be assembled, assuming a mission coinciding with their interests.[20] Others might be recruited from Europe or the Middle East.

The latter half of the titular question, "And then what?" is a bold one to raise at this point. Some might claim that if we become reasonably satisfied with the formula for American-led legions in the Middle East we should be prepared to explore its applicability elsewhere. That certainly merits discussion, but judgment should be reserved until we have rather more case-specific experience and insight than we can claim right now.

Nevertheless, we should recognize that there are likely to be many opportunities to assist other countries and forces with common experience training in areas of current stress. Late in 2008 American Special Forces units were deployed to areas in Africa where local forces had been intimidated by hostile Islamic groups. Supported by a $500 million partnership, our State and Defense Departments agreed to provide Algeria, Chad, Mauritania, Mali, Morocco, Nigeria, Senegal, and Tunisia with practical instruction in counter-terrorism techniques and procedures. Libya might wish to join the group at some time in the future. The objective would be to build the countries' capabilities for dealing with Islamic militants who have taken refuge in populated areas. Particularly dangerous in Mali are some two hundred fighters from an offshoot of Al Qaeda, known as "Al Qaeda in the Maghreb," which uses the northern Mali desert as a staging area and a support base. The US Special Forces Group has been reinforced for this cooperative work, and, at times, has been joined with elements of Dutch and German forces.[21]

As we have noted previously, the legion concept has been broadly exercised by others, through both space and time, especially by Switzerland and France. Now the question is of its applicability in the twenty-first century, in combat against foes of significant strength. Circumstances suggest that continued testing and trials are warranted wherever possible. Especially, they suggest its application in a well-known theater of combat before it is attempted in areas in which we have had rather less experience. In short: we may wish to try it first in Iraq. Later we can investigate other possibilities.

Over recent decades we have chosen to rely primarily upon American troops, supplemented where possible by European forces, for the most critical military missions in southern Europe (former Yugoslavia) and the Middle East. At the same time we have undertaken important support missions for the development of indigenous formations in both Iraq and Afghanistan. Where our best judgment has indicated that indigenous units may acquire acceptable combat or security capabilities, we have encouraged the host states to take their forces to the field. While some adjustments have been required, it is evident that progress has been made. Many indigenous units have become organizations of competent professionals, but not without extraordinary expense. In late October 2009 the Congressional Research Service released a statistic: it will cost one million dollars to support one soldier for one year in Afghanistan. This includes the cost of private contractors who have moved into areas of support that have been strictly military in the past. Estimates for the number of contractors have been as high as one contractor for every soldier.[22]

Nevertheless, there is always room for improvement. If we are to expect further professional advancement, and above all, as we consider development of foreign (American-led) legions, it would be appropriate to enlist specialists from the highly professional French Foreign Legion for staff advice; the earlier, the better. As noted before, we currently host one mid-grade French Foreign Legionnaire at our Infantry School at Ft. Benning, Georgia. An expansion of the Ft. Benning program could prove quite helpful, especially to include a sufficient number of junior officers and noncommissioned officers to advise on the preparation of American officers working to develop indigenous (Iraqi and Afghan) legions of regimental size (1,500–2,000 native troops) in the native countries.

Considering the experience which many of our soldiers have already had with Iraqi and Afghan counterparts on a conventional assistance basis, it should not be a great stretch to look for an initial fielding of two or three indigenous regiments (with 3–4 battalions each) of Iraqi legionnaires within a year, perhaps less.

Again, the strongest motivational factor we can expect is the progression of time from the moment the volunteers arrive at camp to, a number of years later, the point when they may apply for US immigration "green cards." With some success in Iraq, it would be sensible to progress with the program into Afghanistan. As the president commented on CBS's *60 Minutes* on the evening of 22 March 2009, in context with his discussion of sending an additional 17,000 troops to Afghanistan, "There's got to be a sense that this is not perpetual drift."[23] He may have noted the unfavorable statistics from that country:

Table 6.1. Statistics from Afghanistan 2009

Category	February 2008	February 2009
2009 U.S. and Other Foreign Troop Deaths	2	24
Afghan Security Forces Deaths	10	75
Civilian Deaths from War	40	200
Opium Production (in tons)	4,287	7,793
Public Favor (for U.S.)	68%	32%
For Afghan Government	80%	48%

Three questions were left outstanding:

1. What is the best way to secure the approval and support of the host governments?
2. Without regard for question no. 1, should legion recruitment commence immediately, or should it be delayed until American and allied forces begin to draw down troop strength by some significant percentage, or to a particular level, before the initiation of recruitment?
3. Should we look to established training centers (e.g., in Iraq and Afghanistan), or should they be established in some other country?

The answer to no. 3 is a technical and political matter. The others are more important. The host government should always feel certain that its interests are first in US plans. This is likely to be of special importance and require delicacy in time of stress. On the one hand, it will be important to protect legion volunteers from calls from their national recruiters; on the other, it will be highly desirable to maintain the personal security of legion volunteers and that of their families. The tactics pursued by legion recruits in wartime must be carefully supervised to ensure that the risks incurred are held to a minimum.

Nevertheless, a lack of cooperation on the part of a government under stress need not automatically rule out efforts to enlist local populations in legionnaire programs. A legionnaire's service can be of substantial value to a family in a war zone, and the fact that the enlistee has chosen service in an American force should not be a matter of public knowledge or record. In some cases, it may be desirable that the host government be aware of local volunteer recruitments, but the family must be protected from unfavorable reactions.

Through much of 2010, and continuing into 2011 and likely 2012, regular American units will be stepping back from their combat responsibilities and preparing for shipment back to the United States. However well (or poorly) the indigenous forces have been prepared for the period of American reductions, the changes will be serious, and the responsibilities of the host government greatly expanded. We should not underestimate the range of measures that many an ambitious political or tribal leader may attempt to employ as American forces fade down Iraqi roads toward Basra and Kuwait in the south, or toward departure airfields in Afghanistan. Nor should there be any hesitation in intergovernmental preparations to shape the necessary structures for the host government's assumption of responsibilities and actions before the American troops depart.

However the dates of US force withdrawal are finally determined, the factors surrounding the creation of legion units should be fully explored with host government representatives. Especially, the host representatives must fully understand the vitality of the command and control systems built into the foreign legion concept and the subsystems tying it together. They must also come to terms with all aspects of the conversion. There may be some parallels with the Iraqi units reconstituted under the interim Iraqi government structure in 2003 and 2004, but while these units reacted primarily to US "advice," in dealing with the indigenous guerilla groups, the new units will be designed to operate under exclusive American control. The principal difference will be manifest in the colors the units will swear to protect: the red, white, and blue of the Stars and Stripes, likely accompanied by local colors if the situation merits it. Fundamentally, a maximum number of the soldiers will be potential Americans-in-the-making. While their loyalties may ultimately be to the United States, they must first learn to be legionnaires.

The troops must understand the vitality of the arrangements for their security. They must also make their own decisions, first to grasp the essential dimensions and benefits of their independence, and second, to join in the negotiations of any special local provisions requiring important decisions on their part, swearing to abide by whatever choices may be made by their group as an entity of the United States abroad.

Personnel recruitment may be quite different from that which the participating countries have experienced in the past, and public information programs will be necessary to assist the participating states in decision-making regarding their own role in the programs. The volunteers must understand that they are enlisting in a foreign military service, the likes of which have been known for decades, but the ramifications of which will be very different from anything they have known. And, most especially, they must understand that the road they are taking likely leads to a world they may only have read about—most likely in a not-necessarily-reliable press—one that has not necessarily been portrayed favorably.

Some volunteers may wish to know "who else in my village has signed up?" In most cases it will not be good policy to answer such questions, and enlistees should be clearly advised that their status will be carefully guarded for as long as they are under US supervision. Any special measures undertaken to protect families will necessarily be performed on a highly exceptional basis or in the course of routine protection of cooperative communities.

Early in 2009, Dr. Anthony Cordesman and his colleagues at the Center for Strategic and International Studies (CSIS) drafted an assessment of the situation in Afghanistan, citing a pessimistic outlook by President Obama for the country at that time, a judgment that the war may be on a losing track. The Taliban, Haggani, and HIG forces had become far more lethal than before, and the American, Afghan National Army, and Afghan National Police have suffered increasing numbers of casualties. US commanders called for 20,000 to 30,000 more troops, but some questioned whether that would be enough.[24] While increased numbers of indigenous troops would ease these problems, few observers are optimistic about the results.

On the other hand, the introduction of high-spirited, American-led and -trained legions, initially assisted by selected native language interpreters and closely coordinated for operations with both US and regular indigenous formations, may be able to turn the tables on the opposition, whatever its strength or local popular appeal. The legion will be led by foreign (to the legionnaires) commissioned and noncommissioned officers, but the hearts will be of native sons and daughters who have come to understand the value of the American programs, both for the country they will be leaving and for the country to which they may pledge their future.

Key to the entire effort will be the host nation's understanding, approval, and support. It must be clear to both governments and the publics of the countries involved that the initiative is not intended to extend American interest or control, but to create the structure for the protection of selected countries or regions, based on principles of international cooperation between the United States and threatened countries, incorporating US skills, armaments, and leaders, on the one hand, and local manpower on the other, together with an opportunity for host nation citizens to earn American citizenship if they so desire. In many cases, such a development will also give rise to a long-term living bridge between the legionnaires' countries of birth and the United States, enriching the cultures of all states involved.

In some cases it may be desirable to form legion units in states with greater understandings of the program. Ideally this may take place in countries neighboring principal target territories. In such a situation it would be important that the resulting force not be perceived as an issue between the United States and the host country—especially not as a threat to any government—but rather as a bridge of understanding and respect for the peoples at both ends.

In other cases military action might not be the first or necessarily the most important function to be performed by the legions. Under conditions in northern Pakistan in mid-2009, for example, the welfare of the population appeared to have suffered under the operation of social and religious dicta. These covered the behavior of property owners under the pressure of multitudes of refugees seeking to escape the dangers of battle or the demands of invading Taliban. Pashtun law (Pashtunwali) obliges its adherents to provide shelter, food, and water to those in need, no matter how many there may be seeking sanctuary, or how long they may stay. It may be much easier for Islamic troops to render care to civilians of the same faith than it would be for Western troops to do so.

In early June 2009, reports assessed the practice as the salvation of the refugees in Madhey Baba, Pakistan, but emphasized the stress and danger it imposed on the "hosts." Early on, displaced families sought shelter in the Mardan and Swabi districts, nearly outnumbering the residents. At the time there were three million refugees in all of Pakistan, while the government agencies had been able to care for no more than two hundred thousand. The United Nations put out a call for $543 million in international assistance, but received only sluggish response. In two of Pakistan's provinces, Sindh and Punjab, the UN cited fears that the lack of support could destabilize the populace. The situation was critical.

Thus we see another important function of American legions in foreign environments—but conditions well known to its membership and to its leadership. American organization, equipment, training, and leadership could provide protection and succor to stressed communities wherever the legions might be deployed. Their strengths would be drawn on to balance the special threats and needs of the regions in which they might operate—Latin America, Africa, the Balkans, the Middle East, or Southeast Asia. The legions would provide closely deployed American forces, or allies, that could offer not only cooperation and assistance, but unique capabilities particular to their origin and character, and to the needs of the moment.

Figure 7.1. Map of Latin America

7

Latin America—Our Backyard

Looking back at Dr. Thomas Barnett's "New Map for the Pentagon," we are reminded of how close his "nonintegrating gap" (beyond the global economy and not bound to international trade regulations) comes to the American heartland. From Key West, Florida, to Havana, Cuba, it is barely a matter of a hundred miles. Coincidentally, this is roughly the same as the distance between the opposing capitals in the American Civil War.

It is unlikely that the Latin American portion of "the gap" will develop as great a threat to the interests of the United States as has North Korea since 1950, or become as troublesome as Africa today, but perhaps there are similarities. The South American strip of "gap" members begins in Paraguay and works its way up through Bolivia to the western coast of South America in Peru and Ecuador, going rather lightly through Colombia, to come down hard on the northern coast in Venezuela to the east and Panama to the west, extending as far to the northwest as El Salvador, Guatemala, and Belize. It also island-hops to the east to embrace Cuba, Haiti, and the Dominican Republic. Venezuela and, to an extent, Colombia are two of the larger and more notable countries in the chain.

Barnett completes his argument by talking about the "gap" countries around the "Caribbean rim" and the "Andes portion of South America," essentially standing somewhere short of the netherworld to which he assigns "virtually all of Africa, the Balkans, the Middle East, and most of Southeast Asia."[1] He describes these places as "the world's bad neighborhoods, where gangs live by their own cruel rule sets, where life somehow seems cheaper." These are the "enter-at-your-own-risk regions," he writes, "you know, the early Oliver Stone movies, like *Midnight Express* and *Salvador*. These are the places where the people tend to go medieval on one another, and the rest of the world simply does not care because it's just too off-line from *the Wonderful World*, where the *good stuff* and the *good life* are to be found."[2]

Having established his netherworld and a strategy to "shrink the gap," Barnett highlights the removal of Saddam Hussein as a model operation for shifting a country from an "uncooperative" stature to that of a "cooperative" one. He offers the explanation that "taking down" Saddam forced the United States to take responsibility for the security environment of the region within its disagreeable "gap" role, and that is why Barnett supported the war. He summarizes his argument in the following way: "By reconnecting Iraq to the world, we are not just rehabilitating a longtime pariah, we are stepping up to the role of gap leviathan in a way no other nation in the core could even dream about." But then he adds, "Of course, that's pretty scary business."[3]

Whether we understand Barnett's argument or not, his "scary business" probably does us a favor. Certainly it helps to set boundaries within his "new Pentagon map." And whether we agree with him or not, we may grasp his concept of the "nonintegrating gap" and identify how it applies to certain territories in the western hemisphere and where we may find the boundaries.

Unfortunately, Barnett does not address the feasibility of the formation of American legions, and he makes only modest suggestions of how the southwestern semi-hemisphere may be aided in slipping from the highly depreciated "gap" category to that of a red-blooded "core" member. He simply notes that the breach is wide. Of twenty-four nation-states in the theater of Latin America, he rates only four—Brazil, Uruguay, Argentina, and Chile—as members of the "functioning core." The rest are all denizens of the "nonintegrating gap."

A typical imbroglio among the "nonintegrating" crowd has been the cheap drama in Venezuela in which FARC[4] left-wing guerrillas have been offering—and contradicting their own offer of—the release of three of its 750-odd hostages. As many as forty-five prisoners, including three American defense contractors, are believed to be among the group to be released, but the outcome of the matter remains opaque.[5]

Another Venezuelan front-pager has been President Hugo Chavez decreeing that a "Chavista militia" unit—an invention of his own—become an official part of the national armed forces. And still another has been the facilitation of government seizure of private companies. In spite of such heavy-handedness, polls continue to reveal that a small majority continue to support the president. Barnett's view of Chavez, like his view of Castro in Cuba and Mugabe in Zimbabwe, is of a "repressive leader inside the Gap who simply refuses to leave power," but holds his neighbors in a "repressive grasp" that denies them opportunities "to escape from the negative investment climate his continued presence generates."[6] Yet the worst of the country's characteristics is the stark rate of murder. Comparing Venezuela's record with that of war-torn Iraq in 2009 reveals a breathtaking murder rate four times that of the Middle Eastern state.[7]

Under Chavez's leadership the country has become known as a terrifying center of crime and mismanagement. More particularly, the home district of the Chavez family, the Barinas district, has a kidnapping rate of 7.2 per 100,000 inhabitants,[8] and armed gangs exploit the police, who apparently are paid to look elsewhere. Police corruption is no less common than crime. In a typical case, a family paid a ransom in the spring of 2009 with no return of the captive. The case was one of 454 reported in Barinas. As one small opposition newspaper wrote, "while the [Chavez] family wraps itself in the rhetoric of socialism, we are descending into a neo-capitalist chaos where all that matters is money."[9]

In September 2009 Chavez traveled to Moscow to encourage the Russians to "stand up" to the United States' "terrorist empire" so it could concentrate on energy and military agreements with Venezuela. In his view, "the United States wants to dominate the entire world." His assessment holds that "the empire of the Yanks will fall" in the next few decades. To help in forwarding the process, Chavez says, he has purchased more than $4 billion worth of Russian arms to update the Venezuelan Armed Forces. He asserted that Venezuela would need to purchase additional Russian tanks to counter the aid which the United States is providing to Colombia.[10]

In late February 2010 the Organization of American States' Commission on Human Rights issued a searing and authoritative report on the destruction of Venezuela's political institutions and the erosion of freedom under President Chavez. "[T]he regime has done away with judicial independence, intimidated or eliminated opposition media, stripped elected opposition leaders of their powers, and used bogus criminal charges to silence human rights groups."[11]

Still later in the year, Roberto Briceno-Leon, of the Venezuelan Observatory of Violence, reported that the national murder rate had almost doubled, from an earlier 49 persons per 100,000 to a current 75 per 100,000. But in the capital city, the numbers had worse than quadrupled: Caracas's record was running at 220 per 100,000. The murder rate in the capital at this writing apparently exceeds that of any other city in the world.[12]

Turning next door to Colombia, we find some other oddities. Often the behavior of government officials would seem more fitting for a pulp mystery novel than for a real republic in the twenty-first century. It is called "parapolitics," especially when it involves the support of government bandits who can be relied upon to throw their weight behind one political party or another. But sometimes it gets out of hand. In 2008 the Colombian armed forces attacked a camp of the illegal FARC based in Ecuador. In the process the forces killed a high-ranking leader, Paul Reyes. Both the governments of Ecuador and Venezuela protested the incursion and ultimately broke diplomatic ties with Colombia. The matter was further inflamed when alleged evidence was reported to be found on FARC computers linking the governments of Ecuador and Venezuela to the guerrilla group.[13] (The dispute is reminiscent of two pots calling the kettle black.)

The game has also involved connections between political leaders and right-wing paramilitary groups, many involved in the drug trade. Apparently, these groups have been fighting leftist guerrillas, imposing a reign of terror on parts of Colombia, while the state president has been trying to persuade the outlaws to demobilize. But the question remains: Which is the "good" side and which is the "bad"? In 2008 the Supreme Court had remanded twenty-nine active or retired lawmakers and was still investigating another thirty-nine over paramilitary connections.[14]

A typical legal action, just the sort which might lead one to question—or, alternatively, to believe—some of the allegations in flight around the capital, was one involving a charge that presidential aides had met with emissaries of a paramilitary warlord offering a video recording of a man they falsely claimed was from the court and offered the warlord bribes to testify against the politicians. (The allegations were so complicated that even the charge is almost too complex to be understood.)

Regarding personal safety, the yearbook *Countries of the World and Their Leaders* describes Colombia as having a high rate of ransom kidnappings, citing the seizure of 370 Americans in 2005. The group included journalists, missionaries, human rights advocates, businessmen, tourists, and children. However, the criminals appeared to hold a special interest in businesspeople involved in contracts concerned with water, oil, gas, and electrical works.[15]

On the other hand, Colombia maintains a special relationship with the United States, including the maintenance of military bases on Colombian territory. Particularly, the United States seeks agreement to increase its anti-drug surveillance flights over Colombia, the world's top producer of cocaine. Depending on how the new agreement is shaped, American troop levels in the country could be substantially increased over the 250 currently stationed there, principally as advisors to Colombian forces. Since the year 2000 the United States has paid Colombia more than five billion dollars for its cooperation.[16]

At the same time, travel in Ecuador is practically forbidden near the national northern border in the provinces of Sucumbios, Orellana, and Carchi. Similarly, the border area of Esmeralda province has been effectively closed because of organized crime, weapons trafficking, and terrorist organizations operating in the area. Ten American visitors were captured in those areas, and one murdered, before 2001.[17] In July 2009, Ecuador's foreign minister, Fander Falconi, remarked that his country's relations with Colombia had never been so bad. A video leaked to the Associated Press and published on July 17 showed the military commander of the FARC, Colombia's largest guerilla group, saying, in 2006, that his organization gave "aid in dollars" to the election campaign of Rafael Correa, Ecuador's president, and had reached "agreements" with Ecuadorean officials.

The FARC commander, Jorge Briceno, was found on a captured video reading a letter to a group of guerrillas referring to the damage done by the leaking of guerrilla secret e-mails. The raid during which the video was seized prompted Mr. Correa to break diplomatic connections with Colombia. Colombian officials, in turn, say that their inability to defeat the FARC is largely the fault of the Ecuadorean officials working with the rebels.[18] Very likely both sides are at fault.

In early September 2009 legal officers in Ecuador said that they would investigate allegations of the Chevron Oil Company against representatives of President Rafael Correa and the judge overseeing a $27 billion contamination lawsuit against Chevron, and that punitive action would be sought for any party guilty of criminal action. The Ecuadorian leadership apparently accepted the investigation, but a presidential aide, Alexis Mera, named in the suit, said that the prosecutors should begin by investigating Chevron's lawyers.[19]

The wars in Peru in the late twentieth century appear to have been even larger than those in its neighbors. Observers estimate that the "internal conflict in Peru" (which appears to be still alive in some districts) has caused the deaths of some 70,000 people. The principal players, besides the government in Lima, have been the "Shining Path" (modeled on Chinese Maoist operations), and the Tupac Amaru Revolutionary Movement (MRTA), another communist group, but one associated more with traditional Latin American (Castroist) thinking than Maoist.[20]

Finally, regarding the mainland, we cannot avoid the Panama War in 1989. While the conflict itself may not have had much to do with the identification of "gap" vs. "core" struggles (as presented by the administration of President George H. W. Bush), Barnett accepts the official US line that the United States invaded Panama for the following reasons:

1. To safeguard the lives of US citizens,
2. To defend democracy and human rights in Panama,
3. To combat drug trafficking, and
4. To protect the integrity of the Torrijos-Carter Treaties.[21]

On September 7, 1977, President Jimmy Carter had joined with Omar Torrijos of Panama to hand responsibility for the inter-ocean canal over to the state of Panama. At that time General Noriega of Panama was a paid agent ($100,000 per year) of the Central Intelligence Agency of the United States, notably for sabotaging the socialist government of Nicaragua and leftist revolutionaries in El Salvador. He also worked to suppress (and possibly simultaneously to promote) drug traffic throughout the area. As commander of the Panama Armed Forces, he enjoyed substantial power.[22]

In March 1989 an attempted coup against the government of Panama was resisted by Manuel Noriega's forces. In May, during the national elections, an alliance of parties opposed to the military dictatorship of Noriega counted results from the country's election precincts before they were sent to the national election district centers. There they showed their candidate, Guillermo Endara, defeating Carlos Duque, candidate of a pro-Noriega coalition, by nearly a 3-to-1 margin. Endara was beaten up by Noriega supporters the next day. Noriega declared the election null and insisted he had won because irregularities had been introduced by US-backed candidates from opposition parties. President G. H. W. Bush called on Noriega to "honor the will of the Panamanian people." When Noriega refused to cede, President Bush decided to use force.

In 1992 the film *The Panama Deception* received the Academy Award for Documentary Feature. The film was critical of the 1989 invasion, depicting the US media as biased. The film also depicted mass graves uncovered after the US troop withdrawal and the suffering of a reported 20,000 Panamanian refugees.[23] The true culprit responsible for the mass graves was not established.

The "nonintegrating" tendency of the states of the region was demonstrated on 28 June 2009 by Honduran President Manuel Zelaya, who announced from San José, Costa Rica, that he was the victim of a military coup and brutal kidnapping by soldiers, and that he was seeking political asylum in San José. Zelaya had attempted to cast a ballot in Tegucigalpa in a constitutional referendum he had called for, despite a ruling by the Supreme Court that the action was illegal. Hundreds of troops, tanks, and armored vehicles were used to ensure public compliance with a contrary decision by the high court. According to the Honduran constitution, the head of Congress is next in line to the presidency, followed by the chief justice of the Supreme Court.[24]

Apparently, Mr. Zelaya had alienated his own party with a decision in 2008 to forge an alliance with Venezuela's Hugo Chavez. Zelaya had decided to organize a referendum on convening a constituent assembly—the very device Mr. Chavez had used to establish an autocracy in Caracas. Had Zelaya been successful with that ploy, he might have managed to replace Honduras's democracy with a Venezuelan-style dictatorship. The *Economist* titled its blurb on the events, "Lousy President, Terrible Precedent."[25]

Turning our focus to the Caribbean, we see the rim of Dr. Barnett's non-integrating island territories composed principally of Cuba, Haiti, and the Dominican Republic. In Haiti the current problems can be traced back to the beginning of the decade when Jean Bertrand Aristide won the presidency by default. In July 2001 gunmen attacked the police in Port-au-Prince as well as in the provinces. Pro-government groups attacked the homes of the opposition leaders, and both sides attacked unpopular figures around the country.

Nevertheless, both Venezuela and Colombia, along with virtually all of the other countries of Central and South America, consider themselves to hold some degree of "alliance," or at least nominal association, with the United States. With the exception of Cuba, they all have taken pride in assigning senior officers to attend the Inter-American Defense College, aimed at the graduate level, in Washington, DC. Thus far almost two thousand students from twenty-eight different countries have graduated from the college, with some 40 percent of the graduates rising to general officer rank or the equivalent level in other forces or civilian branches of government.[26]

It would seem likely that some officers falling within this select group might come to help set the bounds for experimentation with American foreign legion development in their own, or other, states. And, considering the breadth of Spanish language and culture, in both Latin America and the United States, we can reasonably expect to find some number of American commissioned and noncommissioned officers within our existing force suitable to fill requirements for experimentation with a modified legion concept in the western hemisphere. In effect, the US Army almost certainly would find it convenient both to form American foreign legions from among volunteers south of its borders and to partially offset the staff requirements for those legions with US Spanish-speaking officers already familiar with the tongue, and with interested leaders from several of the countries in question. That is to suggest that in some cases, US forces may find it convenient to recruit a number of bilingual leaders from both US and foreign officers. In the latter instance, of course, the leaders themselves might make appropriate candidates for US citizenship.

Such flexibility might even be assumed to offer a convenient arena of initial experimentation for the entire concept. While our first experience with volunteer legions in a particular country may be best initiated with personnel from a single national source (the United States), there is no obvious reason not to consider indigenous bilingual, Spanish- and English-speaking volunteers, interested in American citizenship and service, to participate in exercises designed to develop experience in such activities.

The key would seem to be assurance that both the host (Latin American) and leading (US) states would see utility in the exercise. Officers and NCOs from potential host nations likely to interpret the undertaking as demeaning of its political or security interests would clearly be poor candidates, however attractive it might appear to the potential participants. The key would be to ensure that the full set of advantages would be clear to all participants and to the source states involved.

An important test case would appear to be the 2009 June–July imbroglio in Honduras when President Manuel Zelaya was arrested by Honduran troops in the middle of the night and expelled from the country in his pajamas. The action took place shortly before voting was to begin on a constitutional referendum called by the president, even though the Honduran Supreme Court had ruled it illegal, and significant members of the Honduran military and Congress, together with members of Zelaya's own party, had opposed it.

The drama progressed as both sides appealed to Washington, DC, for backing by the US government. The US administration expressed dismay over the Honduran president's actions but sought to avoid a central role in the dispute by turning the matter over to the Organization of American States, where it was expected that the apparent *coup d'état* would receive serious consideration and result in probable support for the Honduran presidency.[27] As an opener, the US government cut its aid to Honduras by $22 million, including $16 million in military assistance. It also cancelled the visas from a number of the Honduran embassy staff in Washington, DC, and President Obama made some public remarks expressing his disappointment in the coup. His remarks were generally well received throughout Latin America, but there was no strong action to reverse the events.[28]

The appeal to the United States was significant, both as an expression of respect for the United States as a mature democracy and as the most powerful member of the O.A.S. For our purposes these events cast only an ancillary cloak around the concept of deployment of American legion units to countries in the hemisphere seeking the stability such units might afford. But that is not the point.

Here we encounter the question of the legitimacy and utility of an American foreign legion in a country like Honduras. While events have disclosed weaknesses in the operation of the Honduran governmental structure, there is no indication that the structure, per se, lacks the means to conduct public business in a lawful manner. Regardless of whether the expulsion of a president by the army is legal under Honduran law, there is no indication in this case that it has been driven by an outside business or by a player acting on behalf of an illegal group or foreign power. Without clear legitimacy (which may be engendered by treaty with the host government) an American legion would have no basis for action beyond self-defense.

The concept of American legions in foreign lands depends upon a commonality of interests between the United States and the local government.

Only such a relationship can engender the trust and cooperation necessary for maintenance of peace and security in the recipient countries. Political and criminal groups seeking advantage or the overthrow of a government should not expect either alliance or inaction by an American legion based upon what they see as the misrule of the existing system. Likewise, the existing government should not expect the legion to be predisposed to countering legitimate domestic political acts within the customs and laws of the country in question.

In the American capital the *Washington Post* treated the Honduran event as a disaster for Latin American democracy. In the view of the highly influential paper, the real tragedy of the event was the gift it donated to Mr. Hugo Chavez, longtime opponent of United States' interests in Latin America. "Fortunately," it stated, "Mr. Chavez wasted his advantages: his foolish attempt to fly Mr. Zelaya back to Tegucigalpa on Sunday (September 5) flopped, producing a ludicrous televised circus on the ground." In the newspaper's view, the circumstances dealt a defeat to the "populist authoritarianism that Mr. Chavez and Mr. Zelaya represent." The United States chose a middle ground as Secretary of State Hillary Rodham Clinton called for the "restoration of democratic constitutional order," but there was no speedy return to such conditions. Mr. Zelaya was charged with multiple crimes, including refusing to respect court orders and invading a military base with a mob of his supporters. In the view of the reporting editor, there was little chance that he could succeed in changing the constitution or perpetuating himself in office beyond the end of his term in January 2010. Such an outcome, in the *Post*'s view, would be a victory not only for Honduras, but also for the cause of democracy in the region. "Mr. Chavez," it ventured, "dreams of a putsch in Tegucigalpa that would produce another lawless autocracy like his own."[29]

The circumstances would appear highly amenable to the activation of an American legion if such a force had been developed in years past. The people of Honduras clearly seek a settlement compatible with their concepts of democratic government—not one which concedes to the wiles of competing advantage between the army and a less-than-respectable, self-serving chief of state. If the army is to truly represent an organization speaking for the popular aspirations (as it claims) there would be little chance of conflict between the two in a 2011 or 2012 election with fresh candidates for the highest office.

Immediately south of Honduras lies the largest of the Central American states, Nicaragua. Long occupied (1912–1933) by US Marines, the country stagnated under conservative political elements supported by the United States. Events in Nicaragua following the occupation did little to instruct the people along democratic lines. General Anastasio Somoza Garcia, a self-appointed dictator, came to power in 1936 and installed a dictatorship which would last through his assassination, the life of his son, Luis, and his brother, Major General Anastasio Somoza Debayle. In 1981 left-wing Sandinistas overthrew Somoza and established a communist government.

The following years were disappointments to most Nicaraguans. In 1998 a hurricane killed more than 9,000 people, leaving two million others homeless and causing $10 billion in damages to the unfortunate land. Many people fled to the United States, which offered an immigration amnesty program lasting for ten years. But leadership remained a problem. In 2002 the former president, Arnoldo Aleman, was charged with fraud and embezzlement, found guilty, and sentenced to twenty years in prison.

Cuba is a special case. Not only did it adopt a communist form of government, but it has endeavored to spread its philosophy to other countries in Latin America and Africa. However, it would appear that the bulk of Cuba's professed beliefs are associated with the Castro family, especially Fidel, the founder of the socialist state, and at this writing a failing figure. His brother, and successor, is not known to husband as aggressive a form of government as Fidel himself.

Cuba is in the midst of efforts to lift itself in cooperation with many non-communist states. It has undertaken many projects for the improvement of its economy, including the development of Western-style tourist accommodations, the establishment of tax-free trade centers for virtually all interested foreign countries, especially European states, and the consolidation of its military service institutions to permit the conversion of the former naval academy to a center for a five-year medical course for impoverished South American volunteer nurses and health specialists.

Cuba has also undertaken efforts to coordinate anti-drug operations with American forces with similar responsibilities. While neither country has been able to maintain full embassies in the other's capital, each has an "interests" office, with the American component providing a US Coast Guard officer to coordinate anti-drug activities in the Caribbean Sea. It would not be at all surprising to see movement on both sides toward much closer cooperation, especially in trade and tourism, upon the demise of Fidel Castro. Cuban beaches, currently catering to Canadian and European visitors, are among the best in the world. And further, many European countries have invested heavily in accommodations for tourists and yachting visitors. Pressures for accommodation of these developments are close to overwhelming. Cuba, however, would seem to be a stripe of a different color. While there is little admiration for the government in Havana, the society does not harbor the selfish gangs that have been noted to seize the capitals of some of its neighbors. While the Cuban commander of the expedition into Africa was clearly dishonest and suffered capital punishment for his misdeeds, the General Staff in Havana, by all appearances, is a respectable organization, staffed by honest and competent officers. Further, there has been little record of criminal behavior among high-ranking officials, or ignoring local laws for their own benefit. The author has had extensive experience in dealing with leading Cuban officials and senior military officers, and has detected little evidence among such officials. The following chapter presents a more fulsome examination of Cuba, as a special case.

Figure 8.1. Map of Cuba and Its Neighbors

8

Cuba: Our Exceptional Neighbor*

The political atmosphere in Cuba is quite different from that of its fellow Latin American states. While most of them entertain pluralistic governments, Cuba is a kind of "dictatorship of the proletariat," but with an indefinite atmosphere of change. Raul Castro calls it "a new socialist model" which includes extra money enabling those with initiative to make a little more than the state prescribes. In the last few years it has taken to loaning unused state lands to some 82,000 private Cuban farmers in an effort to cut imports, which have in the past made up 60 percent of the country's food supply.

The United States has maintained an economic blockade of the island for almost a half century, with but a $350 million exception in 2001 for beans, rice, and frozen chicken. With the exception of the notorious prison at Guantanamo, for which the supposed century rental has long since expired, the island is largely a vacuum in the Caribbean. Russia, the core of the former Union of Soviet Socialist Republics, along with its half-dozen East European fellow travelers, has long been eased out of its painful era of dictatorship, but Cuba is apparently just so small and lonely that it can't break out of its bad dream.

There can be no certainty of Cuba's future, except, perhaps, that things will be better with or without a full-blown counter-revolution. The populace is not a collection of foolish people, devoted as some may have been to the virtually interminable lectures of a crackpot leader. Fidel Castro is offstage and there is no one with sufficient popular following to take his

---

*This chapter is drawn largely from the author's personal visits to Cuba, previously reported in *ARMY* by the Association of the US Army.

place. His brother carries the name, but not the revolutionary fire. Except for a few elderly officers, the army provides an unlikely pool for continued revolution in anything but name. On the contrary, many of the better officers have been to Western Europe to learn how Cuban industry can be made more efficient. Free trade zones can be plotted on Cuban maps, and the fearsome internal guard force has developed techniques for cooperating with the US Coast Guard and counter-narcotic forces.

In his earlier years the villainous dictator paraded in review in Washington, DC, fouled hotels in New York, invited Russian submarines and nuclear missiles to operate from Cuban bases, and cooperated with Soviet nuclear missile planners to identify launching sites within range of countless American vital targets. Fidel Castro sent hundreds of his countrymen "to the wall" to face firing squads, and bored most of the others with daylong lectures. Beast and comic, he played host for foreign leaders, including the pope. Fidel Castro is hero to millions of his countrymen and a villain to others, but his demise will likely mean a new life for almost all.

Yes, Cuba deserves Dr. Barnett's classification as another "nonintegrating" country, but the title is not so much inaccurate as it is blind to the dynamics of the island, as its villainous and heroic liberator and dictator passes his final days behind the walls of the national palace.

Yes, 1950s Chevrolets still gasp their way through the narrow streets, but Havana also claims Ernest Hemingway's favorite bar, the newly minted waterfront with its freshly painted window frames and polished doors, and the National Cathedral and first-class hotels right behind them. Not far out of town one can visit the free-trade centers managed by Europeans. The hotels are outfitted with up-to-date yacht dockage and beautiful beaches. The workers are Cuban, hand-picked by the foreign managers and approved by the Cuban government.

But many of the café conditions in town are simply silly. The number of chairs is limited to twelve in an unlicensed café. That is as far as socialism can permit free trade to go. Normally, customers will make reservations so they don't have to scramble out of the way if the police make a check. Since many restaurant keepers often have some pretty good leftovers, the police seldom warn of their visits for fear of cutting back the customer count. The solution has been to follow the law closely and make sure that there aren't more chairs in sight. Any number of customers can be in the restaurant. There may be fifteen plates on the tables. They just can't have more than twelve chairs. Of course police often find that the savvy maitre d' has a dinner or two boxed and ready to be carried out—most often by the police.

Still, some events can be shocking. At 3:24 p.m. on 24 February 1996, a Cuban MiG-29 pilot received orders to engage and destroy an unarmed American single-engine Cessna over the Straits of Florida. Within minutes, two allegedly intruding aircraft had plunged into the water, while a third streaked northward, back toward Miami. The incident was followed by charges and counter-charges between Havana and Washington regarding the facts in the case, and the legality of acts on both sides. The Cubans charged that the Cessna had violated their airspace after warnings by the Havana air controller (true, for at least one of the planes), while the United States accused Cuba of "blatant violation of international law" (equally true with respect to the destruction of unarmed aircraft). The episode added another dismal chapter to the prolonged and unhappy chronicles of Cuban-American relations. But for American doubters of all Cuban claims, it would be beneficial to visit the collection of US arms, uniforms, and explosives of the US-based political (anti-Castro) commandos assembled in island museums, as well as photographs of smashed stores and offices.

Oddly enough, just two weeks before the air action, Major General Ulises Rosales del Toro, chief of the Cuban General Staff, had hosted a small group of visitors, retired US military and foreign service officers, during their trip to the island in hopes of developing a security dialogue between the Cuban staff and knowledgeable Americans. Clearly, the general had hoped to repeat similar successful efforts of earlier years, involving officials from the United States on the one hand, and Russia and China on the other.

It was apparent to the general's guests that the Cuban government had come to recognize its isolation since the collapse of the Soviet Union. The country badly needed hard currency to climb out of the economic hole its socialism had helped to dig. Nevertheless, its leaders wanted to protect the revolution. They feared the North American colossus, and strove to demonstrate the country's self-defense capabilities. At the same time, they hoped to earn an acceptance of their nation's independence and the benefits of foreign investment. The Cessna incident could not have stretched the Cubans more tightly over the horns of their own basic dilemma.

In a subsequent report, the undersigned—one of General Rosales's guests—spelled out his impressions of the Cuban military in a Florida paper in 1996 and provided a measure of insight into mainstream Cuban strategic thinking (shown below).

CUBAN DEFENSE STRATEGY IN 2000

Cubans have been living without much lighting and have been tilling much of their soil with ox-drawn plows. Dilapidated Chevrolets dating from the 1950s were still seen on the roadsides, while drivers poked through heaps of ancient parts to get them going again. Toilet seats were luxury items outside the capital city. Soldier-farmers sang the glories of the revolution from the 1950s as they harvested sugar or listened to lectures on "The War of All the People." Citizens "volunteered" their weekends to dig bunkers against the coming Yankee assault. (During the Americans' visit, Raul Castro, now Fidel's successor, had to excuse himself to travel to the far eastern extremity of the island to present an award to a region that had just completed its fiftieth kilometer of tunnels.)

The reception of the guests was warm enough. The senior officer on the tarmac, who would later serve as the group's principal escort throughout the visit, was Brigadier General Annaldo Tomayo Mendez, Cuba's hero cosmonaut who went into space in the halcyon years of the Soviet program. A host of microphone-wielding reporters and television camera crews pinned the visitors to chairs in the reception lounge for the better part of an hour. Did we think this was a breakthrough in Cuban-American relations? (No); Were the visitors happy to be there? (Of course); Would the United States attack Cuba? (Of course not).

The schedule was tight for a four-day visit. Of greatest importance were two extended sessions across the table from General Rosales del Toro and his senior staff. Another such meeting brought the group to the Foreign Ministry, opposite the deputy foreign minister, Senor Bolanos (a graduate of Georgia Military Academy), who was fluent in English.

Other visits included the National Defense College, the Cadet School, the NCO Academy, and an underground defensive installation for a reinforced motorized infantry regiment. The group also visited the barracks of another regiment (formerly occupied by a Soviet brigade), a Youth Labor Army farm, the submarine base at Cienfuegos (another installation formerly used by the Soviets—inactive but maintaining a "dribble" electric charge over dozens of submarine batteries "just in case"), and the Juragua nuclear power plant near Cienfuegos, where most work had been halted over international environmental issues. The group would also meet with the head of the "American Interests Section" (officially part of the Swiss Embassy).

Cuba's concept for defense was explained and discussed by General Rosales del Toro at two sessions at his headquarters and during a social event hosted by the Defense Ministry. The elements have taken shape in the years following the collapse of the Soviet Union. Since that time, and most particularly since the US-led victory over Iraq in 1991 (which Havana interpreted as further evidence of an American inclination to seek solutions to international problems through force), Cuba has come to realize that the victory at the Bay of Pigs was circumstantial. The Cuban defense establishment has allegedly undergone fundamental reorientation and restructuring. The principal results have been a sharp downsizing of the armed forces; adoption of new techniques of deterrence and defense under an umbrella concept called "The War of All the People"; and a new focus on the self-support of the armed forces through farming.

"The War of All the People," General Rosales explained, is composed of six strategic tasks:

1. Training the entire populace for prolonged defensive warfare against superior forces with high technological advantage. Cuban leaders argue that "artificial intelligence should not be confused with human intelligence." They reason that in the final analysis, in war, men must fight men—they must get out of their planes and off their ships and face each other man to man. "The Cuban strategy is based upon the imposition of high human and political cost upon an enemy. . . . And is therefore bound to prevail in the long run." The general went on to assert that Cuba would never make the mistake Saddam Hussein did by leaving his forces in the open, exposed to attack by high-technology weaponry.

2. Preparation of the theater of operations. For the most part, this involves the fortification of Cuba against surprise attack and the development of a capability for protracted defense and guerrilla-type operations. It also involves protection of the entire population through the construction of underground shelters (to be accomplished, as in Abraham Lincoln's formulation, "of, by and for the people").

3. Subjecting all military programs to strict measures for increased efficiency to realize maximum possible savings to the government. This will include the preparation of civilian defenses through "voluntary" participation in shelter construction. Defense Minister Raul Castro (who has since assumed his brother's leadership position) announced that the Eastern Army (the eastern third of the country) had completed seventy kilometers of tunnels.

4. Extending the useful life of military equipment through storage of all matériel not essential for current military training and operations. This includes the encapsulation of equipment in nitrogen-filled plastic bags and their placement in underground facilities. The minimum storage life sought through this technique is five years. At the five-year point the equipment is removed from storage and checked for deterioration. Reportedly, the latest such check in December 1995 found a tank unit to be fully serviceable.

5. Developing island self-sufficiency in terms of feeding its citizens. This includes the complete self-sufficiency of the armed forces through farming, and the objective of providing approximately 40 percent of the needs of the civilian population by the Youth Labor Army. Most foods will be provided by the state cooperative farms, but civilians will assist through the operation of private garden plots. Individuals may sell a designated share of privately grown foods.

6. Maintaining a high level of readiness in armed forces. The United States is perceived as a volatile, intolerant power with a history of aggression against Cuba. Readiness is measured in terms of manning, training, and having authorized equipment on hand.

Cuba cannot afford equipment modernization, and claims to have a strategy that does not require it. General Rosales dismisses modernization as participation in a pointless arms race. According to the annual estimate of the International Institute for Strategic Studies, the active armed forces of Cuba (Fuerzas Armadas Revolucionarias, or FAR) number about 49,000 men and women, with almost as many in the reserves, and over a million paramilitary troops in the active components of the Youth Labor Army (Ejercito Joven Trabajo, or EJT). Conscripts serve in either the active forces or the EJT for a period of two years. Thereafter they may revert to reserve status or serve in the territorial militia. The International Institute for Strategic Studies estimates these forces at 135,000 and 1.3 million, respectively. The General Staff says that it has a special asset in the reserve and militia forces, which are believed to have some 300,000 veterans with combat experience in Angola between 1975 and 1987. Some of these men are expected to remain in the structure until 2017.

The visiting group encountered no units of the FAR (aside from the schools described below) but it had the services of a detachment of particularly sharp-looking guides, wearing red berets, creased trousers, and parachute wings. Unfortunately, the visual impression was not confirmed by the unit's performance, which strongly suggested a Keystone Cops entertainment routine.

The function of the detachment was to clear the way for the visitors' bus transport. The soldiers' approach to this mission was to speed their Russian-made squad car ahead while all four of the occupants waved and shouted out the windows to everyone in sight. This tactic did manage to bring a few lumbering trucks closer to the curb, but, as often as not, it was accomplished on the wrong road. The guides seemed to pay more attention to clearing a path than to pursuing the planned route, necessitating occasional U-turns.

The Youth Labor Army (EJT) was formed in 1973 as part of the Revolutionary Army to perform rural labor and to fulfill local area security missions. The strength of the organization is said to vary from 50,000 to 70,000, depending on the season. The EJT is credited with having harvested as much as one-third of the nation's sugar crop and having contributed 40 percent of the national food production effort when such help was needed. For the most part it operates farms in areas not otherwise under cultivation by the state cooperatives. The Isle of Youth (formerly the Isle of Pines) is said to be a large EJT preserve. While EJT undergoes periodic infantry and guerrilla training, it is probably not well adapted to the area which it serves, since the members are frequently moved according to the seasonal demands for farm labor. The farm visited was unremarkable. The workers wore civilian clothes and appeared to have old but serviceable transport (some horse-drawn) and machinery. The briefing officer gave no numerical strength figures for men working at the farm, but said that the number varied widely from season to season.

The officers also mentioned "frontier brigades," but it was not clear whether these units were associated with the EJT. Some brigades were said to include women, especially in air defense units. A female company was mentioned as serving in the Guantanamo area.

The National Defense College, established in 1990, is located a few miles east of Havana. The institution offers an array of programs, ranging from advanced military branch courses to senior service college (master's) level. The senior course, which lasts for one year and grants a master of arts degree in national defense studies, has a student body of sixty selected from all departments of the government. During an academic year some 250 military and other government officials address the students. Approximately half of the student body is from the armed forces, and as many as fifteen or twenty may be women.

The curriculum is divided into four periods: basic international political theory (8 weeks); Cuban domestic issues, including sixteen days of travel in the country (19 weeks); diplomatic, scientific, international, and geopolitical studies, including a one-week war game (14 weeks); and vacation and research time.

The students write two major papers during the year—an individual thesis and a contribution to a group study project. Judging by the quality of the questions asked of the visitors by the students, the curriculum is probably similar to that of some of the programs offered by the US National Defense University. The students seemed to be well informed on their topics of interest. But, surprisingly, Cuba has no foreign students or faculty members at any of its military educational or training institutions.

Notable in the seminar rooms of the college were numerous instructional panels dealing with guerilla operations in Chinese, Vietnamese, and Korean Wars. Also prominent were maps of the campaigns of Napoleon and Simon Bolivar. Perhaps the conflicts afforded greatest significance in the college were the Cuban Ten-Year War against Spain (1868–1878), led by Carlos Manuel de Cespedes (known as the father of his country), and the subsequent uprising (1895–1898), led by José Marti, who perished in battle.

Cuban history records that in these campaigns an indigenous Cuban force of 25,000 effectively defeated the Spanish Army of 300,000. American forces intervened in 1898, but, while not unwelcome, they were largely seen as interlopers who entered the struggle just in time to steal the Cuban victory. The Cubans remark dolefully that they were cut out of the Treaty of Paris, which settled the war in America's favor and set the stage for thirty-five years of US domination of the island—first as occupiers, and later as economic bullies under the infamous Platt Amendment. The US law authorized military intervention practically on whim until that ability was revoked under President Roosevelt's "Good Neighbor" policy in 1936. In discussions regarding the concept of "The War of All the People," which some seemed to believe to be a likely future event, Cuban officers drew parallels with the campaigns of Manuel de Cespedes and José Marti. In particular, they focused on the decade-long duration of the first conflict.

The Cadet School and NCO Academy were located on an attractive campus southwest of Havana. The NCOs staged an impressive display of close order drill and weapons-handling, culminating in a halftime-style march formation, with one of the women of the group standing on a platform of interwoven rifles, waving the Cuban flag. The group was said to be celebrating completion of its five-month course. The class displayed a spirit and style worthy of any NCO corps.

The Officer Cadet School staged an array of field exercises over a twenty-acre area, circus style. A lieutenant colonel acted as master of ceremonies, pointing out key events to the observers. The participation of women in all but the most strenuous activities was notable. In one routine, students (including women) clasped the ends of bamboo poles and were thrust aloft to the tops of high walls, from which they dropped ropes for others to follow.

Flaming hazards were prominent. At one point, successive pairs of cadets were smeared with grease and set afire to test their fortitude and their ability to extinguish the flames quickly. Others entered a flaming mock village to flush out snipers. Still others rolled beneath tanks (T-55s) bearing down on them and rose afterward to pitch Molotov cocktails on the rear decks of the vehicles. The finale brought the cadets together in a mass formation, singing a patriotic anthem and waving their arms and poles in unison.

The barracks at Bejucal, south of Havana, were reportedly built by Soviet forces to house a reinforced rifle regiment. The original mission of the unit had been to protect the nuclear warheads deployed to the island in 1962. Subsequently, the Soviets became advisors and trainers for the Cuban military, particularly for those units preparing for overseas duty in Africa.

At the time of the visit the garrison appeared to house a similar Cuban unit, but the visitors were not invited to inspect the equipment sheds. From a distance the sheds appeared to be full of mechanized and armored equipment. The six principal buildings of barracks complex each had three floors, apparently designed to accommodate battalion-size units.

The visitors were also invited to inspect a tunnel complex not far from the National Defense College. The plan of the installation, basically, an intersection of twin tunnels, had at least six exits. Four of the exits appeared to lead to external combat positions; three others may have led to other subterranean installations.

The entrances seen were covered by large, heavily camouflaged doors, closely resembling the karst limestone into which the tunnels had been dug. So closely did the camouflage material match the surrounding rock that one had to knock on the surface to determine the difference. In its entirety, the complex may extend over a square kilometer or more. Auxiliary casements in the tunnels were said to hold 290 tons of diesel fuel, 175 tons of gasoline, 90 tons of medical supplies, 160 tons of life support equipment, 30 tons of clothing, and 12,000 liters of water.

The tunnel complex was described as a principal fortification for a territorial motorized infantry regiment. The unit was said to be composed of three infantry battalions, an artillery battalion, a tank company, and antitank, air defense, chemical, and service units. A large portion appeared to be filled with a unit's heavy equipment. Notable were Russian infantry fighting vehicles, D-30 122-mm howitzers, and ZU-23 twin-barrel anti-aircraft guns. Most of the equipment was shrouded in plastic bags.

Also notable in the sections of the facility that could be viewed was the absence of provisions for comfort. If the facility is intended to shelter troops for more than a few days, there must be more spacious areas with better provisions for water, waste disposal, and rest. Baffles to contain the damage in case of explosion were also apparently lacking. Fuel and munitions casements, as with those for other supplies, appeared to lead directly to the main tunnels.

THE CIENFUEGOS NAVAL BASE

The base was removed from active service as part of the drawdown of the FAR. The visitors were shown two piers said to service Soviet submarines and a large warehouse apparently for recharging submarine batteries. The piers were said to accommodate up to eleven submarines at one time. Approximately 300 batteries with Russian markings, each about four feet tall and two-by-three feet in cross section, remained on racks with power connections attached. The base commander said that these were extra batteries left behind by the Soviets when they withdrew. It was not clear whether they were serviceable, since no machinery with which they might be associated was in operation. The only vessel in the area at the time appeared to be a Corvette standing several miles from shore.

THE JURAGUA NUCLEAR POWER PLANT

The Juragua plant is located on Cuba's southern shore, across the bay from the Cienfuego Naval Base. In the past decade or so two planned reactor shells and several associated buildings have been erected. Some large reactor machinery and components are on the site, but are stored in separate sheds as much as a half-mile from the principal structure. No nuclear fuel was on hand. The engineers at the installation expressed considerable frustration at the multiple obstacles to completing the plant.

The engineers estimated that at least $800 million would be required to complete the project. They admitted that as many as eleven safety-related deficiencies may have existed in the structure, but complained that the international community—particularly the United States—had not been helpful in moving the project forward. (The reactor design is described as being similar to that of Chernobyl, but considerably improved. Most objections to the plant appear to relate to its design and its location with respect to Florida.)

The Cuban motive for inviting the group to the island was probably twofold. On the one hand, the government was anxious to impress upon the visitors the viability of the new defensive strategy and the specific military measures adopted since the collapse of the Soviet Union. On the other, it was clearly interested in developing an opening at a professional level that would avoid direct confrontation between Cuba and the United States over ideological issues.

THE GENERAL STAFF

The General Staff seemed to be as concerned about an attack by US forces at the time of the visit as the NATO Alliance was of an attack by the Warsaw Pact nations at the height of the Cold War. While the contingency may not necessarily have been considered likely, it loomed as a definite possibility and was a factor coloring much government decision-making.

The Staff also showed concern about the relocation of the US Southern Command Headquarters from Panama to Miami. It apparently viewed the latter as the epicenter of hostile Cuban émigré influence. Some members expressed a fear of the coordination of US military and émigré policies and the possibility of hostile actions. Further, the appointment of the former US commander-in-chief, General Barry R. McCaffrey, as director of the Office of National Drug Control Policy was interpreted by some, without explanation, as a potentially anti-Cuban measure.

With respect to narcotics control, a number of General Staff officials argued that Cuba could assist the United States substantially, particularly in the coordination of anti-drug sea and air patrols. They pointed out that the execution of a prominent Cuban leader for drug dealing demonstrated the government's attitude toward the drug trade. At the time Cuba cooperated with Argentina, Canada, Mexico, and other hemispheric countries in operations to block trade in illegal substances. Cuban officials assert that the US Drug Enforcement Administration expressed interest in cooperation with Cuba in 1994, but was blocked by the US Department of State. What the Cubans wanted at that point was the removal of the US economic embargoes of the island, which they termed a blockade—hence an act of war. They also wanted the respect of the United States for their revolution and help in completing their nuclear power plant.

Other issues, heard less frequently or in more subdued tones, included the return of the Guantanamo Naval Base to Cuban control; discontinuance of US hostile reconnaissance and bomber flights near the island; curtailment of private anti-Castro operations and demonstrations by Cuban-American groups based in Miami; free trade between Cuba and the United States; and the amelioration of perceived American "arrogance and hegemony."

While the visitors observed no combat units, the high spirit of the students and the members of the faculties at the National Defense College and the Cadet and NCO Schools was palpable. These Cuban elite were clearly enthusiastic and proud of what they were doing. Further, while socialism is a prominent theme in public moral engineering, one gains the impression that the revolution is much more than simple Marxist-Leninism—if, indeed, it is even seriously connected. The revolution of which many military officers speak appears to be rooted deeper in Cuban history. The Ten-Year War, Marti's uprising, and the overthrow of the Batiste regime come to the surface far more readily than do Marxist calls for the union of the workers of the world.

Mao Tse-tung's wars and the Vietnam War enjoy a focus more for their lessons regarding peoples' uprisings and techniques for inflicting political damage on a superior force than for their ideological message. One gains the impression that even when Fidel Castro disappears the revolution will remain as a national institution—shorn, perhaps, of much of its communist dressing.

On the other hand, it is the very socialist dimension of the revolution that appears to be the greatest restraint on Cuba's progress. Desperate for foreign investment, the leadership seems incredulous at the reluctance of free-market managers to sink more money into a society in which the laws can be made or unmade for political purposes by the stroke of a pen. Such arbitrary restrictions as the limit of twelve chairs in a private restaurant are not unusual. That particular law was apparently drafted in the wake of a Castro remark that it might be all right to have that many seats, but that private interests should not dominate the restaurant business. It is quite likely that Cuba's inability to attract more foreign investment is due more to such arbitrary regulation than to US embargo.

In sum, through Cuban eyes, the national story is a history of prolonged suffering at foreign hands and of proud struggle for independence. Fidel Castro is seen by the military as a living liberator, but he is not necessarily considered greater than others in the past. His specialty, and his brother's, is socialism, and Cubans are quick to point out institutions for orphans, the blind, the infirm, and the elderly that have been erected during their leadership. But the revolution is more than the radical left. It is the national heritage, and even while mired in poverty, the Fuerzas Armadas Revolucionarias will probably remain a faithful, if limited, force for the system's defense.

FIDEL CASTRO

It was almost two years later that a group of a half-dozen American officers was invited to make a second visit to Cuba, this time as personal guests of

El Commandante en Jefe. The dinner to which we were invited was scheduled for 7:00 p.m. Castro appeared precisely 15 minutes later. After a round of handshaking, some drinks, and introductions, he led us into a beautifully appointed dining room. He and a few from his staff sat down on one side of a room-long table. We took our appointed seats on the other. As the senior officer in our group I found myself directly opposite his hypnotic gaze.

Sitting with his head cocked to one side, he stared right into my face, in part as if to question why I should be there, but mostly to lecture me about what a "wonderful" place Cuba was becoming. His first objective was clearly to tell me how he was outliving all of his significant enemies, foreign and domestic. He was by then a septuagenarian with plentiful war stories to hold his guests' attention. This was to be his evening, and his big chance to keep Fuerzas Armadas Revolucionarias before his guests as they enjoyed their dinner.

He asked no questions. This permitted him a full nine-hour talkathon, with topics almost entirely in his hands. He had used these hands frequently before we had come to the table, mostly to tap our lapels to reinforce points he wanted to make at the outset. Now they were theatrical properties he used for pointing to his temple, or to the ceiling—always upward. This was his place, his dining room, and his conversation.

It took patience and courage on the part of any of the five on our side of the table to seek, however infrequently, clarification of a point or to pose a question. When one of my colleagues, or I, did so, he would react with surprise and a rather mystified look. Apparently, that did not happen to him very often. He took no visible offense. He was just not accustomed to such behavior by his guests—or by anyone else.

He knew that our group had been making occasional visits to Cuba of the last four or five years, and he was aware of the US military air doctrine for raining smart bombs on practically all of an opponent's military equipment. As a result he had supported the military's program to get their gear underground for years. When questioned as to whether the army still used "volunteer" labor for this work, an officer from the Operations Section of the General Staff replied bluntly, "No. We assign quotas."

On another trip we had driven into the mountains of Villa Clara Province to visit an explosives plant that produces shotgun cartridges and .22 caliber ammunition (longs), as well as military ammunition, rockets, and mines. Our vision, however, had been carefully limited to the civilian side of the facility. We had been to a youth farm, a national hospital, and the Che Guevara boarding school. We had held extensive talks with the General Staff, the Ministry of Foreign Affairs, and individual members of the National Assembly.

From these earlier visits we had gathered the principal subliminal message intended by our hosts: Cuba will not be caught unprepared for an assault from abroad. It may have lost its principal patron when the Soviet Union collapsed, but it is not going to follow the path of either the USSR or its satellites into a new orbit around the Western powers. "If an aggressor chooses to attack Cuba," we were advised by the chief of the General Staff, "the aggressor will have to come down from his aircraft and ashore from his ships and face us man-to-man in the countryside."

Castro, our loquacious host, was aware of all this and wasted no time repeating the point. He had other matters on his mind. Most particularly, he seemed disturbed that some officials in Washington were attempting to paint Cuba as a willing participant in the drug smuggling business with Colombian and Spanish accomplices. We would not hear that such a charge had appeared in many newspapers that morning (28 October 1999 in Robert D. Novak's syndicated column). It is very likely that Fidel had been advised of the accusation, and our visit was an opportunity for him to present his side of the story. He had at his elbow a complete portfolio of text and photographs showing a cavernous steel shipping crate with a false inner shell, alleged to have harbored an enormous cache of cocaine.

Our host's story was as follows: Two apparently well-heeled Spaniards had entered into a joint venture with the government of Cuba for the acquisition and sale of foreign goods through one of the island's new free-trade zones. The two used their plentiful financial resources to entrench themselves in one of the best hotels in Havana and to entertain lavishly many of the top people in town. They were generous to a fault, apparently oblivious of the risk of raising suspicions within the Cuban apparatus.

Meanwhile, Colombian police were investigating a consignment of cocaine in their port at Cartagena ready to be shipped to Cuba, apparently intended for further transference to Spain. The Colombians informed the Cuban government, but not quickly enough for the Cubans to arrest the Spaniards before they fled. They were arrested in their own country, but they could not be charged for lack of evidence. (Just why they could not be returned to Cuba for trial or why the evidence could not be shipped to Spain was not explained. Again, our host's vocal style shaded clarity.)

The story itself may have important legal ramifications for policy, but the interesting point for us was the extraordinary length to which Castro went with his tutorial for us, his guests. For almost an hour, he held us at a side table, showing us pictures and samples of the nominal contents of the shipment: poor imitations of Lladro and Hummel figurines. They had been carefully set out for our inspection. This was not a matter he wanted us to forget. "Cuba is not—repeat not," he insisted, "involved in drug or any other form of smuggling."

However, that was not to say that Cuban air and sea spaces are not used regularly by drug smugglers in their nefarious efforts to deliver such goods to the US market. The Commandante painted a picture of frequent flights by small private aircraft violating Cuban sovereign territory, disposing their packages in the water to be picked up by high-speed boats operating from "mother" ships traversing the Straits of Florida. At any moment, he said, there may be as many as a hundred ships in the narrows, which at night or in fog are difficult to identify. The lack of Cuban-US cooperation in tracking and arresting these players, he continued, makes the game a reasonably safe bet for the perpetrators. Cuba's shortage of fuel, he insisted, prevents effective defense operations against the hostile aircraft. Wordlessly, but with a meaningful twist of his mobile features and a half-wink of an eye, the president indicated that we should understand whose fault that was.

He went on to outline another aspect of the drug operations that he thought we ought to understand. The fast boats used to pick up the drug shipments are occasionally used (for a fat fee) to deliver illegal emigrants from Cuba to the neighboring Florida coast. If the emigrants could make it to the neighboring Florida shore, he advised us, they were considered "home free." Only if they were intercepted at sea by the US Coast Guard were they arrested or turned back. Sometimes the boats did double duty by delivering both drugs and illegal emigrants to their destination, he said. Again, by implication, the fault lay in the lack of US-Cuban governmental coordination because of "irrational" US law and policy.

Having made the political points that in his mind probably justified our being there, the *Commandante en Jefe* fell back into the monologue in which he apparently felt most comfortable—Cuban history, old war stories, and a close interrogation of his guests. He was delighted to learn that my grandfather had been there aboard a warship in the Spanish-American War, and somewhat less pleased that my father had served as commandant of the Guantanamo Naval Base in the 1950s. He waxed loquacious about his time in the mountains, first fighting bandits and later the Batiste dictatorship. One could almost hear the bullets sing past his ears as he described some of his exchanges.

He showed no special pride in having trained three guerrilla fighters to kill twenty-four soldiers in the back of a truck with forty rounds of ammunition. (A high rate of fire and a good distribution do the trick.) His troops practiced on dummies with coconut heads. He commented that smashed coconuts were everywhere following the exercise.

On the other hand, he seemed to regret having ordered the execution of one of his trusted lieutenants, Arnaldo Ochoa. He recalled in one nocturnal, near fratricidal engagement, how two guerrilla groups surprised each other in the bush. There was a furious exchange of fire before the two sides realized that they were each dealing with a friendly unit. He described how Ochoa remained on his feet during the entire incident, and it was he who saved the rest from killing each other. "He was fearless, and would become the Cuban commander in Africa."

"But he was also greedy. He embezzled large quantities of funds before he was caught." Ochoa was tried by military court (in which Castro appeared for the prosecution), found guilty, and sentenced to death. Castro approved the sentence, and by all appearances has regretted it ever since. No tears came to his eyes as he told the story, but his voice betrayed emotion. One senses that there may be more to the story than either the official government reports or Castro himself chose to disclose.

The Commandante patted his guests on the arm and tapped their lapels with his index finger. He looked them straight in the eye and conveyed as much by the extraordinary mobility of his brows and mouth as he did with his unceasing flow of words. He had a lot on his mind and seemed to need every form of communication—both audible and visible—that he could muster to get his points across. His superb interpreter had undoubtedly heard much of it before and had no difficulty in providing virtually simultaneous translation. At times she even finished lines before her chief.

Castro clearly enjoys lecturing his guests on proper care of their health: exercise, lots of vegetables, red wine, no bread, and no tobacco. He had given up cigars years before, but distributed top-of-the-line boxes simply because they were important Cuban products.

Surprisingly, Castro expressed no particular sense of his place in history. He stated that he had many fine men with him in the mountains, and a number of them died. He could have died, too, he argued, in which case someone else would be sitting in his place. It was just the luck of the draw. The implication was that he has never had a sense of destiny through any mystical power. As an atheist, he takes things as they come.

The argument appears to be supported by the absence of any sign of idolatry of the ruling group. There are posters aplenty of such "saints" as Che Guevara, Camilo Cienfuegos, and José Marti, but on the streets there was no visible cult devoted to the current leadership as is normally so prominent in communist states.

To one question Castro replied that he sees himself more as a political leader than as a military man. He would have liked to have gone to a military academy, but he never had a chance (as did his younger brother, Raul, who at the time of our visit was minister of defense). Fidel said that war is an art, and that he loves to read about the campaigns of Napoleon, Hannibal, and the Romans. He had an early fascination with weapons. Robert E. Quirk, one of his many biographers, tells of his turning a shotgun on his mother's chickens at age ten.

Castro said that he felt obliged to wear fatigues and a beard in honor of the old days. One may notice, however, that the fatigues are well-tailored and fashioned from high-grade material. With respect to his management of Cuba's economy since the Soviet collapse, Castro said he believed that the country had seen its worst days. Placing his faith in the discipline of his officers a few years back, he dispatched a number of them to Europe to study how businesses operate in a capitalist environment. The officers returned to Cuba to introduce the techniques that seemed most applicable to the industries controlled by the military (such as the ammunition plant we visited).

Castro said that he believed that that phase of his program had been successfully accomplished. Now, he said, he would be moving the officers' efforts to focus on the civilian sector to complete the transformation of the economy. The appointment of General Ulises Rosales del Toro, formerly chief of the General Staff, to head the sugar industry was typical of the current state of the effort. Castro said that he was generally satisfied with the management of Cuban enterprises, but there were some exceptions. He believed that he would have to make some personnel changes as he went along.

Finally, our host remarked on the role the United States had been playing in international affairs in the past decade. He said he believes that the president of the United States had been delegated too much authority for making war.

Although he did not elaborate, one might assume that he had in mind the virtual suspension of the constitutional provision for the US Congress to be the instrument for declaring war. The United States is now so powerful, he argued, that there should be a better means for controlling the actions of the president. One might have wished to ask his opinion of the war powers of leaders in communist states, but the opportunity did not arise.

Fidel Castro is clearly a man of talent and ambition for his country. He is proud of the socialist system he has created, and he appears confidant that in the end it will provide a high quality of life for the people of Cuba, whom he professes to champion. He points to the near extermination of illiteracy in the country; the system for medical care he has introduced, particularly in rural areas; and the equality of opportunity among the citizenry. He looks for foreign capital to invigorate the economy through the formation of joint ventures and the designation of free-trade zones in which regular manufacturing, as well as storage of goods, can take place.

While he made no predictions, he clearly believes that in time the United States will eventually amend its laws to permit unencumbered investment, tourism, and trade to flourish. He also believes that the United States will come to realize that Cuban-American cooperation is essential to the control of drug traffic and the migration of people between the two countries. He believes he is on the right track—and he likes to talk about it.

Whatever one may make of the elderly Castro in his waning years, he makes little difference today. He has "strut and fret his hour upon the stage," and is unlikely to be heard much more. His brother, Raul, is doing his best to keep things going, but whatever becomes of the country, it is not likely to be quite as troublesome a problem for the United States as it has been in previous times. Communism may remain part of the official line, for a decade or more, but other dynamics are likely to have greater influence.

In late July 2009 the Cuban Communist Party declared the indefinite suspension of plans for its next congress, and lowered its projection of 2009 economic growth for the second time, this time nearly a full percentage point. President Raul Castro referred to the economy as being in "a very serious" crisis. One very damaging factor has been three hurricanes on the island in one summer, creating more than $10 billion in damage, and conditions have been made worse by the global financial crisis and the recession.

The president commented to the press that "the principal matter is the economy: what we have done and what we have to perfect and even eliminate as we are up against an imperative to make full accounts of what the country really has available, of what we have to live and for development." The official statement also announced that the sixth party congress would be postponed until the current "critical phase" had been overcome, but no date was given for that event.[1]

Stricken by three hurricanes in 2008, as well as the global recession, the "socialist" government has chosen to lend its under-employed land to farmers wishing to expand their modest incomes. Sugar, the former queen of agriculture, has had its day: the demand has given way to many substitutes. The result has been a system invented somewhere else in the West. It is not that the farmers have defeated the system, but that the government has come to better understand the incentive of private enterprise.

The government now "lends" its vast under-exploited lands to farmers wishing to work for themselves. As one farmer commented, upon being assigned twenty acres, "This is a big change. Everyone wants in." The state still sets the price but the more the farmer produces the more he sells. In their own interest, farmers try to grow better-quality produce, which fetches a higher price. They are paid in cash. "Right now," one farmer said, "there are shortages of everything, so there is no risk of overproduction."

The first hint of positive movement in the "critical phase" may have come on 17 September 2009. For the first time in thirty-six years US and Cuban officials met in Havana to discuss the possibility of reestablishing direct mail service between the two countries. While the agenda was a narrow one, the step was important, very possibly marking major changes in the attitudes of both governments. If successful, the measure could signal a breakthrough and likely reconnection of former ties between the governments.[2]

In terms of Thomas Barnett's "functioning core" (the West) and the "nonintegrating gap" (much of the South and East of the world), the meeting of Cuban and American officials would send a strong signal of Cuban movement from the latter group in the direction of the former, and a significant improvement of many conditions for both Cuba and the United States. Further, in terms of the need for development of an American legion for Cuba, considering the advanced level of Cuba's national security apparatus, the requirement would be virtually nil. While Cuba may require a new supply of weaponry for its own defense, it has a highly coherent armed force with a generous skein of competent officers and enthusiastic troops devoted to the welfare of the state.

While the reintroduction of anti-Castro Cubans from the United States may stimulate some problems, including formal reconstruction of the government, there is little reason to believe that public law and order would deteriorate to the point that American-led troops would be necessary. The Cuban army, while small, is a good one, and it should be able to enforce the directives of a more democratic government.

Most recently, the United Nations has voted overwhelmingly to condemn the American trade embargo against Cuba, with speeches by the American ambassador and Cuba's foreign minister reflecting, as the *New York Times* writer has pointed out, that little has changed despite an expected shift under the Obama administration. An annual nonbinding resolution comes before the national representatives of the UN every year in hopes of recognizing the changes that have overtaken Cuban policy since the wicked days of high communism in that impoverished land. But recognition of change has been difficult for both the United States and the General Assembly. The vote on 21 October 2009 was 187 in support of change, 3 opposed, and 2 abstaining. One can only imagine how embarrassing the process must be for our representatives, year after year, to play with cold stone. Few who are at all knowledgeable of conditions on the island do not support the measure. All others must simply wait for the Washington bureaucracy to clear its intestines of the ancient bile.[3]

As a direct result of President Bush's strategic blunder in 2004, Cuban dissidents have experienced a significant reduction in material and humanitarian assistance. They are subject to a ban on receiving cash remittances that help them and their families survive. Those who have escaped Cuba continue to be isolated from the land of their birth. But that is not the only Bush blunder to complicate life for Americans and Cubans. The Bush wars in the Middle East have drawn much of the strength out of American foreign initiatives around the world.

With respect to Cuban-American affairs, it will likely be up to either the current or next US president to put a stop to America's spectator approach in the Caribbean. The status quo is unacceptable to either party, and change will have to be extracted from both Cuba and the United States. The US side must:

- Restore official relations;
- Restore free (or reasonably fair) trade with Cuba;

- Change the rules that make it impossible to send cash abroad—considering the number of Cubans taking refuge in the US, we need to quickly allow direct, substantial, and unfettered aid to Cuba's dissidents;
- Lift the 2004 restrictions on travel and remittances by Cuban Americans—removing the handcuffs that have prevented us from becoming active participants in the development of Cuban civil society will make us agents of change;
- Seek to establish cooperative actions with Cuba for control of the drug trade in the Caribbean.

As the time for a change of attitudes between the United States and Cuba draws closer, it may become useful to seek a degree of cooperative training between the two armies, and an arrangement incorporating certain features of a binational legion may become useful. In spite of the differences between a democratic and a socialist state, the absence of any third player, such as crime-ridden states elsewhere in the hemisphere, may permit a degree of cooperation on the island. It would be premature to declare communism dead, but cooperative programs between the two countries' forces are more feasible than one might imagine. The principal commonality between the two armed forces is a sense of professionalism, which may be cultured as long as the political environments are not hostile to one another.

On 7 July 2010 the Cuban government announced that it would release fifty-two political prisoners over the following few months. The announcement could affect as many as a third of the total number of noncriminal prisoners held under the government's control. Especially important was Mr. Guillermo Fariñas, who fasted for seven months until it appeared that the government would also release twenty-six other prisoners of conscience who were seriously ill. Fariñas was released and awarded the Sakharov Prize for Freedom of Thought by the European Parliament, but resumed his hunger strike in June 2011 in response to the death of a fellow dissident.[4]

The Roman Catholic Church appears to be playing a role in the changing Cuban government policy. Cardinal Jaime Ortega, the archbishop of Havana, has been in touch with both Cuban and Spanish officials, and the prisoner release appears to be advancing under diplomatic coordination with the Church and the Cuban government.[5]

Figure 9.1. Map of Africa

9

Africa—the Dark Continent

From the beginning of recorded history Africa has probably been the most exploited continent in the world. While the riches of the land have been sufficient to support its kings, bandits, and entrepreneurs, much of the exploitation has been achieved by those born elsewhere. Slaves, gold, precious stones, and fuels have long attracted foreign traders with their seagoing ships. Slaves, in particular, were hot items. Between 1451 and 1870, some nine million slaves were forced to cross the Atlantic under barely life-supporting conditions. Another million or more did not survive the voyage, while untold additional numbers never made it to the coast to board the ships.[1]

In recent times there has been intra-continental combat among royalty, competitive kinsmen, culture groups, foreign aggressors, and political leaders. Following World War II, for instance, Angola fought a liberation war (with Portugal) and a civil war (over socialism) for fourteen years. Martin Meredith's monumental volume, *The Fate of Africa*, provides us with as pertinent and concise a review of the development of the continent over the last two centuries as is to be found in most any modern library in the Western world. Here we may learn of the meetings in London, Paris, Berlin, and other capitals, of diplomats prepared to bargain over the separate spheres of interest they intended to establish on the little-known, and even less-well-understood, "dark continent."

Some began with rather well-developed databases regarding the islands and coastal areas of the mammoth continent, but soon found themselves bargaining over immense tracts of land of which they knew very little. As Meredith points out, much of the interior had to be labeled terra incognita, even as the negotiators projected boundaries, largely on blank maps, by simply extending straight lines inward until they met other boundary extensions which, in turn, helped to divide the expected spoils among the representatives of the "civilized world."[2]

"In some cases," Meredith points out, "African societies were rent apart: the Bakongo [people] for instance, were partitioned between French Congo, Belgian Congo and Portuguese Angola; Somaliland was carved up between Britain, Italy and France. In other cases the new Europeans' boundaries cut through some 190 culture groups. In still other cases, Europe's new colonial territories enclosed hundreds of diverse and independent groups, with no common history, culture, language or religion. Nigeria, for example, contained as many as 250 linguistic groups. Officials sent to the Belgian Congo eventually identified six thousand chiefdoms there."[3] Meredith writes of Prime Minister Salisbury of Great Britain "haggling in Europe over African territory, land and peoples [which would become] little more than pieces on a chessboard." Britain traded the North Sea Helgoland with the Germans for Zanzibar, and parts of northern Nigeria with the French for fishing rights off Newfoundland. Paris, in turn, exchanged parts of Cameroon with Germany in return for German recognition of the French protectorate over Morocco. By the time the "scramble" for Africa was over, some 10,000 African polities had been amalgamated into forty European colonies and protectorates.[4]

"In the concluding act of the partition of Africa," Meredith continues,

> Britain, at the height of its imperial power, set out to take over two independent Boer republics, the Transvaal and the Orange Free State, and to incorporate them into the British Empire, assuming that a war of conquest would take at most a matter of months. It turned into a grueling campaign lasting three years, requiring nearly half a million imperial troops to finish, and left a legacy of bitterness and hatred among Afrikaners which would endure for generations. Faced with guerrilla warfare, for which they were unprepared, British military commanders resorted to scorched-earth tactics, destroying thousands of farmsteads, razing villages to the ground and slaughtering livestock on a massive scale, reducing the Boers to an impoverished people.[5]

French interest in Africa early in the nineteenth century tended to focus on the Sudan and the African shores of the Red Sea. The Somali and Afar tribes in the region were notable as the first on the African continent to adopt Islam. But Islam did not imply immediate hostility. By 1862 the sultans of Raheita and Tadjoura signed an agreement with the French for the sale of the key anchorage at Obock at the southern extremity of the Red Sea.

As the British were sinking their roots into Egypt, both England and France developed an interest in the feasibility of a Suez Canal. In 1897 the French extended their protectorate along the northwestern coast of Somaliland. They also reached an agreement with Emperor Menelik II of Ethiopia regarding their western border, and strengthened their claims by further agreements with Emperor Haile Selassi I after World War II, in 1945 and 1954. In 1977 the French granted Djibouti its independence, but they were not able to solidify their relationship until 2000.[6]

In the post–World War II era of East-West competition, the communist Cuban leadership sought to ensure its standing in Moscow by dispatching some 30,000 troops to Angola to support the far-left Movimento Popular de Libertação de Angola (MPLA), battling for control of the government.[7]

Notably, many of the rank and file of the Cuban forces were black, which facilitated their commitment. The greater part of the former African slave population in Cuba had been involuntary immigrants in the eighteenth and nineteenth centuries. Thus, many of their offspring could readily identify with their hosts in Angola against the Portugese landowners and their supporters. Not as substantial were Castro's contributions to the Algerian war against France in 1961, to the secret war between Havana and Washington in Zaire (1964–1965), and to the Guinea-Bissau war for independence from 1966 to 1974.[8]

And the British at one point looked for the establishment of a colonial "colossus of Rhodes" in Africa, stretching from the Cape of Good Hope in the south, northward across Rhodesia (now Zimbabwe), the "great lakes," and Sudan, to the Mediterranean shores of Egypt. To their credit, they had moved much earlier to abolish slavery on both sides of the Atlantic.

The United States was a relative latecomer to both universal human freedom and the African continent, the source of much of its manpower before the Civil War (1861–1865). One hopeful spot in America's early record had come in 1822 when it raised an effort to ship freed slaves to a lightly inhabited new home on the western coast of the African continent. Their freedom lift effort lasted for about twenty-five years, facilitating the foundation of the state of "Liberia." The settlers found some stability under the novel regime, but external pressures from neighboring colonial states and financial problems were endemic. The settlers from the United States, speaking a dialect of English, enjoyed an element of prestige during an early period, but often they could not read, and they certainly could not compete with European settlers in neighboring countries.[9] Nor did they have capital or technical savvy.

Nevertheless, for all the ambitions and activities of European powers in Africa in the nineteenth and much of the twentieth century, it would be largely the United States in the approach to the twenty-first that would begin to counterbalance the demons that seemed to infest many of the unhappy lands. As with most of the European countries involved, the "white man's burden" in Africa would not prove much easier for Americans than it had for the earlier explorers and men searching for riches.

Probably one of the most confusing territorial situations in Africa was that of Somalia, or Somaliland, frequently depicted on maps as either one or two countries. At the last mid-century they were colonies of Great Britain and Italy, respectively. In 1960 they merged to form a new Somalia. However, the union never sat well, primarily due to historic differences, including military aggression.

Somaliland gained independence from the colonizers on 26 June 1960 and announced a merger with Somalia the following day. But the independent state of Somalia never accepted the merger. The following decade was notable for open warfare between the states. Some 50,000 people were killed in the fighting while another 750,000 fled to Ethiopia.

More recently, Australia, which has critical marine traffic interests in the approaches to the Red Sea, has indicated that if Somalian leadership cannot settle the matter with its own diplomatic and other governmental instruments, Australia will do so unilaterally.[10]

In January 1991, President Mohamed Siad Barre, of Somalia, was overthrown by a coalition of opposing clans called "the United Somalia Congress." Through most of the year the various groups involved struggled with one another for leadership of the country. Feelings ran high and some 20,000 persons were slain in local battles before another leader, Mohammed Farah Aidid, could seize power. The international community tried to alleviate some of the tragedy, but bandits stole large quantities of relief goods. Food was short, and some half-million people starved to death. China wasted little time stepping in with lucrative arms sales.

The United States dispatched a light military force to stabilize the situation, as did Pakistan and Malaysia. Unfortunately, the operations were not well coordinated, and clear mistakes of policy soon translated into human losses as local citizens turned against the foreigners. This should not have been a big surprise. Enormous differences in cultures, languages, and expectations all took a toll.

On 3 October 1993 the curtains of peaceful debate in Somalia were rent with the onset of the Battles of Mogadishu. The American-led "Operation Gothic Serpent" would bring US Ranger teams, an air element of the 160th Special Operations Aviation Regiment, Navy SEAL operators, and Air Force Pararescue/Combat Controllers into action in an effort to capture high-ranking Somali officials. The force had some 160 troops aboard nineteen aircraft and twelve vehicles, and (late in the operation) was reinforced with small Malaysian and Pakistani detachments.

The objective was the capture of General Mohammed Farah Aidid, the commander of indigenous, anti-Western bandits. But, in the operation, two US MH-60 Black Hawk helicopters were shot down by rocket-propelled grenades, and three others were damaged. US personnel were trapped in native built-up areas and could not be rescued until the following day, and a number of the Americans were killed or wounded, including one captured by the locals. The body of another was dragged through the streets to the din of celebrating thugs.[11]

In Washington, in the wake of the action, President Bill Clinton directed Admiral David E. Jeremiah, the acting chairman of the Joint Chiefs of Staff, to stop all military action against Aidid, and to remove US forces by 31 March 1994. Already by December 15, the secretary of defense, Les Aspin, had stepped down, taking much of the blame for what was deemed a failed policy. Notably, there was no indigenous force with which basic coordination could have been effected.[12] As critics remarked, "The Eagle lost some of its tail feathers." Less gentle commentators resorted to less gentle terminology.

Since then Somalia has bubbled on as a troublesome area. Central Africa, to the southwest, especially the heartland of jungles and lakes, is home to tribes with murderous reputations. Since 1994 the Hutu tribal Democratic Forces for the Liberation of Rwanda (known for its French initials, FDLR) has been fighting and killing some 800,000 Tutsis and moderate Hutus. The Tutsi Rwanda Patriotic Front, however, was successful in turning the tables and driving the Hutus back into the Congolese jungle. As the Tutsis pressed further, however, they provoked reaction from surrounding countries: Angola, Burundi, Chad, Sudan, Uganda, and Zimbabwe.

In the process, the reactors toppled the Congo's dictator, Mobutu Sese Seko, and replaced him with their own candidate, Laurent Kabila. The complex mix of battles, raids, and related pandemics killed some four million people, an event cited by the *Economist* as "the biggest single bloodletting since the Second World War." The editor cited more recent events in the area as marginal improvements which could lead to peace, but there has been no real settlement, and resumption of the killing could occur at any time.[13]

Whatever the paths being studied (and, perhaps, mined) by the hostile groups today, it is apparent that only an outside power is likely to bring order and stability to the region in any period short of the horizon. The classic patterns of common racial identity, or tribal superiority, provide no guarantees of real peace in the region. The resident UN contingent is too small and cannot balance the fanaticism of some of the tribal groups. Most "best expectations" for the region today really amount to hopes. And that is where matters stand as the United States contemplates its various withdrawal efforts from the Middle East and its future role in counterbalancing terrorism worldwide.

Yes, force may be necessary, but not one of a self-inflative nature. Ideally, any military requirements could be met by professional, politically disinterested organizations with insight and understanding of the most troublesome issues. In short, one or more unbiased organizations with the power to ensure the compliance of all parties with rules laid down by an authority with unbiased insight. In other words, American foreign legions with men of the ranks drawn from volunteers from local interest groups, but likely disconnected from their former associates in the region. The first regiment of the American-African Foreign Legion, under the command and control of the US African Command commander, should be prepared for deployment as quickly as possible, not later than 2012.

An almost opposite case is to be found over three thousand miles away in the northwest corner of the continent, in the (poorly named) region of "Central Africa." There, since the mid-1980s, the Arabian Kingdom of Morocco has fended off guerrilla attacks by the mixed racial bands of the "Polisario Front" through the construction of a huge berm, well to the south of the southern political boundary between Mauritania and Senegal. The line is manned by UN troops, but contrary to events in Somalia, the arrangements have been moderately successful, however limited the grounds for continued confidence in the peace.[14]

In early fall 2009, fighting between soldiers of the transitional government and insurgents of an extremist Islamic group, called al-Shabab, broke out in Somalia again. And again the Islamists took control of the capital, Mogadishu. The US Federal Bureau of Investigation identified dozens of Somali-Americans who had previously joined African groups with links to Al Qaeda. Reportedly, eight people were killed when the insurgents attacked an African Union base at a former military academy. The best a deputy mayor of Mogadishu could offer was a promise that the government would drive the insurgents out of the capital city—as soon as the holy month of Ramadan was over.[15]

On 1 October 2009, President Sharif Ahmed of Somalia told the press that he urgently needed help to beat back the Al Qaeda insurgency in the country, noting that he had received only a fraction of the $200 million pledged in support of his security forces at a UN-sponsored donors' conference the previous spring. Ahmed's government nearly fell in mid-year under attack by the terrorist organization al-Shabab. The United States rushed in about forty tons of ammunition and weapons and more than $1 million in cash. Ahmed said that he had pressed Washington for thousands more peacekeepers, in addition to the 5,300 African Union troops already in the country.[16]

Much of the problem, of course, was the quality of the pro-government forces available in Somalia. Compared to modern forces elsewhere in the world, they were often of limited reliability and effectiveness, with questionable leadership. Unfortunately, no Western power assisted them with sufficient quality equipment, training, or leadership. Nor are such assets likely to develop in the country without the benefits of a well-cast foreign legion.

Healthy, dedicated volunteers with high-class tactical leadership would clearly be the best answer to Somalia's problem. Without them, radical Islam and international crime pose the most likely future for the country.

Looking for some of the worst terminology in Africa, reporter Nicholas Kristof ran across "autocannibalism." He suggested that "it describes what happens when a militia here in eastern Congo's endless war cuts flesh from living victims and forces the victim to eat it. Another [term] is 're-rape.' The need for that," he reported, "arose because doctors were seeing women and girls raped, re-raped and re-raped again, here in the capital of murder, rape and mutilation."

A reader of Kristof's writing wrote a response to complain about the use of common street terminology in a newspaper. "'Yes,'" he wrote, "'there are terrible things happening in Africa, [but] none of them are anything we can do anything about by ourselves.' Do we really need to say that we can't address suffering in Congo . . . because we have our own needs? Particularly when the Congo war has claimed so many lives (perhaps more than six million), isn't it time for the U.S. to lead a major, global diplomatic push for peace?" Then he added, "A United Nations official estimates that the population here in South Kivu Province is 55 percent female because so many men have been executed. Women are less likely to be killed, but more likely to be tortured."[17]

But one must keep an eye on Kenya, too, for matters jumping off track. In early September 2009 President Mwai Kibaki had to fire his chief of police commissioners, Mohammed Hussein Ali, for having committed illegal executions and rapes. But then, having done that, he immediately rehired the chief to head the postal service. The United Nations alleged that Ali had run death squads after hundreds of bodies were found dumped in the countryside. Ali denied the allegations, saying only that during his tour as police chief the police were vilified as a national pastime.[18]

Kenya certainly had enough other problems to get very deeply involved in Somalia. In 2008 more than a thousand Kenyans died in post-election violence. No one has yet been identified as the mastermind of the bloodshed. However, in the fall an investigation commission came up with a list of top suspects, widely believed to include some of the nation's most powerful men. The names were selected and handed over to Kofi Annan, the former secretary-general of the United Nations, who had taken the role of peacemaker. But at this writing none of Kenya's leaders have moved to bring the names to the International Criminal Court at The Hague. The Kenyan cabinet (which has more than sixty ministers and assistant ministers) called an emergency meeting to decide what to do, but no one seemed capable of (or interested in) bringing the issue to a point of decision.[19]

Complicating the matter was a United Nations move warning peace-keeping officials "not to participate in combat operations with the Congolese Army if there was a risk that Congolese soldiers might abuse human rights. . . . But the mission went forward—and the abuses took place as feared." A few months after the warning, Congolese soldiers, "who had been supplied with ammunition and food by the UN peacekeepers, killed hundreds of civilians, gang-raped girls, and cut the heads off young men," according to reports.[20]

And still further complicating the problem, the Saudi terrorist, Osama bin Laden, moved his operational base to Sudan, prompting the United States to designate it a "state sponsor of terrorism." The UN Security Council followed suit in 1996. The US action forced the withdrawal of US companies from Sudan in 1997. By 2008, Beijing had taken advantage of the situation to the point that thirteen of the largest fifteen foreign companies in the country were Chinese.[21]

Matters improved for a while for the West, but by 2009 Somalia was back in the headlines, this time regarding struggles involving both native groups and foreign jihadists. The government declared a state of emergency and appealed to neighboring countries for assistance, but the problem was so extensive—the government controlled just a few neighborhoods in Mogadishu—that the capital was in danger of collapse.

Ethiopia, which had sent troops during the 2006 fighting, announced that it "would act within the framework of the decision of the international community," but its actions during the crisis were unpopular, so it may be slow to react in the future. Kenya stated that it would not stand by and allow the situation in Somalia to deteriorate further. The Islamist militia attacking the Somali capital warned Kenya not to intervene, saying that it would attack Nairobi, the Kenyan capital, if the Kenyans interfered in Somalia. Kenya probably has enough problems without getting very deeply involved in Somalia.

Mr. Maina Kiai, a former human rights official, noted that gangs across the nation were arming themselves with guns rather than the machetes employed in the past. He said that unless the culprits were punished for the 2008 killings the people would be emboldened to wreak havoc again. Kenya is still dealing with some problems that go back decades, and the tribunal crisis is wrapped in sweeping land reform and constitutional reform issues. Another official commented that the parliament would not pass a tribunal unless it was sure the tribunal would prove dysfunctional.

Further, according to a lawyer at the Kenya National Commission on Human Rights, the parliament would not pass the legislation because the murderers themselves were in the government. People worried that punishment for past crimes would simply provoke more killings.

What appears to be clearer is the advisability of the prompt formation in the country of a native legion that is organized, paid, and led by US officers, if the government is to survive the ongoing assaults. And the same probably applies to some of the other states in Africa if they expect to remain independent under the various threats posed by Al Qaeda and similar Islamic fundamentalist forces.[22]

More recently, Ahmedou Ould-Abdallah, the UN special representative for Somalia, weighed in with an appeal for "The World's Duty to Somalia." He claimed that action was "not a classic civil war but an externally funded attempt to overthrow a legitimate, reorganized government." "In contrast," Ould-Abdallah asserted, "those who attacked Mogadishu [in 2009] were extremists with no common agenda except to seize power by force. They included individuals on UN Security Council's list of al Qaeda and Taliban members, and a few hundred experienced fighters from other areas of Africa, as well as Arabs and Asians. While the world focuses elsewhere, groups of foreign extremists are liable to take control of the country. . . . The United States, France and Norway are those among the countries in the UN that have condemned the attempted coups."[23]

Fierce fighting continued into September between troops of Somalia's transition government and insurgent forces under al-Shabab. Both sides seemed to fight with spirit, but the al-Shabab recovered the territory it had initially lost and continued to maintain its strong position in most of Mogadishu. Surprisingly, one of the Islamist soldiers was an American from Minnesota. According to the FBI, dozens of Somali-Americans may have joined the Shahab jihadist movement, which official American observers have accused of having links to Al Qaeda.

In an earlier engagement, witnesses said that eight people had been killed. One may discern the casual attitude of the government by its statement that as soon as the Ramadan holy month was over it would endeavor to recapture all of the land previously lost.[24] That may yet happen, but many doubts persist.

Whatever outcome may appear most desirable to the United States, there can be no assurance of its achievement while large numbers of US forces remain tied up in the Middle East and elsewhere. It would appear more likely that the current situation in Somalia, like the one in 1994, could have been much better if the United States had negotiated and delivered a foreign legion of a half-dozen American-led indigenous volunteer brigades for protection of the Somali capital and seat of government.

Another east coast conflict reinforced the problem in a state critical to international peace in Africa and to seafaring traffic approaching or departing the Suez Canal. The situation has cried out for a solution, which could most economically and effectively be achieved by one or more major units of American-trained, -led, and -financed legions—especially ones composed primarily of Somali soldiers who know the territory, can become skilled in modern battle equipment and techniques, and possibly look forward to American citizenship, if desired, at the completion of their voluntary term of service. Success in this critical region could establish a model for organization and the assembly of like forces throughout most of the continent—but forces unlike anything assembled in the Middle East in the last decade.

On 1 November 2009, the news added to earlier reports about the fate of a British couple sailing in the Indian Ocean. They had been captured by Somali pirates, halfway up the Somali coast, in the vicinity of the town of Xaradheere. The spot had been marked earlier by a freighter, dead in the water, for which the pirates had been negotiating for some $7 million in ransom. According to a pirate chieftain, "Red Teeth," the couple was being evacuated to a more secure spot inland, near Baxdo, some 100 miles to the north. The international news dispatch relating the incident noted that even "while dozens of foreign warships were cruising Somalia's waters . . . trying to crack down on the stubborn piracy problem, there are very few, if any, foreign military personnel on shore."[25]

But before this most personal conflict had developed, other sharp differences were building in the "Lake District" between the Hutu tribal "Democratic forces for the Liberation of Rwanda," known by its French initials, FDLR, and the Tutsi Rwanda Patriotic Front. In spite of early Hutu successes (including the murder of some 800,000 Tutsis and moderate Hutus), the Tutsis managed to turn the tables, driving the Hutus back into the Congolese jungle as we have noted.

What can be done? Clearly, pacification by existing players has not worked. Few outside powers have indicated much interest—or even understanding of the issues. Imperial forces are a century late, and a final solution by the recent players is more sanguinary than anyone wants to contemplate.

In the west a cease-fire between the Polisario and Morocco, monitored by UN troops, has been in effect since 1991. At one point the parties had agreed to a referendum to settle the border, but the matter got bogged down over details, and no peace agreement was reached. The situation has been described as "neither peace nor war." Negotiations have continued well into the new century, but with no observable reason for optimism on either side. One press report, apparently referring to the region to its south, read, "Much of the brutality was captured in a 183 page 'Chronicle of Horrors,' dealing with gang rapes, massacres, village burnings and civilians being tied together before their throats were slit—many such incidents carried out by a Congolese army being fed, transported and otherwise supported by the United Nations."[26]

At least the report called for the UN mission "to 'immediately cease all support' to the Congolese army until the army removes commanders with known records of human rights abuses and otherwise ensures the operation complies with international humanitarian laws. 'Continued killing and rape by all sides in eastern Congo shows that the UN Security Council needs a new approach to protect civilians.'"[27]

For its part, the Robert Mugabe regime in Zimbabwe began to show signs of serious differences when Prime Minister Morgan Tsvangirai, speaking of the chief of state, Mugabe, said, "It is our right to disengage from a dishonest and unreliable partner." The government had jailed the prime minister's deputy agriculture minister-designate, adding to a list of alleged crimes and misdemeanors, including putting 16,000 members of the youth militia on the payroll, torturing a human rights activist, and warning villagers that their heads would be cut off if they opposed a new version of the constitution favorable to the president's party and his powers.[28] To virtually no one's surprise, Zimbabwe was rated fifty-first out of fifty-three African countries by the Mo Ibrahim Foundation in its index of governance, especially for economic opportunity, safety, human rights, and development.[29] *Parade* rated Mugabe the world's worst dictator in its edition of March 22, 2009.[30]

In December 2009 the Red Cross sought $32 million to feed more than 200,000 Zimbabweans who had no access to hard currency in their country's collapsed economy. At the same time the United Nations was seeking over ten times as much for all types of aid for the people. The Red Cross reported that the markets had food, but that the people had no money to buy it. As an interim measure the organization issued food vouchers that presumably could be exchanged for cash.

One faint hope for peace in Central Africa is a motion in the United Nations General Assembly for "Responsibility to Protect (R2P)"—persons against war crimes and ethnic cleansing by one tribe against another—to which 150 world leaders pledged support in 2005. Ban Ki-moon, secretary-general of the UN General Assembly, attempted on 22 July 2009 to set the tone for possible action, to begin the next day. Ambassador Susan Rice, US representative to the Assembly, furnished support to the motion and argued strongly for the UN to "respond to the worst outrages." She argued that "we must work to ensure that there will also be more justice and fewer bystanders." Few expected any useful conclusion to the motion.[31]

On the continent a strong possibility for civilization is the apparent development of a free-trade zone incorporating a total population of 130 million in Burundi, Kenya, Rwanda, Tanzania, and Uganda. Following that in the same countries is a cup of interest in the formation of a monetary union. There is also a possibility of a political federation at some point in the foggier, more distant future.

The emerging structure encompasses the five countries in an East African Community (EAC) with a headquarters in the Tanzanian city of Arusha. For all its population, the EAC's $75 billion is barely one-sixth of Belgium's financial base. It is hoped that the community's proximity to Africa's larger traders, such as the Congo, Ethiopia, and Sudan, will help it to begin making deals with at least the "cheap stuff" from China. Clearly, Kenya, which has the region's strongest manufacturers, retailers, and banks, has the best chance of significant profit.[32] But, for all the good news, in late March 2010, "The Lord's Resistance Army," one of the most infamous armed groups in Africa, was reported to have killed hundreds of villagers in the remote Tapili area of the southern Congo while kidnapping hundreds of others and marching them off in a vast human chain.[33]

Thus affairs have gone in most countries with large Islamist populations. In an effort to strengthen American power in the eastern hemisphere, Washington has created the United States Africa Command (US AFRICOM), a new unified combatant command of the US Department of Defense, responsible for military relations with fifty-three African nations, covering all of Africa except Egypt (which is included under the US Middle Eastern Command).

The headquarters was established on 1 October 2007 as a temporary subunified command under the US European Command with a staff of about 1,300 people. For lack of a suitable base in Africa, the headquarters has been co-located with the headquarters for US European Command (EUCOM) in Stuttgart, Germany. The new organization springs from concerns for international terror, the importance of African oil, and the dramatic expansion and improvement of Sino-African relationships in the new century.

The US Congress had previously approved US $500 million for a "trans-Saharan counterterrorism initiative" (TSCTI) over a six-year period to support countries involved in counter-terrorism against threats by Al Qaeda in Algeria, Chad, Mali, Mauritania, Niger, Senegal, Nigeria, and Morocco. The effort was designed to counter weapons and drug trafficking, as well as terrorism.

Much US experience in North Africa flows from tactical operations across Morocco, Algeria, and Tunisia in World War II, and from Sub-Saharan Africa in more recent years, with Special Forces in association with Joint Combined Exchange Training and Forward Operating Sites across the African continent. It is expected that these facilities, along with Camp Lemonier, in Djibouti, will form the basis for many of AFRICOM's activities on the continent. Thus far, only Liberia has publicly expressed a willingness to host the AFRICOM headquarters. Three states—Nigeria, South Africa, and Libya—have made it known that they have no interest in hosting the headquarters on their territory.

On 18 February 2008, the US AFRICOM commander, General William E. Ward, stated that the deployment of at least some part of the headquarters staff to Africa would be "a positive factor in helping us to deliver programs," but he also remarked that there were no definite plans to move any part of the headquarters at any time. Nevertheless, for the foreseeable future, it appears that the United States will maintain a base in Djibouti, with some 2,300 troops.

The conversion of the former French base (Camp Lemonier) to joint US-French administration and its occupation of Djibouti soil provides a significant footprint on the continent from which US forces might be able to undertake broad programs for the establishment of legion activities elsewhere throughout Africa as circumstances may permit. As an independent state on infertile soil, Djibouti has little natural wealth for its population, but as an operational base for American forces, and for the support of American-led legions throughout the continent, the site is of extraordinary value. Quite obviously, it enjoys high strategic value for controlling Suez-Canal traffic, if that should become an important factor, or for operations across the twelve-mile-wide Bab el Mandeb to the Yemeni coast line.

In any event, it appears likely that some US Army and Navy components may be temporarily forward deployed to bases in Italy, especially in Vincenza and Naples. In particular, the US Army has taken a step to fulfill a major part of the concept. Before the end of 2011, the existing Army Southern European Task Force (SETAF), heretofore carrying responsibilities in southern Europe, assumed ground force responsibilities in Africa under the direction of Headquarters US AFRICOM. The record shows that Headquarters SETAF had already assumed responsibility for directing African operations on five occasions in the last decade and a half. Now, under new orders, it will assume responsibility for helping African states with the development of long-range (ten-year) plans for ground forces.

Major General William B. Garrett, the SETAF commander, denies that the US Army is interested in "a big US Army footprint in Africa," unless there is a major crisis in the future. Instead he anticipates "small, agile teams of instructors, trainers, doctors, lawyers, technicians, professors and teachers" visiting countries interested in the programs to "train the trainers." The total number of US Army personnel in Africa, in late 2009, stood at about 800.

The general supposes that these tasks may result in the "establishment of a training center initially run by US personnel, then by local instructors." "The key issue," he says, "is that we want to provide them with self-reliance. We don't want to do this for them." But the true purpose of the program, it would appear, includes considerably more than conveyed in that simple formula. The general added that there were already four US Army lieutenant colonels teaching at the Ethiopian War College, while many African students from other countries are in attendance at military education institutions in the United States.[34]

Recognizing that AFRICOM's responsibilities may be stretched beyond strictly military matters, planners anticipate that in some respects the organization may focus more heavily upon interagency concerns, to include intelligence, diplomatic, health, economic, and technical aid affairs. In addition to its territorial responsibilities on the continent, the command will have responsibilities involving the continent's seven island groups:

Cape Verde
Seychelles
Madagascar
Equatorial Guinean Islands
Comoros
Mauritius
Sao Tome and Principe

Perhaps the most difficult matters with which the command may ultimately be called upon to deal are some of the long-running, headline-grabbing conflicts, such as that between Rwanda and the Congo, with serious crosscurrents between the Tutsi and Hutu tribes, or the high-speed water-borne pirates operating, for the most part, off the Somalian coast.

The Rwanda-Congo conflict has been running since the fall of 2008. By November of that year, US and UN envoys had crisscrossed the "Great Lakes" district[35] in efforts to relieve thousands of civilians caught in a Tutsi rebellion in the eastern Congolese camps around their homes in Rutshuru. Fighting between troops loyal to General Laurent Nkunda and other renegades, and their rape of the countryside, turned a difficult situation into circumstances deemed "catastrophic." Officials feared that the borderlands would turn into a rerun of the Congo's 1998–2000 war. The 17,000-man UN force in the area has been totally inadequate to prevent combat escalation. It is quite difficult at this writing to detect a clear preponderance of fault on one side or the other.[36]

What can be done? Clearly, pacification by existing players has had marginal effect (either positive or negative), and outside powers have not indicated a great interest in or even understanding of the issues. Imperial forces were unwelcome instruments of past centuries, and players for absentee rulers rather than for the peoples of the land. More recent attempts at governance by local leaders have proven more sanguinary than many want to admit.

The United Nations Security Council took action shortly before the last week in 2009 to extend the mandate for the 20,000-man Congo force for five months (rather than a year) to focus attention on the problem, to protect civilians in the eastern Congo, and to respond to President Joseph Kabila's request that the UN develop an exit strategy for the peacekeeping force, the world's largest, which has been active for over three years. The new resolution was apparently designed to limit UN military actions to the protection of civilians. Some previous maneuvers are believed to have spurred the massacre of civilians.[37]

In the meanwhile, major problems have returned to Somalia. Early in 2009 Osama bin Laden issued a statement on how the land should develop, and now it appears that a fresh flow of foreign fighters is responding to the call. Even the new president, a moderate, Sharif Ahmed, has moved to introduce *sharia* law. Hundreds of people have been shot dead on the streets, and tens of thousands are being displaced. Fighters and their "technicals" (pick-up trucks usually loaded with heavy machine guns and ammo) have been spotted near the Ethiopian border, which could provoke another invasion and war.[38]

Yes, force may be necessary, but not the brutal "kill them all" forms of the past, underpinning the self-serving interests of a single leader, tribe, or people. Military requirements for the pacification of troubled states should be met by professional elements, assembled for the welfare of the region and its value to the global community, with insight and understanding of the most troublesome issues and historical transgressions. In short, the need is for a capable and respected organization with power and a sense of responsibility to ensure compliance by all parties, with rules set forth by authorities with unbiased insight. Clearly, the interests of the United Nations, the peoples of the continent, and the United States lie with the development of an international (US-financed and -led) legion with the men and women of the ranks drawn from local volunteers, but disconnected from former associates in the region.

The initial regiments of an American-African foreign legion, under the direction of the US AFRICOM commander, should be established with calls issued for volunteers. Interested political leaders should be invited to participate in the formation of advisory bodies to assist the commander, but not to develop separate interpretations of such orders or to form personal connections with legion volunteers. Rather, they would be expected to provide aid and advice to selected native leaders in context with established legion goals. An initial target of pacification might be the "Great Lakes" area. Ideally, the necessary backbone legions for the initial areas of operation should be crafted for deployment before the end of the decade.

But possibly more pressing will be the problems now emerging regarding the governance of Darfur province and coastal matters in Sudan. Over the last eight years a bestial ethnic war has exploded there, with fatalities stretching from six thousand in 2005 to almost a million in the latest count. In 2007 the International Criminal Court issued arrest warrants against the former minister of state for the interior, Ahmed Haroun, and a militia Janjaweed leader, Ali Kishayb, for crimes against humanity and war crimes. On 14 July 2008 the prosecutor filed charges against the Sudanese president, Omar al-Bashir, including three counts of genocide, five of crimes against humanity, and two of murder. The prosecutor has publicly warned that authorities could arrest the president if he enters international airspace. That announcement prompted the Sudanese government to announce that henceforth the presidential aircraft will be accompanied by jet fighters.[39]

Shortly thereafter, armed tribesmen attacked a fishing village in southeast Sudan where hundreds of displaced people were camped near a river. One hundred and eighty-five people, mostly women and children, were found dead in the worst violence in three months. An epidemic of tribal clashes through the first half of the year slaughtered more than one thousand people, but this carnage does not appear to be necessarily connected with other strife in the Darfur (western) region.

In an attempt to stem the mayhem, in 2008 the United Nations raised its troop strength in Africa to four times that which it had dispatched around the world to noncombat areas in the previous ten years. Its total of such deployments reached beyond 90,000, with Africa absorbing 65 percent. One of the principal tasks was to protect some two million people in camps around the Darfur district. The UN estimated that 300,000 people had been killed in the recent past in the area.

Counter-action by Sudanese forces and militias included air and ground attacks on towns in west Darfur, aimed at pushing back the opposing Justice and Equity (JEM) group, but the action resulted in driving additional noncombatants out of the country, and further overloading facilities already strained by the quarter of a million refugees already there. To the east, the European Union assumed responsibility for protecting the displaced population of more than 460,000, mostly refugees from Darfur and the Central African Republic. On 28 February 2009, US Secretary of State Clinton remarked, "The genocide in Darfur must be brought to an end, and the U.S. has a responsibility as a world leader." Especially notable was Mrs. Clinton's notation of the *responsibility of the United States as a world leader* for the suppression of genocide in an underdeveloped country.[40]

In June 2009 some forty southern Sudanese soldiers were killed when tribal fighters ambushed boats carrying food aid to the rival Lou Nuer tribe from the United Nations food program. Women and children were also in the boats and died in the fusillade or by drowning after jumping into the river. The United Nations expressed special dismay and the denial of badly needed food to displaced people in the town of Alcobo, on the Ethiopian border. The UN agency immediately encouraged flying in emergency rations but could not make up for the tons of food that had been stolen or destroyed in the attack on the supply boats.[41]

Secretary Clinton would add strength to her argument for the suppression of genocide in Sudan when, eight months later, she announced a policy featuring rewards and punishments for Sudanese leaders based on whether they met benchmarks in three areas: Darfur, the north-south agreement, and counter-terrorism. Still, she has appeared less accommodating toward the Sudanese government than the approach suggested by the US envoy, retired Air Force Major General J. Scott Gration. The strategy which he suggested, normalization, has not sat well with those in the US government who continue to refuse to deal with Sudan's president, Omar Hassa al-Bashir. It is he who has been indicted on war crimes before the International Criminal Court for killings in Darfur. US officials have emphasized that Sudan would not be rewarded if it simply made progress in one area, such as counter-terrorism, but would have to show advances across the board.[42]

For its part, Mauritania endured a year under the dictatorship of a retired general, Mohamed Ould Abdel Aziz, only to select him president in July 2009. For all his military background and his manner of coming to power in a coup in 2005, Mr. Aziz insisted that he simply acted to prevent the country from slipping back into the repressive rule of the past. Bouhoube Yni, a lawyer with the nation's independent electoral commission, insisted that no serious complaints or proof of fraud had been received so far. While it may be true that he fabricated false identity cards and illegally inflated voter lists, Mr. Aziz has promised to eradicate terrorism and ensure that the army is well equipped so that it may protect the people's interests. Washington has never recognized Mr. Aziz's junta, but it hopes that Mauritania will stand as a bulwark against Al Qaeda and prevent the moderate Muslim nation from sliding toward extremism.[43]

Beyond Mauritania's eastern border are the equally bleak deserts of Mali. In June 2009 Al Qaeda was accused of the murder of a Mali army officer in his home and the ambush of a colony of two dozen Algerian paramilitary troopers. Then, in early July, "Al Qaeda in the Islamic Maghreb" attacked a Malian army patrol in the northern desert, killing about a dozen soldiers and capturing most of the rest. Reportedly, several of the militants were killed in the exchange.

The Al Qaeda affiliate in Algeria is considered to be largely a criminal gang engaged in the kidnapping of Westerners for millions of dollars to finance its operations. Some officials assert that it has plans for substantial expansion, just as it has grown from its experience in anti-government insurgency in Algeria.[44]

Barely 300 miles south of Mauritania is the wretched state of Guinea-Bissau, the world's fifth-poorest nation, with no prisons and few police. Sitting astride the shortest cocaine route from South America, across the Atlantic delivery route to Europe, it harbors a few filthy rich super-barons within its destitute population. The value of the drug trade exceeds the national income. Some say that living in Guinea-Bissau is like moving into an empty house. Government supervision is limited to the patrol of one rusty ship along 350 km of shore and eighty islands. Reportedly, the police have few cars and no petrol, radios, telephones, or handcuffs. On 9 September 2009, Conakry, the capital of Guinea, experienced "a brutal rampage at an opposition rally, shooting, stabbing, raping, assaulting dozens of men and women in a packed stadium."

Reportedly, hospitals were full of the wounded from what opponents of the military government termed a massacre. By the next day 157 people had been declared dead. Over a thousand suffered gunshot wounds or other injuries, reporting groups said. In addition, soldiers were seen ransacking the homes and shops of opponents of the government. The next day, newspapers commented that "even with Guinea's long history of government brutality, killings and torture, the violence of Monday came as a shock."[45]

To the surprise of but a few, shooting broke out again in December between military factions in Conakry. One shot wounded the country's nominal ruler, Captain Moussa Dadis Camara. Reportedly, it was a disgruntled member of the captain's staff who attempted to kill him. Shortly afterward, the captain was flown out of the country of ten million, without leaving behind a clear leader. Camara's deputy, Lieutenant Diakite, was out of the country at the time, but some observers expressed suspicions that Diakite was somehow involved in a plan to get rid of Camara.[46]

Of course, the military does not have all the power or glory. Mr. Teodoro Nguema Obiang, the forest and agriculture minister, has a $35 million estate in Malibu, Florida, which he visits several times a year. Reportedly, he has a "fleet" of luxury cars, speedboats, and a private jet at his call. These are paid for through corruption connected with gas and oil reserves, according to internal Justice Department and Immigration and Customs documents.[47]

Only time will tell if this comfortable life can continue under a military junta. The Nigerians have ended their military rule, but replaced it with an Islamic legal system. While the Christian minority feared for the institution of certain extreme Muslim penalties (the amputation of men's hands and stoning of women) for infractions of certain religious laws, there have been no such penalties imposed in the last decade.[48]

These internal problems come in conjunction with others which have developed along the western African coast, between the chaotic Nigerian port at Lagos and Equitorial Guinea. The Nigerian government launched attacks on militants' camps in late May 2009, killing many people and upsetting an extended period of calm in the area. The militants had threatened to place a British hostage, whom they had held since September 2008, in the area to ward off further government attacks. They also advised oil workers to leave the area for their own safety.[49]

In mid-2009 Nigeria developed two areas of disorder, both underscored by Islamic leaders. The decades-long (and still growing) Niger River delta insurgency has damaged the country's oil and gas production and foreign investment from abroad. To the north, the Boko Haram ("Western Forbidden") movement armed itself with weapons seized from under-manned police stations and spread its reach forcefully into three states: Borno, Kano, and Yobe. The death toll probably exceeded 600 by July 30, 2009. Complicating the problem were growing concerns that the honesty and efficiency of the national police had been badly undermined. The problems grew more complex as people lost confidence in their security forces. Boko Haram began by planning attacks on private schools, believed by the terrorists to preach the corruption of Nigerian society. Fortunately, an intelligence officer discovered the group's plans just before July 26, when they were to be implemented. The Nigerian intelligence service also acquired some evidence that Boko Haram had received financial support from Libyan leader Muammar al-Qaddafi. The most recent concern among honest leaders in the country is that the Nigerian police will diminish in effectiveness and the entire machinery of state will collapse.[50]

But the country remains notorious for its deep corruption. During a visit to Nigeria in August 2009, US Secretary of State Hillary Rodham Clinton commented that the reason the people were so poor was "a failure of government at the federal, state and local levels." She spoke openly about "flawed elections and a lack of public trust that had seriously eroded the credibility of the Nigerian Government."[51] Significantly, there was no mention of child abuse. In a comparison of the death rate of children under five years of age in Nigeria with the next worst state in Africa (Ethiopia), Nigeria wins, hands down, with 700,000 infant deaths per year.[52]

In late 2009 a group of African bishops meeting in Rome issued, without names, a strong statement calling for the resignation of corrupt Catholic politicians on the home continent. There was little necessity for names; just about everybody in the various states—and certainly the principal figures—knew who they were talking about and how they had misused their offices. The *New York Times* singled out Presidents Robert Mugabe of Zimbabwe and José Edwardo dos Santos of Angola as being figures "to have led their countries to economic ruin," with the latter having been called "one of the most corrupt in the world."[53]

In March 2010 the *New York Times* reported that "things are again falling apart in Nigeria." A predawn massacre entailed the murder of Christians, many of them women and children, who were then laid out in mass graves, according to Chinua Achebe, a prominent writer in the country. In his view it was the fault of Nigerian authorities for not exercising their powers of law and order. Nigeria's acting president, Goodluck Jonathan, he said, is too weak to handle his responsibilities.[54]

"Many Catholics in high office," an *LA Times* report related, "have fallen woefully short in their performance in office." The impact of the document may well have a significant audience among the 153 million Catholics on the African continent. It is expected that by 2025 Africa will be home to some 230 million Catholics and a very large percentage of the world's priests.[55]

Ghana, also on the west coast, and a close friend of the United States, has recently discovered oil. Since January 2009 the US Navy has maintained a 17,000-ton amphibious transport offshore in the neighborhood, providing Ghanians and other friendlies with instruction on oil rigs, pipelines, and security. The US effort is coordinated through US AFRICOM headquarters, but suffers to some extent because of the continued mis-location of its headquarters in Europe.[56]

With a further glance southward, we encounter another oil-rich (but quite small) fiefdom, Equatorial Guinea. The president's son (and unofficial crown prince), Teodoro Nguema Obiang, makes frequent visits to his $35 million estate in Malibu, California. He has only to be concerned with a few details back home as minister of forestry and agriculture. American newspapers report that "most, if not all of his wealth comes from corruption related to the extensive oil and gas reserves discovered more than a decade and a half ago off the coast of his tiny West African country, according to internal Justice Department and Immigration and Customs Enforcement documents."[57]

Across the continent, on the eastern shore, the Somali coast is an exceptionally difficult stretch. There, pirates are operating. The situation endangers ships and their crews. Early in 2009 the US and French Navies were able to rescue men captured from ships flying their flags, but the piracy practice continues and threatens to turn more difficult as the pirates seem to have less regard for human life. Some 20,000 ships a year navigate the dangerous waters, so important is the path to trade approaching or exiting the Suez Canal. The International Maritime Bureau reported 293 piracy incidents in 2008, an increase of 11 percent from the year before. Forty-nine vessels were hijacked and 889 crew members were taken hostage. Eleven were killed and twenty-one were reported missing, presumed dead.[58]

Another string of events grabbed the headlines in Algeria, Mauritania, and Mali, in the northwest region of the continent, beginning in late spring 2009. It appears that Al Qaeda has established a branch in North Africa intent upon expelling or killing Westerners and African security forces. One view is that Islamic foreign fighters have returned from the battlefields in Iraq where they likely would have developed skills for making bombs.

The news reports indicate that the attacks probably reflect Al Qaeda's "growing tentacles" in the northern tier of Africa, reaching far beyond the group's main sanctuaries in Pakistan's tribal areas. In a six-week period, through June and July, the group claimed responsibility for killing one British hostage in Mali, an American aid worker in Mauritania, a Malian army officer, and nearly two dozen Algerian paramilitary guards. The principal objective appears to be ransom in the cases of Westerners. To date, bandits are estimated to have received millions of dollars from their operations while Nigeria has been producing 1.6 million barrels of oil a day, barely two-thirds of its quota established by the Organization of Petroleum Exporting Countries (OPEC).[59]

Inasmuch as US AFRICOM has been limited in access to its assigned region of responsibility, and considering its distance from the action, it is not immediately apparent that the headquarters would be the most likely focal point for near-term coordination of future air, land, or sea operations off the Somali coast (nor, we should add, is such a development necessarily unlikely). In any event, the problem illustrates the desirability of moving the headquarters to its designated region of responsibility without further delay. Considering our misadventures in the past, it would certainly be better to develop solutions to likely problems before those problems escalate.

Further, the situation in Somalia also illustrates the high desirability for the development of American foreign legions in fulfillment of objectives shared by both the local authorities and the United States. It should not be surprising to find many areas of common security concern between African host governments and the United States (i.e., Departments of State and Defense and the headquarters of US AFRICOM). One should not overlook the high value and enthusiasm selected host governments may come to attach to the formation of US legions on their territory. Clearly, the assembly and formation of a geographically oriented legion would convey a message of harmony between the leadership of the host state and that of the United States of America.

The likely benefits are not limited to the military capabilities of the resident legion, but include the clear political prestige of working in concert with the most powerful country in the world. Among the less harmonious countries that afford Africa much of its reputation for instability, a military association and understanding with the most mighty of the Western world can be an especially precious asset.

If the United States wished to begin the program in a few countries with a reasonable chance of success, it would be wise to follow the indices afforded by international organizations that assess countries for the quality of their public policies. Typical of such assessments is the Mo Ibrahim Foundation Index of Assessment of Governance, noted previously above. With this as a guide, the first five countries to be offered opportunities to participate in the formation of American-sponsored legions would be Mauritius, Cape Verde, the Seychelles, Botswana, and South Africa.

Still further, the legion itself may be expected to make important contributions to the development of the host state, its security and its welfare. Not only would it serve as a deterrent to hostile action by terrorists or unfriendly neighboring states, but, through its programs entailing recognition of cooperative actions and the award of prizes and citizenship to local supporters, the states would be likely, over time, to create (1) a proud group of persons, knowledgeable in military affairs, with friends and associates in both native and US camps, and (2) those who elect to accept training and legion appointment, and eventually US citizenship, may expect to become members of a highly esteemed interest group within the United States, wherever they may ultimately settle.

The program should not be perceived as one of invasion by the United States, but rather as one of opportunity for the natives to aspire to a higher quality of life, while not necessarily forsaking their interests in the "old" country. Whatever the choice made by an American legionnaire upon his or her honorable completion of the minimal required service for US citizenship, it will be up to the member to select one of an attractive set of options open for the next phase of life. The principal choices would likely include the following:

- Continued service in the legion with substantial prospects for advancement in either noncommissioned or commissioned rank through attendance of noncommissioned schooling or graduation from an officer candidate school, with comfortable retirement after a given number of years' service in the legion.
- US citizenship with travel and settlement arranged for the member and family to the state and municipality of choice.
- Free medical care for life for members and their families while in service or retirement (after twenty years' service).
- Opportunities for free education for the member and his or her family.

Other opportunities that are likely to develop for qualified veteran legion-naires include comfortable post-service pursuits, either in the country of origin or in the United States. Few men or women of modest means are likely to find themselves in more advantageous positions than men and women who have served the US foreign legion either in the United States or in their land of origin.

Figure 10.1.   Map of the Balkans

10

The Balkans: The Slippery Slope[1]

Following Dr. Barnett's "nonintegrating gap" northward from Africa on "the Pentagon's new map" brings an observer to another conglomeration of difficult states, with some seventeen combat symbols, and a half-dozen others, conveying the troublesome experiences of modern times. The focal point in this region is the former territory of the Kingdom of Yugoslavia, a collection of dissimilar provinces created in the wake of the First World War (1929), and now the broadly disclaimed "settlements" of national boundaries of remaining territories.

The official monarch, King Alexander I, abolished the historical internal regional boundaries and designated administrative borders without great consideration of marked differences among the populace—religious, cultural, or linguistic. Much of the territory composing Yugoslavia was Islamic as a result of years of Turkish rule, while the political center, Serbia, was Slavic, hence Christian, and closer to Russia. Most of the rest of the country was traditionally under Austrian control. And, indeed, it was the assassination of the ruling archduke of Austria by a Serb, during a visit by the royal figure to the Serbian capital, that effectively triggered the First World War.

After the war the country remained under King Alexander I, but not for long. He was assassinated in Marseilles during an official visit to France in 1934. The crime ended the royal period, and the path lay open to the country's rise of communism under the leadership of Marshal Broz Tito. But Tito was not inclined to take orders from Moscow. Instead, Yugoslavia became the lead state under a "third bloc" theory that would emerge during the Cold War.[2] Communism was the state "religion," but not to the point that the state would faithfully follow orders from Moscow. Aided by financial donations from the West, a "distinctly Yugoslavian 'road to socialism' took shape over the following decades."[3] By 1990 economic problems—rising inflation and massive foreign debt, plus unemployment at 15 percent while inflation zoomed to 150 percent—threatened to kill the state. Government efforts to tame the crisis stimulated strikes and demonstrations involving more than a half-million workers. Then came ethnic tensions, especially in Slovenia, in the northern part of the country, which locally enjoyed a much stronger economy. Kosovo was pressing for independence to permit its Albanian (Muslim) majority to go their own way. Serbia reacted sharply, with killer groups to the north, to the west, and to the south. The whole concept of Yugoslavia as a nation under Serbian leadership was at stake. Ancient hatreds ran high from other capitals. Pleas were made to the United Nations and abroad to stop the killing.

On 10 February 1993, the US secretary of state, Warren M. Christopher, announced the diplomatic engagement of the United States in the ongoing conflict. While there was no initiative ordering military units into the fray, the secretary clearly laid the groundwork for the deployment of forces. They would be dispatched, he said, either for enforcement of a political agreement, once attained, or for participation in hostilities if the conflict were to spread to either the Kosovo district of Serbia or to the newly independent state of Macedonia.

Since one or more of the conditions was bound to occur eventually, the announcement amounted to a wake-up call for the US Armed Forces. Two weeks later, President Clinton ordered US military aircraft to begin parachuting food and medicines into isolated communities in Bosnia-Herzegovina. While the Yugoslav (Serbian) Foreign Minister Ilija Djukic protested that the airdrop was a "risky and unilateral" operation by the United States, a senior US Defense Department official insisted that the operation would be "absolutely evenhanded among Bosnians, Croats and Serbs."[4]

The idea of parachuting in supplies sprang from a complex mixture of promises, threats, and physical interference with UN relief shipments, primarily by the Serbs, to embattled cities cut off in hostile areas and a desire by the US government to demonstrate concern for victims of war.

Throughout 1995 and 1996, large areas of the former Socialist Federal Republic of Yugoslavia were turned into a theater of conflict, and more than 100,000 people died either in, or as a result of, the fighting. The principal theater was centered on two Yugoslav provinces, Croatia and Bosnia-Herzegovina. Slovenia and Serbia were involved over the course of the struggle—or series of struggles—and there was considerable danger that other provinces (each of which claimed some degree of independence) could be drawn into the melee at any time.

There was also reason for concern that neighboring countries could become involved, especially Albania, Greece, Bulgaria, or Turkey. A number of the neighbors sought reassurance from each other that foreign intervention would be avoided if at all possible.

Romania and Greece signed a bilateral accord on 14 February 1993 that "the Balkan countries should participate in case of an outside military intervention in Yugoslavia" (but the identity of the aggressor was not clear). On the same day Albania and Bulgaria signed an agreement on stability and cooperation in the region, but, like the participants of the other accord, they were not specific about the intervention they were most concerned about.

More disturbing may have been the risks of larger power involvement. Ukraine and Russia had historic and ethnic interests at stake, which could spur them to move in support of one or more of the warring groups. As Slavic states, their most natural client would be Serbia, but they might also be moved to intervene on behalf of the ethnic Serbs of Bosnia or Croatia. The Balkans' reputation as a catalyst for major wars is well deserved and must be borne in mind by policymakers and analysts dealing with such problems.

A large part of the theater of conflict is a mountainous, relatively thinly populated region with a restricted transportation net. The backbone of the region is defined by the Dinaric Alps, an extension of Swiss and Austrian ranges. The most rugged mountains, with peaks over 7,000 feet, cover a triangular area, narrow in the north, wide in the south around Sarajevo, and extending into southern Serbia and Montenegro.

The principal mountain range runs from northwest to southeast. While this has offered the peoples of the area a potential refuge from invaders, it did nothing in World War II to protect the vitals of the lowlands from Nazi occupation. The great majority of the population and industry of the former Yugoslav Republic lies on the northern side of the mountains.

United Nations Protection Forces (UNPROFOR) intended to suppress the hostilities, using the port city of Split, on the Adriatic coast, as the principal base for operations carrying supplies to Sarajevo. The route from the port is more than 200 miles long and passes through rugged terrain. A senior US Army official testified to Congress in 1992 that it would require a corps-size force (some 50,000 troops) to secure the road in the face of determined guerilla opposition. Western forces attempting to make an opposed entry into central Bosnia from the Adriatic would probably have to rely heavily on airlifts for both their initial deployment and continued support. The security of the land routes of supply through the mountains would be a major problem under almost any circumstances.

In early 1991, several of the provinces of the former Yugoslav state began to seek independence. Slovenia and Croatia led the movement. Fighting broke out, principally over land issues between Serbs and Croatians in Croatia. The Croatians wanted full control of their province, and status as an independent state. The Serbs, who had lived in the province for centuries and constituted 11.6 percent of the population, did not want to be separated from their federal state, nor did they want to live as a minority people under Croatian sovereignty. In March they declared the independence of their district, Krajina.

The federal Yugoslav army was ordered to suppress the fighting, but with most key positions in the military hierarchy held by Serbs, the Croatians looked upon the organization more as an army of occupation than as an unbiased instrument of pacification. The fighting continued and gradually the Serbs gained control of about 30 percent of the province.

In spite of a number of UN-brokered cease-fires, civil peace continued to deteriorate wherever different groups lived in proximity to one another. Bosnia-Herzegovina and Macedonia followed Croatia and Slovenia in declarations of independence. Serbian representation within the population of Bosnia (31.5 percent) was much larger than that in Croatia, and the reaction was proportionately more violent.

In March 1992, President Slobodan Milosevic of Serbia joined with allies in the former Yugoslav Peoples' Army and the Serbian Democratic Party of Bosnia-Herzegovina to seize large tracts of territory in the multiethnic republic. His aim was to carve out a "greater Serbia" from the former Yugoslav state.

Thanks in part to the minimalist role allowed the Muslims of their defenses within multiethnic republics, the Serbs were able in a short period of time to gain control of about 70 percent of Bosnia-Herzegovina. By mid-August, they had essentially won their war in the province. Thereafter, the fighting continued as the Serbs sought to clear out pockets of other ethnic groups, and as they attacked Croatian forces attempting to enlarge their holdings.

All three ethnic groups—Serbs, Croatians, and Muslims—had numerous settlements and villages scattered over the former province of Bosnia-Herzegovina, and most of the fighting in the period 1992–1993 was done by militiamen from various townships. Unfortunately, there were large concentrations of Serbs and Croats that straddled each other geographically, with Muslim centers in between, greatly complicating the efforts of peacemakers to devise a plan for dividing the territory fairly. In Croatia, the fighting was bilateral, between Serbs and Croats, but it was not confined to military units. Besides the regular military contingents of both the Serbian-controlled Yugoslav Republic Army and the embryonic Croatian army, there were many small detachments of guerilla fighters of all stripes seeking blood from their neighbors.

The principal objective of the Serbs was the "cleansing" (subjugation, imprisonment, removal, or murder) of the populace within the areas of Croatia and Bosnia-Herzegovina that they wished to control. While the Serbian government had not officially laid claim to these territories, it had supported the actions of local Serbs seeking to establish independent sovereignty.

The presence of a large Serb population astride the Croatian-Bosnian border and in eastern Bosnia, adjacent to Serbia, facilitated this "cleansing" action. Logistical support from Serbia, particularly from the army, contributed to the success of local Serbian operations. Clearly, the Serbs had the upper hand, and they probably could have conquered the full range of sub-states composing the former Yugoslavia, but in 1996 a coalition of unrelated states (some, such as Russia, were recently considered enemies) resolved to bring the hostilities to a halt. The United States dispatched two brigades of its First Armored Division while Russia, Turkey, Poland, and some two dozen other countries prepared to send detachments. The total pacifying force would be composed of some 60,000 troops from all sources.

General Wesley K. Clark, US Army, who was appointed supreme commander of Allied Forces Europe in 1997, provided insightful views of the conflict during his tour of duty until 2000. However violent the civil war among the Serb, Kosovar, and Bosnian peoples became, the United States and its allies avoided major intrusion on the ground until most of the fighting had been suppressed. While the general employed his air power assets effectively for political purposes, he was unable to secure sufficient ground forces to freeze much of the fighting on the territory. He had envisioned the use of combat helicopters to enhance the allied ground force capabilities, but they were not made available when they might have been of the greatest value.

The best he could do was to employ strategic bombers over Serbia to punish the Serbs for their invasion of states wishing to withdraw from the Yugoslav federation. In General Clark's view, the United States never developed a coherent strategy for the conflict, and most of the penalties suffered by NATO and the non-Serbian forces were due to that oversight.[5]

As we have noted elsewhere, opportunities for intercession were apparent, but no power center was inclined to take significant action or to block any particular local power. Both NATO and Russia were confident that they each had sufficient power to influence the action, especially with regard to the key "double-crossing" Posavina Corridor, connecting both Serbian-held Croatia with the Serbian homeland and the Bosnia-Herzegovina heartlands with Croatia to the north. But there was little agreement among the major powers on which indigenous side to support. The issue of how the intersection would be managed was put off for another day—or era—when a solution might emerge. Meanwhile, the Russian force, a brigade composed of elements of two airborne divisions, reinforced with light armor but reportedly including "a lot" of tanks, was matched for coordination with the US First Armored Division. To all appearances, both sides were ready for battle, but also in quite correct military mode—even friendly mode—for the pacification duties ordered by Moscow and Washington, DC.

Probably most dangerous would have been intervention by Turkey on behalf of the Kosovo Islamics against Serbia. That could have stimulated greater action along the US-USSR axis, or possibly unilateral intervention by either of the nuclear-armed powers in pursuit of its own objectives. The outcome of such an event would have been difficult to foresee, but most any such action could at least expose a costly guerilla conflict involving large numbers of people. In the wake of the Yugoslavian civil conflict in the early 1990s a multilateral agreement was developed providing for the restoration of peace among the principal parties which made up the Yugoslavian state.

For years the Serbian general, Ratko Mladic, who directed much of the government brutality during the civil war, has been sought after by international investigators for many of the war crimes with which he has been charged, especially for the murder of 8,000 people, mostly Muslims, in the town of Srebrenica in 1995, the worst massacre in Europe since the Second World War. Some officials also charged him with responsibility for provoking the NATO bombing of Sarajevo, which flattened the city and killed some 10,000 Serbs.

In spite of the Serb losses in the war, the new leadership in Belgrade has turned to the European Union in an effort to escape the country's criminal past and renew its leading position in southeast Europe. Unfortunately, the country's inability (or lack of motivation) to locate and capture Mladic continues to poison the brew. The UN force designated to isolate the Bosnia-Herzegovina army element at Srebrenica during the war was threatened by General Mladic with destruction if it were to interfere with its operations. Accordingly, the UN force withdrew with an understanding that the Serbs intended simply to disarm the opposing group.

Instead, General Mladic ordered the extinction of the civilians as soon as the UN (Dutch) unit was out of the way. Hence, the European Union was ill disposed to act favorably regarding the Serbian request. For their part, the Serbs wished only that Mladic would go to The Hague and die there, without a trial. As of this writing, he is still a fugitive from justice.[6]

Another remaining poisonous figure is Agim Çeku, the former prime minister of Kosovo, and a rebel commander. He is wanted in Serbia on war crimes charges, and he was arrested in Bulgaria in June 2001 for alleged war crimes during the 1998–1999 war in Kosovo. That state declared its independence from Serbia in 2008, but Serbia has continued to claim ownership of the territory years later. Similarly, Kosovo has continued to claim independence from former sister states. Suspected war criminals take advantage of the confusion.[7] While peace has come to the former territory of Yugoslavia, it does not appear that the alleged crimes have been either forgiven or forgotten. The new territories are aware of this confusion and orient themselves for independence in the next decade. Achieving real independence, with justice for all, will require a new formula for security with careful oversight by the most powerful, if less interested, states—a tall and unlikely order.

Perhaps the most favorable development in the region in the last two decades has been a sense of common experience among the various states, however horrible the wars were in their detail. In recent years many companies in the region have come to realize that they are too small to compete in the European market without greater cooperation among themselves.

Some writers have pointed out that from Slovenia in the north to Macedonia in the south, most people still have a great deal in common, even if they do not talk about it very much. They are coming to understand that while Yugoslavia is dead, it has been replaced by a sense of "Yugosphere." Notably a southeast European–style firefighting center has developed for training men and women for action anywhere in the region. Most former Yugoslavs—Bosnians, Serbs, Montenegrins, and Croats—speak the same language, with minor variations, while many Macedonians and Slovenes still speak, or at least understand, what used to be called Serbo-Croat as a second language.

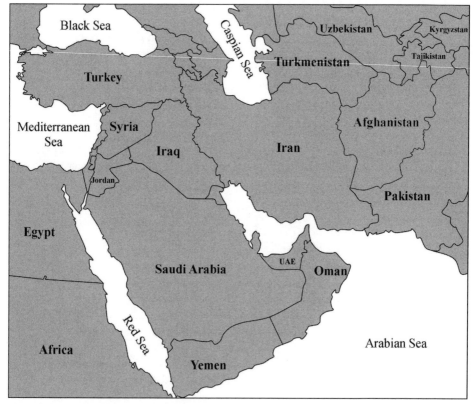

Figure 11.1. Map of the Middle East

11

The Islamic World— and the "Strong Horse"

[S]trange as it sounds, the attacks on New York and Washington were not about us . . . these conflicts are just part of wars that involve the entire Middle East. We are now incontrovertibly a part of these wars, but their causes and sources are to be found in the region itself and not the lower end of Manhattan, or even in the halls of the Pentagon. September 11 is the day we woke up to find ourselves in the middle of a clash of Arab civilizations, a war that used American cities as yet another venue for Arabs to fight each other.[1]

One need not venture far into a volume on world history to encounter maps of pre-Christian settlements of the "Fertile Crescent," reaching from the Land of Goshen in the west, northward along the eastern shores of the Great Sea, and into what would later become neighboring farmlands: Israel, Syria, and Mesopotamia (Iraq), plus the better parts of their neighbors, including Saudi Arabia.

To Americans, this region has seemed like a distant world, although many have read about it, including those educated in one-room schoolhouses. Even if the earliest inhabitants of those communities could have understood where they were (and that is not sure), it is unlikely that they could have grasped the fact that they existed six to eight thousand years ahead of most written histories. It was still another three thousand years before the "Great Deluge" would engulf much of the same territory from the Nile in the west to the Tigris and Euphrates in the east.

As catastrophic (and tale-enhancing) as the floods certainly were (note especially the story of Noah and his ark, with pairs of all living things to ensure the survival of life), the same areas eventually emerged as Neolithic cultural centers, with polished stone and metal tools, poetry, weaving, livestock rearing, and agriculture. To its detriment, however, it was probably a change of climate that led to the dehydration of large areas, with desert belts stretching from the great Sahara in North Africa to present day Saudi Arabia in the south and Iraq, Iran, and Afghanistan to the north and east. The changes are believed to have spurred much of the populace to organize farming in more limited areas, generally along the fertile river valleys.

Such concentration, coupled with improved farming techniques, permitted increasing numbers of people—especially men—to devote themselves to other tasks (crafts, defense, religious life, administration, and technology). It also led to the stratification of society along the various levels of occupation and to differentiation among families. Trade specialization and political stratification were particularly notable. Town, city, and higher aggregations began to take root in this fuzzily dated period. Increasingly, figures with greater power than their associates began to exercise important directive functions within communities. In what would eventually become "Mesopotamia," priest-kings here and there would eventually assume representative roles of gods, or whatever powers were believed to exist beyond the view of most of mankind. The quick-witted souls around them also began to take on the cloaks of various civic functions. Increasingly, even among the common folk, there could be high callings providing service to, or defense of, a revered administrator.[2]

Increasingly powerful figures began to emerge, taking charge of common affairs. Some thousand miles further east, along the path dictated by Barnett's new Pentagon map, we now encounter the troublesome region that has captured so much of the American national attention over most of the last decade. Humorists describe it as the "land of sand, sun, sandals, and suicide bombs." Even the modern region is a distant world from that familiar to most Westerners—or Far (Asiatic) Easterners, for that matter.

But as the presently constituted states—Iraq, Iran, and Afghanistan—congealed in their places on maps, there was created the *umma*—the Muslim community, the supertribe—held together by religious concepts that rationalized and motivated Arab conquests, and distinguished between the elite tribes of believers and all other comers ("infidels" and non-Sunni Muslims). To the supreme author, Mohammed, the struggle of struggles was that between believers and non-believers, and, according to one modern literary guide (author Lee Smith), any belief or any interpretation of Mohammed other than that of the Sunni majority was deemed false. Smith points out, "the Arabic speaking Middle East is not just a sea of 300 million Arabs who have common interests, but a region with 70 percent Sunni population and dozens of minorities."[3] Hence, selective American friendship with any minority Arabian group with faith other than that of the Sunni (the "Strong Horse") has a predetermined likelihood of success.[4]

It is not American or allied policy, or that of non-Sunni Muslims, to seal themselves off from such indigenous groups, or to attempt to pick a winner among the most important denizens of the deserts. But we do well to recognize the strengths and weaknesses of each national community and to adjust our affairs to make as many friends and as few enemies as possible.

For all the efforts of Saddam Hussein (a Sunni) toward war-making at the close of the twentieth century and the onset of the twenty-first, his skills fell short, especially as he provoked multiple enemies to combine their forces against him. While he was able to muster domestic Shia support for his campaign against Iran in 1980–1988, it did not hold over the longer term when he turned against Kuwait and Saudi Arabia, provoking action by a multiplicity of outside (Western) forces. It was simply too much.

The wars in the Middle East in the following decades have run a variety of different courses, with extensive US and broad allied participation. As many as twelve other NATO-related nations have each sent a thousand or more troops, while thirty-four others have dispatched representational contingents. If no solution is found before 7 October 2011, when a substantial departure of Americans is scheduled to occur, the lead conflict (in Iraq) will have lasted a full decade. Not since the great continental Indian Wars has the United States pursued hostilities against a foe for so long.

The reasons for reaching a conclusion, with or without a victory, are many, but the United States has great internal difficulties in bringing hostile situations to a close after prolonged hostilities. As closely and as deeply involved as the United States was with the battles in Korea and Vietnam, neither provided either great military or politically useful experience in near-decade-long combat. Not since the Second Seminole War in the swamps of Florida (1835–1842) has the United States government faced an enemy on his own soil for so long a period, confident that it could ultimately triumph in the dispute.[5] Of course, in that case, the government had the dynamics of an expanding population, with occupation in mind, to seal the outcome of the struggle in its favor.

Unlike the strong Arabian horses of ancient stories, the mounts of the Arabian leaders are not always found to be of such quality that their command accomplishments match all human vocal promises. Further, short of quality leadership, spirited troops are not always ready for action. Advanced automatic weapons skills and electronic search and communications devices are often over the heads of less-well-educated tribesmen. Simple marksmanship may be a minor problem, but private marketing of soldiers' weapons and ammunition to the public is a serious concern. Illegal sales of American-supplied rocket-propelled grenades are even more worrisome. Some of the local soldiers have been known to stage fake firefights so they can explain their ammunition shortages to their superiors. In one case involving the Afghan police, the troopers reported having fired more than $322 million worth of ammunition in a training period. So much equipment is so sloppily accounted for that it should be no surprise to find that fewer than 12 percent of the country's police units are capable of operating on their own.

Ambassador Richard Holbrooke, the US State Department's principal representative in the region, has publicly called the Afghan police "an inadequate organization, riddled with corruption." That it is the police who are primarily involved is especially disheartening. They have the closest uniformed, and armed, ties with the people. As one observer has commented, "The US-backed government in Kabul will never have proper support if it can't keep the people safe in their own homes and streets. Yet in a UN poll in the fall of 2009, more than half of the Afghan respondents said that the police were corrupt. . . . [and] in the town of Aynak . . . villagers accused the local police of extortion, assault, and rape."[6] The community had no "Strong Horse" in its stable. Half-breeds filled the stalls.

But the "Strong Horse" concept has another meaning which bears more careful inspection. Just as the Strong Horse attracts strong riders, it also tends to focus attention on the stable, and away from the palace. Figuratively, the Strong Horse keeps the owner's competitors out of his house— and business—and protects the master's treasury at the expense of the stables. Following this analogy, one might guess that part of the disregard that the Middle East leaders have evidenced for basic matters (like the security of police arms and ammunition) may have been conceived in the context of larger issues between the indigenous Arabs (the horse owners) and the action seekers (the Americans). It would appear that the former may seek to divert the latter from some of their interests in order to go easy on matters of lesser Arab interest.

In this context, it could be suggested that even the 9/11 attack on the United States may have been concocted with the knowledge of a few senior Arab statesmen who were concerned that their more aggressive young countrymen might hold them responsible if they did not countenance attacks on the wealthy West. As Lee Smith points out, "what was extraordinary about the attacks on lower Manhattan and the Pentagon was not the carnage—certainly not compared with some of the most vicious intra-Arab campaigns over the last several decades—but that the Arabs had shifted the field of battle to the continental United States. Washington's response was to try to fix a political system that it thought was broken [in the Middle East] when in fact it was functioning just as it always had, for hundreds, perhaps thousands of years."[7]

Reporters have noted that "America has spent more than $6 billion since 2002 in an effort to create an effective Afghan police force, buying weapons, building police academies, and hiring defense contractors to train recruits"—but the program, they assess, is a disaster: "Fewer than 12 percent of the country's police units are capable of operating on their own." The Americans wondered which was worse: the Afghan police that were there, or the Taliban that wanted to be.[8]

The concept of a "Strong Horse" involves one advantaged group which believers may pursue to improve their own positions with respect to competitors and opponents. The Strong Horse carries the rider faster, further, and more reliably than lesser breeds. Strong Horses do not readily give way to lesser solutions. They are the mounts of strong men on battle missions. Some believe them to include such men as Osama bin Laden.

A critic of the concept (and reviewer of a book on this subject) points out that others who do not grasp the equestrian model may still pursue the principle that "there is no alternative to the Strong Horse."[9] In these individuals' view, victories are won by agencies that strictly control the people and their lives. They can find no Strong Horse in full-blown democracy.

The scheduled drawdown of American forces began in July 2010. A senior American commander pointed out that barely a quarter of the 98,000-member Afghan National Police Force had received any formal instructions in their responsibilities. Most recruits were unemployed youth with little education and few other prospects.

In the last few years the police have suffered some 2,000 deaths in their duty—more than twice the figure for Afghan army soldiers, but as many as half of those are believed to have resulted from firearms accidents and traffic collisions. Further, of the 170,000 Afghans supposedly trained under the US-backed program, only 30,000 remain on duty. There appears to be no Strong Horse in the Afghan National Police.

A cogent case in the region of neglect of the Strong Horse model was the observation of Lieutenant General William Caldwell, chief of the US program to expand and improve Afghanistan's security forces in November 2009, who commented, "It's inconceivable, but in fact for eight years we weren't training the police . . . All we did was give them a uniform." President Obama, to whom he was speaking, looked stunned. The general went on to point out that barely a quarter of the 98,000 member police force had received formal instruction. Amazingly, no single American agency or individual had ever had control of the training program for more than a short period.[10] The war has been long. Without a good "Strong Horse" it may prove to be even longer.

The situation brings us back to the fundamental problem of limiting our support to needy countries—especially those under attack—to logistical and training programs. In some cases that may be sufficient (as with NATO countries), but in those cases where the supported state falls outside the bounds of Thomas Barnett's "functioning core," a very different approach must be invoked. In the *Washington Post* in April 2010, the former editor (and Pulitzer Prize winner) Henry Allen wrote, "[We] invad[ed Afghanistan] it to bring truth, justice and the American way to Afghans, who responded by hating us. We gave them money, food, all kinds of goodies. They hated us. We begged them to let us build a road that would link them with the outside world. They hated the road. And when we didn't get the point, they blew away six members of the road-building crew. They hated us so much that we had to bribe them to let us leave—6,000 gallons of fuel and a crane—without killing us for the sheer joy of it. . . . Ronald Reagan called us 'a city on a hill,' with the eyes of the world on us. . . . Yet Captain Mark Moretti, commander of our forces in Karongal, put it this way: 'I think leaving is the right thing to do.' The dream is dying. No resuscitation, please."[11]

If a local government desires American aid and is not capable of raising its forces to American or other first-class standards, it must be prepared to accept (at best) an assistance program under mutually convenient arrangements. In particular, while strategic direction may be developed between the local government and that of the United States field command, leadership must be provided by US commissioned and noncommissioned officers. In effect, separate legions, staffed dominantly (and initially exclusively) by American combat leaders, should be designed to maximize the combat potential of those willing to undergo first-class training with American-directed operations. The principal objective is both to strengthen the ties of professional respect between US and local commanders and to maximize the combat power of allied forces. The best indigenous officers should be selected for training and operational employment in conjunction with America's leaders and legions. In time, and as the situation develops, individuals and small units may be selected for reversion to host nation control. So much the better for both parties.

The Strong Horse contains a complex formula for Islamic leaders which affords their leaders partially self-contradicting formulae for dealing with potentially dangerous figures within their own societies, in part by turning them on foreign governments and potentially hostile domestic political leaders:

> Democracies must fight their enemies in order to preserve the state, but Arab regimes are caught in a perpetual pincer movement, squeezed by foreign enemies on one side and by their much more dangerous and always present domestic challenges on the other. . . . On September 11, 2001 the United States was one of those foreign lands, a dumping ground for jihadis.[12]

From this is derived both a *conclusion* and a *requirement*: (1) The West does not understand the Islamic tactic of guiding enemies toward different targets not otherwise involved in specific disputes, and (2) a readiness to promote conflict between potential enemies to deter action against the manipulating power. The author of *The Strong Horse* suggests that the concept of the 9/11 attack was not just to injure the United States, but to deflect the actions of *jihadis*, who otherwise might have been free to vent their wrath upon their own governments or other responsible Middle Eastern administrations.

For the United States it provided an enemy for a hawkish American administration seeking to unite the people behind a campaign shifting its weight from rational domestic political and economic concerns to dramatic action against foreign evil-doer, especially one involving a vital resource (oil). The conditions were especially favorable inasmuch as they involved agents with beliefs unsympathetic to either the Old or the New Testaments of the Bible.

About six months before the 9/11 attack, President Saddam Hussein was assessed as desiring to lead Iraq into a "revolution aiming at destroying the bases of imperialism, to shine over the whole Arab world to make it a new power on the world scene." He was already on record as claiming, "We don't look on this piece of land here in Iraq as the ultimate limit of our struggle. It is part of the larger area of the Arab homeland and the aims of the Arab struggle."[13]

His attitude appeared to be one of virtually open-ended expansion, giving good cause for those concerned about the security of the Arabian Peninsula and beyond. Further, like Adolf Hitler before him, he appeared quite willing to risk the lives and fortunes of his people to secure his place in history.

Of high interest at that point was the fact that the armed forces of Iraq, whatever their commanders had said about them, had never encountered an opposition of the caliber they faced at that time. The US forces, especially, had been equipped and trained to engage a far more sophisticated enemy, and was much better trained to fight a fast-moving, high-technology engagement in Europe. While the Iraqis had been substantially reinforced since their war with Iran, including large numbers of Soviet aircraft, they had not had much opportunity to ensure the integration of all of the elements required to recreate "blitzkrieg" in the desert.

There was no question about it: The Iraqis had received large shipments of Soviet matériel, almost tripling their inventory of tanks. They had twenty-two squadrons of ground attack aircraft, including some ninety MiG Floger and sixty SU-25 Frogfoot high performance machines. In total, they had some 275 fighters organized in seventeen squadrons. Most important were the thirty MiG-29 Fulcrums, with advanced air-to-air missiles. Nevertheless, early in the combat with the United States and its allies, almost 100 Iraqi aircraft escaped the battle by flying to Iran, Iraq's most recent enemy.[14]

But Iraq was not the only Islamic state to harbor a populace with anti-Western dispositions. Certainly Afghanistan, whose historic records of enemies included both Great Britain and the Soviet Union, played an active role in opposing the United States' interests. American troops were first deployed to Afghanistan shortly after the 9/11 terror attacks on American cities.

Figure 12.1.   Map of Southeast Asia

12

Southeast Asia— Part of America's History

Our final region of special interest appears on Thomas Barnett's map like the shadow of an ox head, extending southeast from the East Asian mainland some three thousand miles, from Myanmar (Burma) to the western half of the binational island of New Guinea. There it seems to hang like a cloud over the north cape of Australia. Spread over this region are seven nations of significance, with almost as many "seas" shared among them. The total pattern also resembles a football, with the long axis about twice that of the short one. Of special significance in the region is the narrow Strait of Malacca, between Malaysia and the Indonesian island of Sumatra, accommodating the great bulk of sea-borne trade running from China and Japan to Europe and Africa, and back. The region makes no great claim to peace, as the name of its neighboring Pacific Ocean might suggest. At least it doesn't seem able to enjoy much more than any other region in our study.

MYANMAR[1]

Myanmar (previously Burma) has 1,200 miles of coastline, providing ample access to the sea. The forests, covering half the country, include dense tropical growth and valuable teak. As part of a trade route between the enormous population centers of India and China, the land of what is currently Myanmar has been a gateway for centuries. In "modern" times (since the invention of gunpowder) merchant ships have converged at its ports to bring or take treasures back and forth between various ports. Surrounded on three sides by mountain walls and on the fourth by the sea, the land has always been insular; as a consequence, Burmese culture, in spite of many foreign influences, has largely remained distinct and separate. But not entirely so. For some sixty years, between 1824 and 1885, the British mounted border attacks from India to gain a foothold on the territory, but, after succeeding, they granted the country its independence in 1937.

When the Japanese army occupied the land in World War II, 300,000 refugees fled through the jungles to India, but 10 percent of the group never made it. The Japanese were finally driven out by a combined British-Burmese-US ("Merrill's Marauders") army in 1945.[2] An independent Burmese group, the Araka National Army, had initially cooperated with the Japanese to rid the country of British control, but switched sides in 1942 to help expel the Japanese troops, again with hopes of independence—but this time from Tokyo rather than London.[3]

The switch worked. In 1948 the nation became an independent state, with officials Sao Shwe Thaik as president and U Nu as the first prime minister. Multiparty elections were held in 1951, 1956, and 1960. In 1961 U Thant (no relation to U Nu) was elevated to worldwide notoriety, becoming secretary-general of the United Nations. But a year later the Burmese general, Ne Win, led a military coup d'état, displacing the democratic leadership of the distinguished former official, U Nu, and seizing control of the country. He would hold power for the next three decades.

To help solidify the action, many officers resigned their commissions to take civilian posts, and in 1974 they assisted the conversion of the state to one governed by a single-party system. Meanwhile, Burma sank economically to become one of the world's most impoverished countries. Three hundred thousand Burmese Indians fled the country, and a new constitution of the "Socialist Republic of Myanmar" was instituted.[4]

With cooperating locals in a number of the parliamentary seats, the military backed the National Party, which had earned no more than 2 percent of the seats in a surprising postwar election. Nevertheless, the army dismissed the legitimate returns and seized total power throughout the country.[5] Myanmar might have become a candidate for a house-cleaning by a volunteer legion of liberal persuasion, but instead the country went into gridlock under military control, making it virtually impossible to improve anything with a detectable air of liberalism anywhere about it.

Major western countries pressed the Myanmar government to recognize the popular returns and to release all political prisoners. Many prisoners were granted freedom, but the military government continued to exercise all governmental powers. Most particularly, it was noted that the country would come to stand 178th of 180 countries worldwide in the Corruption Perceptions Index.[6]

Mrs. Laura Bush, wife of the younger US Republican president, after a visit to the country, said that she found the administration of Myanmar in frightful condition. She compared the treatment of citizens by the government to the post-2007 period of "genocide-racked Darfur" (in Africa), with the observation that more villages had been destroyed in Burma than had been torched in the African community (some 3,000) over a similar period.

The military administration of the last four decades has been hopelessly entrenched in practices more common in the middle ages than in the twenty-first century, albeit with a cold-blooded confidence in long-range, hard-nosed exploitation of the land's natural endowments. In one writer's opinion the government deserved "dishonorable mention," if not membership in "the axis of evil in the world."[7] On 8 August 1988 the army opened fire on demonstrators (in what has come to be known as the "8888 Uprising"[8]) and imposed martial law. The subsequent election named the liberal National League for Democracy, with 80 percent of the parliament seats, the clear winner.

The government attempted to hold free elections in 1990, but "misplaced" the returns, so it was obliged to annul the vote to remain in power. The majority groups attempted to place their leader, Madam Aung San Suu Kyi, in the government palace, but found the doors locked. The announced explanation: "Women do not belong in public office." Since that time she has been confined under house arrest. Madam Suu Kyi was born in the United States in 1966 to Burmese parents. Her grandfather, U Thant, was then serving as the secretary-general to the United Nations in New York. After graduating from college in 1989 she took to working with Burmese dissidents and refugees. In 2009 she was sentenced to an additional 18 months confinement for allowing an uninvited visitor into her house. But for her valor in the face of government (military) pressure, Madam Suu Kyi was awarded the Nobel Peace Prize in 1991. She was officially criticized by her own (military) government for discouraging visitors from visiting the country after the army seized control of the state.

For her part, Madam Suu Kyi has declined invitations which would oblige her to leave the country. She has come to understand the attitude of the government and its likely move to prevent her from returning to her home if she leaves the country at any time. Her life has been made as uncomfortable as possible in hopes of getting her out of Myanmar.

Much of the land is completely off-limits to tourists in any event. Military leaders exercise very tight control over all important interactions between nongovernment Burmese and foreigners, largely through the military-led "State Peace and Development Council."

But mishap and disorder have continued. In May 2008, the 135-knot cyclone "Nargis" blew through much of the populated coastal sections of the country, leaving 130,000 people dead or missing. The military isolationist regime complicated rescue efforts by delaying the arrival and unloading of UN disaster relief aircraft and ships. The United States dispatched four naval vessels, led by the aircraft carrier *Essex*, all loaded with relief supplies including ambulances, medicines, food, drinking water, and medical equipment. The admiral in charge made many appeals to Myanmar officials for dock space to unload, but was refused each time. A final report said that the ships withdrew after waiting for four weeks for permission to unload.[9]

The foregoing notwithstanding, the armed forces of Myanmar are not particularly suited for the size and strategic location of the country (between India and China). But there is no question that they are equipped and broadly employed to further the interests of the leadership. Large numbers of Burmese citizens, including some five thousand eastern peoples (tribal "Karen"), have fled to Thailand. More than a quarter of all Shan (ethnic Chinese) families have been forcibly relocated, while at least one member of most families has been taken for forced labor, and 9 percent of households have been injured by land mines, the highest percentage of such accidents ever documented among civilians.[10]

These incidents have been followed by the placement of bombs in Rangoon in mid-April 2010, to spread terror during the public's New Year's festivities. The weapons killed nine people and wounded ninety-four others. There was no indication of who was behind the crime, but, again, the instability of the society was clearly highlighted.

Reportedly, Aung San Suu Kyi remains the junta's most formidable opponent. In recent years she has attempted to reach out to the generals, offering to discuss lending her moral authority in return for a drive to lift a "catalogue" of sanctions that are economically crippling and personally embarrassing for a military that still struggles for legitimacy almost fifty years after it toppled the last civilian government.[11]

In sum, there has been little interest in US foreign policy regarding support of Burmese independence or security, and, considering the depth of military control of the country, little reason for the United States to expend effort on behalf of the Burmese government as many have proposed. On the other hand, there may be cause for extraordinary surveillance over the country. During a trip to Southeast Asia, in July 2009, US Secretary of State Hillary Rodham Clinton remarked on possible nuclear links between Myanmar and North Korea.

Were the connections to develop into a serious threat to world peace, she suggested, the United States might be obliged to extend a "defense umbrella" over much of Southeast Asia. She indicated that she was not necessarily signaling an extension of US security policy, but observers noted that clearly it was a matter of such weight that it might quickly become a major issue of state.[12]

China, on the other hand, evidences no particular concern for Burma's internal policies, but it is far more alert to bilateral economic interests. Beijing is expected to begin construction of a gas pipeline from the Andaman Sea, south of Rangoon, to the impoverished province of Yunnan.[13] China's most immediate security concerns in the region are its running sores with Tibet and India. China has exercised governmental control over Tibet since 1951, but India has been moving troops into the nearby Twang area, straddling the border reaches of adjacent Bhutan and Arunachal and Pradesh. This is where Tibetan culture runs strongest—the sixth Dali Lama was born there in the seventeenth century.

It seems unlikely that Myanmar will become involved in border skirmishes in the region, and it should be borne in mind that the country's military leadership has made an effort to strengthen its ties with China, and that could have an effect on the country's other interests.

Recently, Myanmar troops have pressed northeastward toward the border with China. Reportedly, they moved into the area in an effort to ensure that certain ethnic groups remain under Myanmar control and participate in key elections. One of the groups currently in exile says that fighting broke out after the Myanmar military took control of facilities run by the Myanmar Democratic Alliance Army in Laogai, the capital of Shan Province. Many males identified themselves as "soldiers of the Kokang Army," an independent group which had to give up open resistance to the Myanmar force. An observer commented that the Kokang troops were humiliated by the Myanmar soldiers, identifying his group as Wa Chinese, rather than Burmese. He went on to say that the Chinese were far more supportive of the refugees than were the Myanmar troops.[14]

The US assistant secretary of state for East Asian and Pacific affairs, Mr. Kurt M. Campbell, remarked after a visit to Myanmar that "the United States is prepared to take steps to improve the relationship, but that the process must be based on reciprocal and concrete efforts by the Burmese government." Notably, however, he met with the prime minister, General Thein Sein, but not with the senior general, Than Shwe, the leader of the ruling junta.[15] It will likely be some time before Myanmar and the United States are ready to deal with one another as sovereign states.

Analysts suggest that most of the current public assaults have been part of the ruling junta's strategy for the 2010 elections. In addition, the leadership is believed to be forcing some ethnic minority groups into service as border patrol forces to participate in the show. Most of the larger ethnic groups and political parties have rejected such initiatives.[16]

Thousands were killed during a failed anti-government uprising. Madam Suu Kyi was placed under house arrest, and the ruling junta, after losing an election, refused to give up power. By the early 1990s most Western aid to Burma had been terminated, and the country's access to the World Bank and the International Monetary Fund had been blocked. Over the following years, all sorts of boycotts and embargoes were put in place. Nearly all economic ties with the United States and Europe were broken. The country sank slowly into embargos, boycotts, and economic bungling. For the last twenty years, Western countries, including the United States, have lectured and criticized Burma's military governments. Clearly, one of the high-profile misdeeds by the leaders has been the continued confinement of Nobel laureate Madam Suu Kyi to her residence. But the government also holds some two thousand other political prisoners under lock and key.

However, as a number of knowledgeable writers have pointed out, Myanmar is in little danger of economic disintegration. The problem is that without Western engagement, Myanmar's people risk becoming a virtual colony of China. One writer argues that the Western position may be justified to a certain extent, but it may be leading the United States and its supporters down an undesired path. The time may well have arrived for a reexamination of the entire situation.

As inhumanely as the military administration runs the country, and as poorly as it has been managing the economy, it is easy to forget the nation's natural strengths. First, it is the largest country in mainland Southeast Asia, and the fortieth largest in the world, with over a quarter of a million well-watered square miles of rivers and forests. It has 1,200 miles of coastline, providing ample access to the sea. The forests, covering half of the country, include dense tropical growth and valuable teak in the southern sections. The population numbers more than 47 million, with armed forces currently totaling some four hundred thousand in all services.

In early October 2009 the military government permitted a rare meeting of Madam Aung San Suu Kyi with Western diplomats. The British ambassador, Andrew Heyn, remarked that he had had a very interesting meeting with her, focused on the matter of international sanctions. "She was very clear," the ambassador commented, "that it was to be a fact-finding session," but Madame Suu Kyi gave no indication of her thoughts about sanctions.[17]

She did, however, ask about the circumstances under which Western countries might lift sanctions, bringing the fate of the 2,100 political prisoners in Burmese jails into the conversation, along with the possibility of free and fair elections. The United States has severe restrictions on doing business with Myanmar, while the European Union has targeted members of the regime, their families, and their business associates. The United States has recently undertaken a major review of its Myanmar policies and concluded that it will leave its sanctions in place, but end the country's diplomatic isolation.

The army exercises very tight control over interactions between nongovernment Burmese and all foreigners. As it has remained in power, it has depressed most hopes for a more liberal governmental attitude toward the populace. The best thing that can be said about it today is that it has been almost forty years since it killed fifteen students involved in political demonstrations; however, it has threatened thousands of others.

THAILAND

Next door, in Thailand, former Prime Minister Thaksin Shinawatra, an authoritarian populist, dogged by allegations of corruption before being removed from office in a military coup, has mustered a popular movement for his return. As writers have pointed out, the country has lived through a military coup, six prime ministers, and widespread civil unrest in just the last three years. Protesters have occupied two international airports, and disturbances have culminated in violent clashes in Bangkok.[18]

Thaksin fled the country in 2006, and now must await a royal decision regarding his deeds—or misdeeds—before he can venture back across the border to his native land. Convicted of conflicts of interest, he struggles between being a crowd-pleasing "champion" and the hard requirements of honest administration. A motion supporting his return has been judged "illegal" by the succeeding government.

Behind much of the trouble is increasing evidence of religious problems, including the development of an "Islamist agenda" and concern for political and social "unease." Increasingly, attacks have focused on interfaith tensions such as those between Buddhists and Muslims, but the difficulties project into the economic sphere as the disturbances drive tourists away and depress the economy.

The surge in troops is evident across both international and intra-national (state) borders. Teachers and other obvious symbols of the Thai state have been prime targets in the insurgency, with almost fifty killed every year in the last four years. Recent fatalities in the three southernmost provinces have exceeded 3,500. The insurgency is different from many other civil conflicts of this kind in that the participants tend to seek secrecy rather than boasting of their "accomplishments." Further, Amnesty International has published a report that security forces have placed nine peaceful protesters at "high risk of torture or other ill-treatment."[19]

In late 2009 the Thai government initiated action to expel an estimated 4,200 ethnic Hmong, many of whom fought with secret elements of US forces during the Vietnam War in Laos, or were related to soldiers who worked with Americans (particularly the CIA). The problem with returning them to Laos is that they face likely political persecution at the hands of the Laotian government.

Most recently the Thai government dispatched more than thirty trucks to Lao camps and closed off satellite and cell phone service to the areas in apparent preparation for blocking any appeal by the refugees to international authority. At the same time it was suspected that the Thais intended to expel a separate group of some 158 Hmong from another camp site on Thai territory. These moves were expected to parallel the expulsion of twenty ethnic

Uighur refugees back to China, where they face punishment for participation in violent protests in northwestern China.[20]

As these events have developed, the Obama administration sent Assistant Secretary of State Eric Schwartz to Thailand with a letter committing the United States and other Western countries (especially the Netherlands and Australia) to resettle any Hmong deemed to be refugees. Notably, the United States has already accepted 150,000 such refugees.

But the letter did not satisfy all Thai concerns. Not irrationally, the Thais expressed concern that the arrangement would tempt large numbers of additional Hmong to seek infiltration into Thailand in hopes of further movement to Western countries. At this writing, no full solution has been developed for the problem, and the forced deportation of the Hmong has begun. The Thai government has notified the United States that it has assurances of appropriate care for the refugees from the Laotian government, but there is much skepticism for both the Thai and Laotian statements and promises.[21]

As time has progressed, Thai problems have increased in several ways. Contrary to traditional laws, the role of the monarchy has come into increasing question, and in April 2010 the country suffered its worst political violence in nearly twenty years. Soldiers and protesters clashed on the streets, leaving 21 people dead and nearly 900 wounded. A few days later protesters rioted in Bangkok, forcing the closure of stores and banks and severely impacting business in major hotels. The foreign minister, Kasit Piromya, speaking to an American audience, remarked, "I do not know the outcome, but I remain optimistic that we will be able to have [the various political groups] coming to the negotiating table in the course of the next few days and talk to one another."[22]

Another disrupting force for the government is the telecommunications billionaire Thaksin Shinawatra, noted above. Thaksin is a former prime minister and influential absentee leader of the "Red Shirt" movement, which appears to target the abolition of Thailand's constitutional monarchy and its replacement with a republic. After six weeks of paralyzing demonstrations, the Red Shirts brought the country to a point of crisis.

But Mr. Thaksin has not been an easy target for arrest. Rumors have had him in dozens of countries, from China to Nicaragua, escaping arrest for charges of graft following his service as prime minister. Thus far he has kept vital space between himself and the Thai police by traveling on false passports issued by friends in Nicaragua, Uganda, and Montenegro.[23]

LAOS

In their guidebook, Andrew Burke and Justine Vaisutis recite some of the attractions of the southern extremity of the country (by Burke) and the northern territory (by Vaisutis).[24] Both make important contributions about land which has developed a long-term buffer status (between Thailand on its west and Vietnam to its east).

Best guesses have the Thai peoples migrating southward sometime in the eighth century, settling themselves along the Nam Ou and Nam Khan rivers, until such time as they finally found the Great River—the Mekong. Their principal deity was the Ngeuk, or a particularly powerful species of snake with which the Mekong was well endowed. Inadequate attention to the god-serpent was deemed sure to tip over canoes and drown the occupants. Reportedly, most Lao peasants still believe in the rule of the Ngeuk.

Other stories recount the myths of the Lao people, including great gourds from which emerged the city of Dien Bien Phu, on one side, with its darker skinned people, and the Tai-Lao, or lowlands Lao, who sprang from the second gourd.[25]

Whatever their origins, years of conflict between Thais and Laotians was a repetitive pattern. The territory fell under Japanese control in World War II, and afterward was under French control until 1954, when Laos gained independence as a constitutional monarchy. The French maintained a military training group in the area until 1955. The US Department of Defense created a "Special Programs Group" to replace the French team in preparing the Royal Lao Army to deal with the growing communist Pathet Lao units. The United States pumped $120 million into the country—four times that which France had invested—but when American political support was removed in 1958, the native government collapsed.

Of course, the United States would later attempt to reinforce anti-communist forces and states in the region as part of its overall Southeast Asia effort, but, considering the overall weakness in the national military strategy (principally inadequate blockage of hostile land and sea approaches to South Vietnam), that effort was doomed.

Throughout the Vietnam War the Pathet Lao opposed the Royal Lao Army and supported the movement of North Vietnamese troops southward through Laos to South Vietnam. After taking control of the country, the "Lao People's Democratic Republic" signed agreements granting the (forcefully united) Vietnam the right to station armed forces and to appoint advisors "to assist in over-seeing the Lao country." At the conclusion of the war in the late 1970s, Laos was requested by Vietnam to end its relations with both China and the United States. Much later, however, Laos was able to renew socialization with Western countries, and tourism began to grow. Expectations of national income have reached $250–$300 million by 2010.[26]

But that is only a part of the story. At this writing, students in Vientiane, the capital of the country, attend classes under poster-size portraits of Marx and Lenin. Practical communism competes even more with practical capitalism. The country is expected to open its first stock exchange in a few years, while still permitting only the Communist Lao Peoples' Revolutionary Party members to run for election. The system of governance is clearly authoritarian.[27]

CAMBODIA

Formerly a land of "Kampucheans," Cambodia today is home to some fourteen million people, with Phnom Penh as their capital. The country borders Thailand to the west, Laos to the northeast, and Vietnam to the east. Its dominant terrain feature is the Mekong, which both feeds and drains the Tonle Sap, the great freshwater lake which supports the important fishing industry. Most citizens who do not fish till the soil, but that may change in the next decade. Significant oil and natural gas deposits have been discovered beneath Cambodia's territorial waters.

An early protectorate of France, occupied by Japan in World War II, the country gained its independence in 1953, under the rein of King Norodom Sihanouk. During the American involvement in Vietnam the US Air Force bombed communist Cambodian (Khmer Rouge) troops surrounding the capital city. As the war drew to a close, it became apparent that the bombing had been so broad that some 75 percent of the country's draft animals had been destroyed.

Upon acceding to power, the new communist leadership under Pol Pot changed the name of the country to "Democratic Kampuchea." All surviving residents of cities were forced to walk out of their homes and to devote themselves to rural work programs. The apparent aim of the government was to rebuild a model of a land dating back to the eleventh century. Western medicines were discarded; temples, libraries, and almost anything deemed to be of Western origin was destroyed. Over a million people—perhaps as many as three million—died from starvation or were executed.

No peace came to the land until the 1990s, and even then most aspects of national life remained unstable. A new constitution was established in 1993 which provided for a constitutional monarchy. King Norodom Sihamoni assumed the throne in 1994 with the authority to appoint a prime minister, with the approval of the National Assembly. The new Royal Cambodian Armed Forces would serve under the prime minister, who also serves the forces directly as commander-in-chief.

The country has matured into a functioning entity, administering its business as most states are expected to do. It is now a member of the United Nations, the World Bank, and the International Monetary Fund. It is also a member of ASEAN (the Association of Southeast Asian Nations). While the violent eruptions of the 1970s and 1980s have passed, Cambodia is in dispute with a number of its neighbors. There are differences with Vietnam over offshore islands and the location of parts of the common border. Certain undefined maritime boundaries and border areas with Thailand also remain in question.

Cambodian per capita income is still low in comparison with that of most of its neighbors, but recently it has been increasing at an annual rate of 8 percent. Since 1999, the land has enjoyed its first full year of peace in thirty years, and economic growth has resumed. Most national roads are now paved, and the state boasts two operational railroads, with some 380 miles of single-meter track, and four commercial airports.[28]

In sum, there is not very much in the land to be proud of, but times are much better today than they have been in most of the recent past.

VIETNAM

In its unified form, Vietnam enjoys broader access to the South China Sea than any of its mainland neighbors, save China itself. With major urban centers at either end of its thousand-mile stretch, it is well developed for further exploitation of its natural resources. It was not the intention of the United States that it find itself so.

In the 1960s it was Washington's desire that the land remain divided according to the inclinations of the democratic regime in Saigon and the communist leadership in the north. Had Washington's leadership enjoyed a deeper grasp of military affairs, the situation might have developed differently. With little appreciation of the Soviet and Chinese support for the communist sub-state in the north, Washington settled for an extraction of its forces in return for virtually no accommodation on the part of Ho Chi Minh or his successors in Hanoi.

US military planners had developed an interesting planning proposal for high-ranking political leaders' consideration which featured three detailed options under which the war might be pursued. The first two depended primarily upon the strengthening of US and South Vietnamese ground forces. (Option no. 2 included the addition of two US divisions over option no. 1.) Option no. 3 pursued a broader approach to the war, with the occupation of a line across Laos along the east-west Xa Noy River. The third case could have effectively blocked the "Ho Chi Minh Trail" and prevented all but the smallest trickle of arms and reinforcing units from the North to South Vietnam.

Unfortunately, the third option was never effectively pursued. That option was believed to entail some special road and bridge engineering in the mountains, which led some war planners to effectively rule it out of further consideration. That, in turn, led to mistaken understandings of the relative strengths and weaknesses of the proposed options. With key subsequent decisions and orders based upon fallacious assumptions in the early planning, the war was lost. Vietnam today suffers under a rigid communist system, from north to south, after thousands of lives were lost in attempts to escape the frightful invasion from Hanoi.

The unified Vietnam now enjoys a degree of comity with foreign visitors and certain trade progresses, but nothing will ever make up for the terrible human losses suffered as a result of the conquest and subjugation of the people of South Vietnam.[29]

INDONESIA

A columnist noted recently that "countries generally hit the headlines only when the news is bad. In Indonesia it has often been spectacularly bad."[30]

Close to the eastern end of Thomas Barnett's "new Pentagon map" lie the Indonesian Islands. They are home to the criminal Jemaah Islamiah (JI), an extremist group skilled in suicide bombings of first-class business hotels in Jakarta in mid-summer. The terrorist teams are noted for hostile actions against Malaysians, Singaporeans, Indonesians, and Filipinos, but Indonesia has long been the preferred target. Suicide bombings in 2002 killed more than two hundred persons. While the tragedy was obvious, cynics may have also noted that Indonesia has the fourth-largest population in the world, behind only China, India, and the United States.[31]

Since 2002, Indonesian security forces have captured hundreds of Jemaah Islamiah suspects, a sufficient number to alarm political leaders, but also to permit the various governments involved to feel that they are gaining control of the problem. Critical observers have been concerned that they may have let their guard down for a while, but Indonesia is no longer viewed as a weak spot in Southeast Asia's fight against terrorism. A brief glance at the history of the country may reinforce this assertion.

Indonesia is an insular state of some ten thousand components (give or take half again as many). They are spread over 5,200 kilometers of land and water between the Asian mainland and Australia, separating the great continental land masses. It is little wonder that the two hundred million inhabitants speak some five hundred different languages and dialects or that the country has more Muslims than any other nation in the world.

The islands which make up the country are as different as they are distant, and, in some cases, just as dangerous. Physical dangers range from cobras and crocodiles to dehydration and heatstroke. Maluku, a collection of a thousand or more islands, is home for a people known to the outside world longer than any other in Indonesia. The land, dubbed the "Spice Islands" two hundred years ago, prompted European voyages of exploration that would circle the globe for the first time.

Today, Maluku is probably the state most devastated by internecine warfare, and it is clearly addressed in travel literature as an island group to be avoided. Over five thousand people are said to have been killed in the course of local conflicts stemming in part from a poisonous religious mixture of Islam, Catholicism, and Protestantism. What sets the Maluku communities apart is believed to be a unique but dangerous balance of religious groups, each jealous of the others' ability to cope with aggression from one of the others. Oddly enough, most of the rest of the country appears to be comfortable with a breakdown of 85 percent Muslim and 15 percent Christian. It may be that the majority suppose that the distinction is so clear that few favor—or necessarily fear—aggressive action against those of a different faith.

Islam first arrived in Indonesia in the eighth century AD, establishing a kingdom in Java. The first (Christian) Europeans arrived some eight hundred years later. The first of this group came from Portugal, following the trail of Vasco da Gama. In 1580 Portugal had been annexed by Spain, which constricted the former's operations on the far side of the globe. However, the British defeat of the Spanish Armada in 1588 opened the way for the Dutch, themselves part of the Spanish Empire, to explore the East on its own account.

The Dutch negotiated with local powers on Java (now Jakarta) for the establishment of warehouse facilities on the island. But as the private interests of other nations waned, Dutch merchants found that they, too, were becoming increasingly dependent upon government agencies for security. The Dutch government gradually assumed a larger, and ultimately sovereign, role in both private and public affairs. As the nineteenth century unfolded, the Dutch government encouraged the development of a "liberal system" that would strengthen the hands of local farmers. Unfortunately, it coincided with some devastating natural and economic disasters. A coffee-leaf disease and a sugar blight in 1882 sorely tested the foreign management, and did nothing to encourage broad faith in the established government. The early years of the twentieth century also did little to unify Dutch and native leadership on the way toward the Second World War.

Hitler's victory in the Netherlands was initially an encouragement to the native islanders, many of whom had independence on their minds, but the nature of his occupation, reinforced by the Japanese invasion in 1942, provided little support for any movement in Indonesia. Nor were the Dutch ready to grant independence to the islanders. The calendar would reach the end of 1949 before the country received its independence.

But independence did not mean freedom. It wasn't until the late 1950s when Achmed Sukarno rose to power with his concept of "guided democracy" under authoritarian rule. He was an admirer of communism, but just at the moment when he might have seized ultimate power he was ousted by the ambitious General Suharto, who instigated a fearsome counter-revolution leading to the general's seizure of the government. The slaughter of communist sympathizers was the bloodiest episode in the country's history, during which a half-million people were put to death.

Since then, the force was turned to serve primarily the economic desires of the high command, but it has not been without criticism. In one report, the whole arrangement was referred to as "among the world's most corrupt and abusive." The process has included the operations of plantations, logging, hotels, and property development.[32]

A law passed in 2004 instructed the army to surrender its businesses to the government by October 2009. Nothing much happened until President Susilo Bambang Yudhoyono created a panel of experts to investigate the firms. The defense minister, Juwono Sudarsono, says the panel has identified about 1,500 military firms, but most of them have gone bust, been bought up by the private sector, or are close to collapse. Only six viable firms with assets over $50 thousand have been found. The government panel's findings concur with figures determined by a branch of the Brookings Institution, a US think tank.[33]

The militant Islamic group Jemaah Islamiah was once called "Al Qaeda's Southeast Asia Wing" and was regarded as Osama bin Laden's most dangerous ally. Today, after six years of aid to the country from the United States, the situation is more stable, if not less Islamist. Most members of the original JI have been arrested or killed off.

Today, with the departure of the majority of the original JI terrorists, special importance in the counter-crime effort has turned to the formation of a secret "Detachment 88" in the police force, with millions of dollars for fulsome support. The detachment is armed with high-powered sniper rifles and assault vehicles. Along with SWAT teams for raiding hostile hiding places on short notice, Detachment 88 swept up some 400 militants and uncovered a number of large weapons caches. The number of outstanding terrorists has been reduced to a few hundred, including all but a few of the most capable leaders.

The remnants of JI have largely split into two factions since 2005. The first is a smaller group, made up of young die-hards and a few of the older, first-generation leaders. Not disturbed by friendly fatalities, this is the team most likely to risk everything to stage a large-scale attack. The other, much larger group spends much of its time spreading literature and building up groups of sympathizers. In the long run, with a better base, it could turn out to be the more effective of the two.

Significantly, it is the larger group that has the flexibility to attempt de-radicalization of captured terrorists. They have the clout to arrange for visits by prisoners' wives and trips by their children to Mecca in exchange for assurances that released prisoners will cooperate with government needs and wishes.[34] Thus far it has been more successful than many had feared.

The *Economist* summarizes its assessment of modern Indonesia with the words, "On good terms with all countries." It may have some differences with Singapore, which Indonesia considers "a bolt hole for fugitives from Indonesian justice," and Malaysia, "with which it squabbles over practically everything." But, for all its petty problems, the country is an active player in the Association of Southeast Asian Nations (ASEAN), which essentially makes them all close allies. US Secretary of State Hillary Clinton included Indonesia on her first official foreign tour abroad.

International respect for Indonesia is not confined to the United States or its neighbors. The country has shown remarkable powers of recovery after a long period of dictatorship and economic collapse. It is recognized for its emphasis on democratic processes, Muslim tolerance, poverty eradication, and rapid economic development. Every day it seems to make advances in these areas, and, as one writer notes, "Its chances of getting there have never been better."[35]

As another reporter has written,

[P]resent-day Indonesia seems almost a miracle; it is a stable, largely peaceful democracy with a resilient economy growing at a respectable lick. Despite a July [2009] suicide-bombing in Jakarta, Islamist extremism has been marginalized and, in the world's largest Muslim-majority country, moderation rules.

In stark contrast to its shipwreck during the Asian financial crisis of 1997–98, Indonesia has sailed through the credit crunch without leaking much water. In 2009 the GDP grew more than four percent in 2009. Fiscal restraint and sustained domestic demand have given the economy solidity. With its huge domestic market—some 240 million people—Indonesia ought to be the domestic hub for businesses seeking a regional niche in South-East Asia.[36]

One area unaffected by modernity is the shopping and night life of Bandung on the western end of the island of Java. It is well known as "the Paris of the island." It is especially known for its universities, its cuisine, and its fashion displays. The only counterweights are its red light districts and the island's small, but influential, Islamist political parties.

Reportedly, the power of religious and political conservatives has grown in Indonesia in the past ten years, and they have declared the intent of "taking the Paris out of Bandung." Still, as long as the larger and most influential Western states in the world are involved in disputes with important Islamic groups, as we have seen in the Middle East, it is important to keep in mind that Indonesia not only has the fourth-largest population in the world, but it has more Muslims than any other country: over 200 million of its total of 240 million people.[37]

MALAYSIA

For two years the Thailand army has been engaged in struggles with the country's Maylay Muslims in three of its seven provinces. The strength of the army, police, and militia involved has grown to about 60,000, according to the dean at Prince of Songkla University in Pattani. A large increase in security forces reduced government losses for a while, but the number of killings appeared to be on the increase again in the first nine months of 2009.

Since 2004 there have been about 3,500 deaths in the Islamic provinces. Teachers, as symbols of the Thai state, have been prime targets. On the other side, soldiers have been accused of inappropriate behavior around both Buddhist temples and Islamic mosques.

The insurgency is noted for its deployment of shadowy, ill-defined groups that do not claim responsibility for the violence. The apparent objectives of two groups, the Pattani Islamic Mujahedin Movement and the National Revolutionary Front, are to coordinate their actions to drive the government out of power and to put in place strict Islamic laws.

The Maylay Muslims have an apparent edge in the struggle, making up, as they do, some 80 percent of all peoples living in the three southern provinces close to Malaysia. Buddhist volunteers (some 71,000) form village guard units, according to one reporter, for the International Crisis Group, a nonprofit organization that aims to prevent deadly conflicts.

Observers have had difficulty in assessing the effectiveness of either party because the participating groups are often more interested in taking pictures than they are in fighting their opponents.[38]

PHILIPPINE ISLANDS

The Philippines constitute a state with an emerging economy and a democratic government, but one beset by dangerous groups harboring distinct agendas and behavioral habits quite unlike those of members of mature democracies. It also has a high proportion of extremely poor citizens—those living on less than $1 a day. Islamists, largely concentrated on the southern islands, continue to challenge the Manila government with periodic attacks on official personnel and property, largely on the islands to which they lay claim. In August 2009 the government responded with a "major offensive" against the hostile Muslim organization Abu Sayyaf Group (ASG). Serious losses were sustained by both sides.

Four hundred government troops, mostly Philippine Marines, attacked the main rebel camp on Basilan Island, securing the site southwest of the troublesome landmass of Mindanao, and captured large quantities of explosives. But they suffered the loss of twenty-three men killed in action while ASG losses were no greater. The government had military aircraft and heavy weapons available for employment in the operation, but the close quarters in which most of the fighting took place prevented much use of the arms. The next step is expected to be a government attack on Jolo Island, lying some fifty miles to the southwest, further down the island chain. That territory is thought to be held by another 300 of the ASG rebels, and it may hold additional surprises for the government.[39] A recent article in the *Economist* commented that it was becoming difficult to imagine Philippine politics without "guns and goons." The government has both reconnaissance and attack aircraft and heavier ground equipment than its opponents, but much of the fighting takes place at close quarters, substantially limiting its natural advantages.

An independent Philippine commission was formed early in January 2010 to oversee the disbanding of the politicians' private armies before the most recent election in May. The formation of the commission was a reaction to the earlier massacre of fifty-seven people in the southern province of Maguindanao, the worst election-related violence in Philippine history.[40] The authorities accused a local politician and his armed thugs of the public crime, but he denied any wrongdoing and few dared to testify differently. The secretary of national defense, Noberto Gonzalez, said that there were 132 private armed groups with a combined force of some 10,000 men. Hence, there is considerable doubt that the commission can complete its task very soon.

In the past, private armies have been employed to assist official security forces and to help defend communities threatened by communist or Muslim separatist guerillas. Also, local warlords have been known to use their forces to reinforce national security troops when they have felt threatened by competing armed groups. Most recently, in June 2010, a radio political commentator was shot and killed on his way home after rendering scathing broadcast attacks on just such criminals.[41]

"Almost always," it has been reported, "they are employed to keep one or more politicians in office, and other ones out." This was especially the case with President Gloria Macapagal-Arroyo, until a massacre occurred and the governing party swiftly ended the operating agreements. It is expected now that the commission will press hard to approve only small security teams and to avoid the larger gangs and private armies, but there is no guarantee that all political groups will cooperate. One reporter has noted the aptness of the old saying that political power "often comes out of the barrel of a gun."[42]

A major event in connection with this report was the murder of some thirty journalists, the deadliest single attack on media workers in the world. The outcry from abroad prompted President Gloria Macapagal-Arroyo to declare martial law for a week in southern Mindanao province and to crack down on a powerful follower, once her key political ally—and head of his own private army.[43]

A witness to the massacre testified that a town mayor had shot several of the victims and that his father, the patriarch of a powerful political clan and an ally of President Gloria Macapagal-Arroyo, had personally directed his son to carry out several of the killings. The son did so personally with at least three of the victims and ordered his colleagues to make sure that none were left alive.

Later that year Muslim militants beheaded a school principal on one of the remote southern islands after holding him (unsuccessfully) for ransom for three weeks. It has been the practice of organizations like the Abu Sayyaf, an affiliate of Al Qaeda, both to kidnap government officials and to execute them when no ransom is paid.[44]

A recent, far less rambunctious candidate than most others was the winner, Benigno S. ("Noynoy") Aquino III, son of the former President Corazon C. Aquino. Part of his appeal was his promise to "recalibrate" his country's relations with the United States. And, indeed, "Noynoy," who had no identified connections with crime, took the majority of votes. Since 2002 American Special Forces, with Philippine governmental approval, have been operating on the southern islands, training the Philippine military to counter Islamic extremists.

Most responsible Filipinos credit the Americans with strengthening the government's forces and capabilities, but Mr. Aquino cautions that "the United States force should not become semi-permanent or permanent." He expresses concern that the "Visiting Forces Agreement," the bilateral treaty that provides for US control of its servicemen, allows a bit more independence for the US troops than most people find comfortable, even when Philippine citizens are involved or affected.

"I get the impression at times," the president has said, "that Americans follow the mold of a corporation that has to report to its stockholders every year, as opposed to thinking about generating a long-term relationship." A prominent supporter has described the successful Aquino campaign as one which "exuded a more quiet self-confidence. [Aquino] exudes a more quiet self-confidence than most. He's not razzmatazz. He's not dancing girls in short skirts."[45]

But what he may be is a cautious figure who understands the security problems his country faces. He knows that Al Qaeda is a growth industry worldwide, and unless one is prepared to live with it, he needs to reexamine his options. Clearly, the country has problems that exceed Manila's capabilities to control. He says he does not want the level of foreign (read, "American") forces he has now. And he does not want private armies controlling

Philippine election campaigns. He wants to lower the visibility of "foreign forces" without reducing the security of the southern islands. What is his solution? His position cries out for the formation of an American-Philippine legion in order to (1) relieve the burden of direct hostile engagements currently carried by US Marines, with minimal Philippine contribution, and (2) establish a legion with US leadership and Philippine volunteer enrollment until such time that the Philippine military is capable of shouldering full responsibilities for the task.

13

A Final Word

As we have noted on these pages, America's "responsibility of power" has proven to be a far-flung, multifaceted, aspect of life (and death) on earth—shared, in many cases, with others, but rarely on a 50-50 basis. The United States is virtually the only country on earth capable of full-bodied response to crises, whatever they be: economic, technical, military, or social. We have fought a number of high-end battles, in different directions, from one side of the globe to another, as well as others confined to a single region, or even to a single country. Notably, unlike some older states, we have rarely ventured with arms into the southern hemisphere. Our sense of personal liberty and self-determination of government have turned our thoughts in different directions. But we are not a people without ambition or sense of aspiration. In the defense area, our ambitions have been enriched by the development of extraordinary technological and operational accomplishment, such as our long-range troop and weapons lift by sea and air. These dimensions may come to be reinforced by ventures into space. Such developments could permit us to deal with challenges in strength and capabilities, from virtually any direction in ever-shorter periods of time.

At this writing the United States is at war—for a sixth or seventh time in living memory, depending upon how one wishes to count the events—especially with the respect to our efforts in the Middle East, and possibly in North Africa. Cynics may add, "It is time to declare victory and order our troops home." But the United States is already realigning available forces, and dispatching additional ones in the Mediterranean. Conceivably, we may have been simply trying to wind down one war in the Middle East to clear the decks for another elsewhere. On March 7, 2011, Thom Shanker wrote in the *New York Times*, "Rebel commanders [in Libya] have begged for American strikes on troops and weapons that have turned on civilians and assaulted strongholds of the resistance."[1]

The US 26th Marine Expeditionary Unit has arrived aboard two amphibious assault ships, the U.S.S. *Kearsarge* and the U.S.S. *Ponce*, forming a modest offensive capability, should one be needed. The team included Harrier jump-jet warplanes with bomb delivery and strafing capabilities, posing increasingly serious threats to Libyan government forces. In addition, the expanding US force has sufficient aerial delivery capabilities for substantial air-drop supply operations to friendly Libyan elements operating on the ground.[2]

Nevertheless, NATO has pledged to assume much of the responsibility for Western interests in Libya and the largest commitment of US forces remains the Middle East. As we have noted, one of the most persuasive arguments from a knowledgeable participant there is that of Colonel Timothy R. Reese, a recent advisor to the Iraqi military's Baghdad Command. One of the colonel's memoranda calls attention to the tensions between American and Iraqi military officers in the late June 2009 period, when American forces were withdrawn from many urban areas to reserve positions in less populated areas.

As we have noted, in the main sector of current military actions documents detail Iraqi military weaknesses, corruption, poor management, and an inability to resist internal Shiite political pressures. Further, it argues that any extension of American diplomatic pressure beyond 2010 would do little to improve our hosts' military performance, but would be more likely to intensify their resentment of Americans' presence on their soil. While not formally endorsed by General Odierno, the US country commanding general, the colonel's memorandum has been seen as the view among a number of senior American officers, and perhaps as a potential instrument for shaping future policy. As we have previously noted, Reese commented, "Our hand is on the back seat holding the Iraqis back from exercising full control over their country," and thus is a strong cause of resentment. "We need to let go before we both tumble to the ground," he argues.[3]

The colonel is a well-qualified and experienced officer. Before deploying to Iraq he served as the director of the Combat Studies Institute at Fort Leavenworth, Kansas, alongside the US Army Command and General Staff College. He had also written an official Army history of the earlier phases of the war. With respect to his views on the need for change in the Army's strategy, he noted that he had read many Army reports that made the same points.

In his summary, the colonel noted that a "sudden coolness" had overcome a number of Iraqi officers working with Americans in the American governmental and military headquarters, as well as an unfortunate Iraqi "forcible takeover" of a checkpoint in the so-called Green Zone (site of international headquarters). The Iraqi Ground Forces Command, he wrote, imposed restrictions on American military operations that violated many basic rules of the alliance, and refused to comply with a number of previously important regulations for coordination of national forces. One matter was of particular concern. The Iraqi legal system was found to be of specific difficulty, for it tended to release captured Iraqis for actions that would normally bring extended incarceration to persons identified as those mounting attacks on US personnel. The implication of attachment of greater value to Americans than to natives was unsettling to Iraqi soldiers.

Under 2009 agreements, the bulk of American forces were to remain in place until after Iraqi national elections scheduled for January the following year. Thereafter the documents called for the reduction of US troops from 130,000 on duty in 2009 to 50,000 by the end of August 2010. However, other senior Americans have argued that this timetable may have been too fast, but it might also have been a view close to that held by the theater commander, General David H. Petraeus.

Whatever the need for US trained forces, or, more particularly, for the skills of leadership so well known among American officers and noncommissioned officers, Iraq would appear to be a singularly suitable place for the creation and establishment of *a first US-recruited, -trained, -equipped, and -led legion for the future security of the Iraqi state and American interests in the region.*

During an appearance at the United States Institute of Peace, in Washington, Mr. Nuri Kamal al-Maliki, the Iraqi prime minster, appeared to contemplate a possible role for American forces after December 2011, even if accomplished within a general concept of removal of all American formations. Coupled with Colonel Reese's argument, however the various remarks may be interpreted, there is a hint of a suggestion for common ground. The United States has clearly assumed too much for too long and involved too many hundreds of thousands of American and allied soldiers to simply walk away from the *responsibility of power.* While he made no mention of an American legion in his remarks, one may find some close similarities.

At this writing, neighboring Iran appears to have chosen to pose the nightmare of nuclear weaponry employment to a number of its neighbors. As serious as the matter is, Tehran must realize that it is not the only—and perhaps not the most threatening—nuclear power in the region. Nor should it be allowed to seriously abuse or attempt to destabilize its neighbors by forcing them to plunge into the nuclear world themselves. To begin with, the United States has the counter-nuclear force *par excellence*, including total suites of intercontinental delivery and defense systems, thus constituting the one most capable of discouraging serious operational planning for resort to nuclear weaponry, even if only by demonstration. Further, nuclear programs in neighboring Israel and Pakistan illustrate the marginality of value of such efforts.

Generally speaking, the practical application of the nuclear dimension in this theater, with these players, would be likely to prove self-defeating to most countries. Iran, an exception, has been seriously testing its finances with a full array of processes necessary for acquisition of reliable weaponry. But the financial and political demands for full development of nuclear arsenals for active warfare (e.g., vis-à-vis the United States) could prove overwhelming.

On the other hand, the acceptance by local states for defensively oriented, US-led legions armed with modern, conventional weapons, operating in conventional roles, and largely financed by the United States, would sharply improve the defenses of the recipient states. Furthermore, the expense to the US (with low-cost manpower, American standard equipment maintained to US standards, etc.) would be substantially less than that for regular US units.

Further, development and deployment of Iraqi-American or Afghan-American foreign legions in the field would suffer no self-limiting restrictions. In both cases, opportunities for solution favor US interests. While it would not be surprising for the United States to encounter a degree of political hesitation and reluctance (such as occurred in the Middle East in 2001) before it might dispatch a fresh group of forces, adequately trained and doctrinally balanced for the challenges they would be likely to face.

Most NATO countries have been represented in the Middle East, with some (mostly minor contributors) showing their flags. While that was politically pleasing, it provided little of the spirit or regional accommodation that could be attained with volunteer national legions, each attuned and tempered for operations within its assigned borders: equipped, trained, supplied, and led by the best in the business, the US Army.

For dealing with many troublesome tribes, bandits and their often overambitious chieftains or dictators around the world, the United States maintains an impressive array of intelligence networks, allies, and ready conventional forces. But under these circumstances, it did not. We must consider that the effect of a resident foreign legion, stationed on or near the target area, could imply both a reassurance and number of deterrents. Clearly, and first of all, it would spell out the continued involvement of the United States. Thus far, in modern history, only Soviet Russia has chosen to pose a serious challenge to the United States at the high end of the spectrum of weapons, including the possible nightmare of global nuclear war. Second, it would indicate a dedication by the host government to a readiness to coordinate its policies and likely operations with those of the United States. Third, it would signify the high quality of a significant number of indigenous forces in the legion units themselves, with specially trained and schooled officers guiding their every step. This would likely include the management and direction of sophisticated weaponry, high-speed communications, and the dedication of back-up US forces (not necessarily deployed) to ensure their success.

While the presence of legion forces might not indicate a certainty of any specific reaction by either the host government or that of the United States, it would substantially increase the risks and complicate the decision-making of the potential aggressor, while increasing the potential efficiency of joint US-local government military coordination.

But especially it should be remembered that on February 25, 2011, Secretary of Defense Robert M. Gates told an assembly of cadets at West Point:

> In my opinion, any defense secretary who advises the president to again send a big American land army into Asia or into the Middle East or Africa should "have his head examined," as General MacArthur so delicately put it.[4]

Mr. Gates does not need to have his head examined. But he does need to keep his eyes open for a strategy matching the responsibilities of the greatest power on earth.

Endnotes

PREFACE

1. General McChrystal was subsequently relieved of command and retired from the Army for a number of critical comments by him and his staff to the press in June 2010 regarding his orders from higher authority.

CHAPTER 1

1. Douglas J. Feith, *War and Decision: Inside the Pentagon at the Dawn of the War on Terrorism* (New York: Harper, 2008), p. 9.

2. Ibid.

3. Ibid.

4. The war in Iraq, "shock and awe," the doctrine of preemptive war, and the subsequent display of a "Mission Accomplished" banner would be cited popularly five years later as the worst ideas of the decade. See "The Worst Ideas of the Decade," *Washington Post*, 27 December 2009, p. B3.

5. "Costs of the War," ProCon.org, 25 August 2008, p. 1. Also see Carol Giacomo, "New Beltway Debate: What to Do about Iran," *New York Times*, 3 November 2008, p. A26.

6. Bob Herbert, "The $2 Trillion Nightmare," *New York Times*, 4 March 2008, p. A25.

7. Edward B. Atkeson, "Our Mesopotamian Foes: Just Who Are They?" *Army*, March 2005, p. 79.

8. "Costs of the War," ProCon.org, 25 August 2008, p. 1.

9. Dana Priest and Walter Pincus, "U.S. 'Almost All Wrong' On Weapons," *Washington Post*, 7 October 2004, p. A1.

10. Williamson Murray and Maj. Gen. Robert H. Scales Jr. *The Iraq War: A Military History* (Cambridge, MA: Belknap Press of Harvard University Press, 2003), p. 255.

11. The White House admitted five years later that "President Bush had paid a price for the 'Mission Accomplished' banner that was flown in triumph . . . but it later became a symbol of

U.S. misjudgments and mistakes in the long and costly war in Iraq." See Terence Hunt, "White House Admits Fault on Banner," *Daily Journal*, San Mateo, CA, 1 May 2008, p. 10.

12. Editorial, *Washington Post*, 27 December 2009, p. B3.

13. Christopher Preble, director, "Exiting Iraq: Why the U.S. Must End the Military Occupation and Renew the War against Al Qaeda," Report of a Special Task Force, Cato Institute, 2004, p. 53. Nicholas D. Kristof, "1 Soldier or 20 Schools," *New York Times*, 29 July 2010, p. A23.

14. Eric Schmitt and Mark Mazzetti, "Secret Order Lets U.S. Raid Al Qaeda in Many Countries," *New York Times*, 10 November 2008, p. A1.

15. Richard J. Whalen, "The Revolt of the Generals," *The Nation*, 16 October 2006, posted on the Internet 28 September 2006.

16. "General William Odom on Iraq: Immediate Withdrawal the Only Option that Makes Sense," Alternet.org, http://www.alternet.org/world/81626?page=entire.

17. "Costs of the Iraq War," Internet ProCon.org, 25 August 2008, p. 1. Also see Jon Ward, "'Whatever It Takes' under Bush, the Cost of Protection, War and Economic Collapse Reach Historic Levels," *Washington Times*, 19 October 2008; and Herbert, "The $2 Trillion Nightmare," p. A2.

18. "Casualties in Iraq," www.Antiwar.com/casualties/8/25/2008, p. 1. Total US war deaths in Afghanistan from 2001 to June 2010 were reported by the Pentagon as 1,108; the total in Iraq from 2003 to June 2010 was 4,410, *Washington Post*, 20 June 2010, p. A11.

19. Bob Herbert, "Help Is on the Way," *New York Times*, 22 November 2008, p. A19.

20. Lizette Alvarez, "Suicides and Soldiers Reach High in Nearly Three Decades, and Army Vows to Bolster Prevention," *New York Times*, 30 January 2009, p. A14.

21. Maureen Dowd, "American President Pleads Guilty to Hopeless Idealism," *New York Times*, 18 June 2008.

22. Fareed Zakaria, "An Iraq Speech for Obama," *New York Times*, 23 June 2008, p. A15.

23. Colonel Craig Trebilcock, "The Modern Seven Pillars of Iraq," *ARMY* 57, no. 2 (February 2007): pp. 25–33.

24. Richard Oppel, "Stolen Oil Profits Keep Iraq's Insurgency Running," *New York Times*, 16 March 2008, p. A1.

25. Ibid.

26. Anna Mulrine, "To Battle Group Think, the Army Trains a Skeptics Corps," *U.S. News and World Report*, 26 May–2 June 2008, p. 30.

27. North Atlantic Treaty Organization / International Security Force / United Nations / Afghan Compact.

28. Anthony H. Cordesman, "Shaping a 'Conditions-based' Strategy and Plan for Staying in Iraq," Center for Strategic and International Studies, Washington, DC, 17 April 2008, pp. 1–2. Compact.

29. Ibid.

30. Ibid., p. 2.

31. Jane Mayer, *The Dark Side* (New York: Doubleday, 2008), p. 123.

32. Scott Shane, "China Inspired Interrogations at Guantanamo," *New York Times*, c. 26 May 2008, pp. 1–14A.

33. William Safire, cited in Mayer, *Dark Side*.

34. Bruce C. Swartz, "Interrogation Tactics Were Challenged by Career Lawyers," *Washington Post*, 22 May 2008. Also online: "Interrogation Tactics Were Challenged by Career Lawyer," *Huffington Post*, 30 May 2008.

35. Mayer, *Dark Side*.

36. Online, "Fire John Yoo!" "Boalt Hall Action: Stop U.C. Complicity in War Crimes," "Fire, Disbar and Prosecute John Yoo!" 19 August 2010. Online, Jack M. Balkin, "Balkinization," 19 February 2010; "Justice Department Will Not Punish Yoo and Bybee Because Most Lawyers Are

Scum Anyway," *Balkanization*, 19 February 2010. See also Eric Lichtblau and Scott Shane, "Report Faults Two Who Wrote Terror Memos," *New York Times*, 20 February 2010, p. A1.

37. Mayer, *Dark Side*, p. 241. Amanda Ripley, "Redefining Torture," *TIME*, 13 June 2004.

38. Pamela Hess, "Interrogator Details Pre-Abu Graib Abuses," *New York Sun*, 26 September 2008.

39. Mayer, *Dark Side*, p. 259. Wikipedia: Richard J. Durbin, "Making Life Easier: Guantanamo Interrogation Controversy," 14 June 2005.

40. Raymond Bonner, "Torture Claim Credible, Court Finds," *New York Times*, 22 August 2008, p. A6.

41. William Glaberson, "U.S. Drops War Crimes for 5 Guantanamo Detainees," *New York Times*, 22 October 2008, p. A1.

42. General Wesley K. Clark, *Waging Modern War* (New York: Public Affairs, 2001). See entire volume, especially page 6: "To successfully 'compel,' I realized the (NATO) force must be much greater than we had been willing to commit at the time."

43. William Glaberson, "Questioning 'Dirty Bomb' Plot, Judge Orders U.S. to Yield Papers on Detainee," *New York Times*, 30 October 2008.

44. William Glaberson, "An Unlikely Antagonist in the Detainees' Corner," *New York Times*, 19 June 2008, p. A1.

45. James Dobbins, "Who Lost Iraq," *Foreign Affairs* 86, no. 5 (Sept./Oct. 2007): pp. 61–62.

46. "So Little Time, So Much Damage," editorial, *New York Times*, 4 November 2008, p. A26.

47. Ibid.

48. Peter Finn, "Complex Issues Surrounding Guantanamo Jail," *Washington Post*, 12 November 2008, p. A6.

49. "Indefinite Detention," editorial, *New York Times*, 25 November 2008, p. 24A.

50. Bob Woodward, "Detainee Tortured Says U.S. Official," *Washington Post*, 14 January 2009, p. A8. Also see "Pulling Back the Blanket," *Economist*, 12 July 2008, p. 69.

51. "Broken Laws, Broken Lives, Medical Evidence of Torture by the U.S.," Physicians for Human Rights Report, preface by John Taguba, 2008, http://brokenlives.info/?page_id=23.

52. Woodward, "Detainee Tortured," 14 January 2009.

53. Campbell Robertson, "Iraq Troops Say Army Is Willing, But Not Ready to Fight Alone," *New York Times*, 6 August 2008, p. A6.

54. Ibid.

55. Bob Woodward, "Outmaneuvered and Outranked, Military Chiefs Become Outsiders," *Washington Post*, 8 September 2008, p. A1.

56. Thom Shanker and Stephen Lee Myers, "U.S. Makes Firmer Commitment to Pullout Date Accord," *New York Times*, 18 October 2008, p. A5. Also see John Nagl and Shawn Brimly, "How to Exit Iraq," *New York Times*, 5 September 2008, p. A27.

57. Anwar J. Ali and Katherine Zoepf, "Car Bombs, Then Sudden Blast, Kill 28 on a Baghdad Street," *New York Times*, 11 November 2008, p. A6.

58. Abeer Mohammed and Alissa J. Rubin, " To Make Female Hearts Flutter in Iraq, Throw a Shoe," *New York Times*, 14 March 2009, p. A8.

59. Anna Mulrine, "Afghan Warlords, Formerly Backed By the CIA, Now Turn Their Guns on U.S. Troops," *U.S. News and World Report*, 11 July 2008.

60. Nathan Hodge, "Pentagon May Send More Troops to Afghanistan," *Jane's Defense Weekly*, 23 July 2008, p. 14.

61. John L. Harper, "Anatomy of a Habit: America's Unnecessary Wars," *Survival, the International Institute of Strategic Studies Quarterly* 47, no. 2 (Summer 2005): p. 63.

62. Ibid., p. 64.

63. Ibid., p. 69.

64. Ibid., p. 78.

65. D. Jehl, "Intelligence Official Cites Wide Terror Threats," *New York Times*, 17 February 2005.

66. Karen De Young, "Pakistan Did Not Agree to New Rules, Officials Say," *Washington Post*, 12 September 2008, p. A10.

67. Eric Schmitt and Mark Mazzetti, "Bush Said to Give Orders Allowing Raids in Pakistan," *New York Times*, 11 September 2008, p. A8.

68. "Downward Spiral," *New York Times*, 15 October 2008, p. A34.

69. Ann Scott Tyson, "Top Military Officer Urges Major Change in Afghanistan Strategy," *Washington Post*, pp. A1 and A13.

70. "Downward Spiral," editorial, *New York Times*, 15 October 2008, p. A30.

71. Charles Bremer and Michael Evans, "British Envoy Says Mission in Afghanistan Is Doomed," *The Times* (London), 2 October 2008, leaked memo (author not identified).

72. "Afghan War Deaths," *Washington Post*, 13 February 2010, p. A12. Also see Philip M. Berkowitz, *New York Times*, 19 November 2007; and "Bush's Mideast Diplomacy: What If . . .," letter to the editor, 29 November 2007. Afghan war deaths approached 1,000 (942 as of January 2010), *Washington Post*, 10 January 2010.

73. Lizette Alvarez, "Army and Agency Will Study Rising Suicide Rate Among Soldiers," *New York Times*, 29 October 2008.

74. Mark Thompson, "Why Are Army Recruiters Killing Themselves?" *TIME*, 4 April 2009.

75. Mark Thompson, "The Dark Side of Recruiting," *TIME*, 13 April 2009, p. 34.

76. James Glanz, "Contractors Outnumber US Troops in Afghanistan," *New York Times*, 2 September 2009, p. A8.

77. F. G. Hoffman, "The Anatomy of the Long War's Failings," *Foreign Policy Research Institute Footnotes* 14, no. 16 (16 June 2009): p. 1 (newsletter of the Wachman Center).

78. Thomas L. Friedman, "Don't Build Up," *New York Times*, 28 October 2009, p. A29.

79. Nicholas D. Kristof, "1 Soldier or 20 Schools," *New York Times*, 29 July 2010, p. A23.

80. Robert M. Gates, speech to Naval War College, 17 April 2009, http://www.defense.gov/speeches/speech.aspx?speechid=1346.

CHAPTER 2

1. "Effects of Hurricane Katrina in New Orleans," Wikipedia, 23 August 2005, http://en.wikipedia.org/wiki/Effects_of_Hurricane_Katrina_in_New_Orleans.

2. Michael Isikoff and David Corn, *Hubris: The Inside Story of Spin, Scandal, and Selling of the Iraq War* (New York: Crown Publishers, 2006), pp. 21–26.

3. Softback cover comments on Thomas P. M. Barnett, *The Pentagon's New Map* (New York: Berkley Books, 2004).

4. Barnett, *The Pentagon's New Map*, p. 3.

5. International Institute of Strategic Studies, *The Military Balance: 2000–2001*, p. 16.

6. Barnett, *The Pentagon's New Map*, p. 4.

7. Ibid., p. 5. Barnett argues that countries of the "functioning core" constitute those which function within globalization that "[accept] the connectivity and can handle the content flows associated with integrating one's national economy to the global economy." *The Pentagon's New Map*, p. 125.

8. Ibid., p. 29.

9. James A. Baker III and Lee H. Hamilton, *The Iraq Study Group Report* (New York: Vintage Books, Random House, 2006).

10. Ibid, p. xiv.

11. Ibid. p. xvi.

12. Ibid. p. xvii.

13. Major General Robert H. Scales, USA (Retired), "Infantry and National Priorities," *Armed Forces Journal*, December 2007, p. 17.

14. Michael Kamber and James Glanz, "Iraqi Crackdown on Shiite Forces Sets Off Fighting," *New York Times*, 26 March 2008, pp. A1 and A11.

15. Thom Shanker and Nicholas Kulish, "U.S. Ties Europe's Safety to Afghanistan," *New York Times*, 11 February 2008, p. A6.

16. Charles Krauthammer, "A Rank Falsehood," *Washington Post*, 28 March 2008, p. A19.

17. Bob Herbert, "The $2 Trillion Nightmare," *New York Times*, 4 March 2008, p. A25.

18. Ibid.

19. Ibid.

20. Zachary A. Goldfarb, "The Talk," *Washington Post*, 31 March 2008, p. A3.

21. Ambassador Chas W. Freeman Jr. (USFS, Retired), "Why Not Try Diplomacy?" Remarks to the University Continuing Education Association, New Orleans, LA, 28 March 2008.

22. Robert D. Kaplan, "Equal Alliance, Unequal Roles," *New York Times*, 27 March 2008 (reprinted online).

23. Ibid.

24. Colonel Douglas MacGregor, "Washington's War," *Armed Forces Journal*, October 2007, p. 16.

25. Walter Bagehot, "The Forgotten War," *Economist*, 22 March 2008.

26. Ibid.

27. Benjamin H. Friedman, Harvey M. Sapolsky, and Christopher Preble, "Learning the Right Lessons from Iraq," *Cato Institute Policy Analysis* no. 610, 13 February 2008, Executive Summary.

28. Five Army and Marine Corps general officers were included in the "Revolt of the Generals": General Anthony Zinni (M.C.), Lieutenant General Gregory Newbold (M.C.), Major General John Riggs (USA), Major General Paul Eaton (USA), and Major General Charles J. Swannack (USA).

29. Patrick J. Buchanan, "The General's Revolt," April 15, 2006, antiwar.com.

30. Wolfowitz's appointment to the relatively low-profile International Security Advisory Board (ISAB) sparked questions because of his efforts to push for the invasion of Iraq. In late January 2008, shortly after news of Wolfowitz's ISAB position was announced, the Center for Public Integrity released a study detailing Iraq-related "false statements" made by top Bush administration officials, including Wolfowitz, in the two years after 9/11. By the center's count, Wolfowitz alone made eighty-five public statements reflecting "misinformation about the threat posed by Saddam Hussein's Iraq" (see http://projects.publicintegrity.org/WarCard). Bloomberg News reported, "Wolfowitz was among the senior U.S. officials who warned of Iraq's alleged weapons of mass destruction capabilities, a key justification for invading Iraq and toppling the late dictator Saddam Hussein."

31. DeKaren Young, "Paul Wolfowitz, World Bank Just Didn't Fit," *Washington Post*, 20 May 2007, p. A1.

32. Mark Mazzetti, "'03 U.S. Memo Approved Harsh Interrogations," *New York Times*, 2 April 2008, p. A1.

33. David C. Hendrickson and Robert W. Tucker, *Revisions in Need of Revising: What Went Wrong in the Iraq War* (Strategic Studies Institute, US Army War College, 2005), p. v.

34. Ibid., p. 24.

35. Kenneth T. Walsh, "Bush Vows to Stay the Course in Iraq," *U.S. News and World Report*, 14 April 2008, p. 16.

36. Nitya Venkataraman and Jonann Brady, "Exclusive: Cheney Cites 'Major Success' in Iraq, Says U.S. Has Hit 'Rough Patch,'" *ABC World News*, 19 March 2008.

37. Steven Simon, "The Price of the Surge," *Foreign Affairs*, May/June 2008, p. 59.

38. Ann Scott Tyson, "Military Waivers for Ex-Convicts Increase," *Washington Post*, 22 April 2008, pp. A1 and A16.

39. Zbigniew Brzezinski, "The Smart Way Out of a Foolish War," *Washington Post*, 30 March 2008, p. B3.

40. Institute for the Study of War, *Iraq Arabic News*, 17 March 2008, http://www.under standingwar.org/arabic-news/iraq-arabic-news-march-17-2008.

41. Brzezinski, "The Smart Way Out of a Foolish War."

42. "Admiral Fallon Resigns as Head of Centcom," Foxnews.com.home > Politics, 11 March 2008.

43. Linda Robinson, "A General's Assessment," *U.S. News and World Report*, January 28–February 4, 2008, p. 24.

44. Iraqi Bloggers Central, "A Look Back at Iraq and the Iraqi Blogosphere: 2008–09," 30 April 2009, http://jarrarsupariver.blogspot.com/2009/04/look-back-at-iraq-and-iraqi-blogo-sphere_30.html.

45. Robinson, "A General's Assessment."

46. Frank E. Smitha, "Timeline: 1991," *Macrohistory and World Report*, http://www.fsmitha.com/time/1991.html.

47. Con Coughlin, *Saddam King of Terror* (New York: ECCO: An Inprint of HarperCollins Publishers, 2002), p. 280.

48. Anthony H. Cordesman, "Iraq and the Crocker-Petraeus Testimony: The Risks That Only Time and a Sustained U.S. Presence Can Deal With," Center for Strategic and International Studies, Washington, DC, 7 April 2008.

49. Elisabeth Bumiller, "General Sees a Longer Stay in Iraq Cities for U.S. Troops," *New York Times*, 9 May 2009, p. A8.

50. Bobby Ghosh, "How to Make Terrorists Talk," *TIME*, 8 June 2009, p. 41.

CHAPTER 3

1. Cordula Meyer, "U.S. Army Lures Foreigners with Promise of Citizenship," *Spiegel Outline*, 19 October 2007.

2. David Katz, "The Army after Bush: Iraq Needs a National Guard," *Armed Forces Journal*, 2007.

3. *Wikipedia*, s.v. "foreign volunteers," p. 1, accessed 15 November 2008.

4. Julia Preston, "U.S. Military Will Offer Path to Citizenship," *New York Times*, 15 February 2009, p. A1.

5. Charles Knight, "Like a Mirage in the Desert," Project on Defense Alternatives, United States Institute on Peace, pp. 3, 4.

6. Task Force for a Responsible Withdrawal from Iraq, "The Necessary Steps for a Responsible Withdrawal from Iraq," June 2008, http://www.comw.org/pda/taskforceresponsible withdrawal.html.

7. Max Boot and Michael O'Hanlon, "A Military Path to Citizenship," *Washington Post*, 19 October 2006.

8. USA Greencard Lottery Service (USAGCLS), http://www.usagcls.com.

9. Boot and O'Hanlon, "A Military Path to Citizenship."

10. Ibid.

11. John M. Broder, "Climate Change Seen as Threat to U.S. Security," *New York Times*, 9 August 2009, p. 1A.

12. Fabius Maximus, "America Needs a Foreign Legion," http://fabiusmaximus.wordpress .com/2008/04/18/legions/.

13. Ibid.

14. Antonia Handler Chayes and George T. Raach, *Peace Operations: Developing an American Strategy* (Washington, DC: National Defense University Press, 1995).

15. "First Bull Run," July 1981 (pp. 3–7), and "Peninsular Campaign," June 1862 (pp. 27–30), *Civil War Atlas*, Department of Military Art and Engineering, US Military Academy, West Point, New York, 1950.

16. Anne Scott Tyson, "Army's Record Suicide Rate 'Horrible,' General Says," *Washington Post*, 18 November 2009, A2.

CHAPTER 4

1. Robert F. Evans, *Soldiers of Rome: Praetorians and Legionnaires* (Washington, DC: Seven Locks Press, 1986), p. 73.

2. Ibid., pp. 76–81.

3. Edward Gibbon, *Gibbon's Decline and Fall of the Roman Empire* (abridged and illustrated) (London: Bison Books, 1979), pp. 11–12.

4. Wikipedia, s.v. "60th Royal American Regiment of Foot, 1755–1760," http://en.wikipedia.org/wiki/60th_%28Royal_American%29_Regiment_of_Foot; *Encyclopaedia Britannica*, vol. 2, 1974, p. 194; and R. Ernest DuPuy and Trevor N. DuPuy, *The Encyclopedia of Military History from 3500 BC to the Present*, 2nd ed. (New York: Harper and Row, 1986), p. 707.

5. Wikipedia, s.v. "Mickiewicz's Legion," http://en.wikipedia.org/wiki/Mickiewicz%27s_Legion, accessed April 2008; and *Encyclopaedia Britannica*, vol. 4, pp. 862–63.

6. Wikipedia, s.v. "International Legion," http://en.wikipedia.org/wiki/International_Legion. The legion was composed of French, Polish, Swiss, German, and other units. Later the force was enhanced with Hungarian, British, and other elements.

7. Byron Farwell, *The Gurkhas* (New York: Norton, 1984), p. 15.

8. Charles Messenger, *The History of the British Army* (Novato, CA: Presidio Press, 1986), pp. 76, 96, 172, 198–201, 208, 209; Farwell, *Gurkhas*, pp. 276–88; Wikipedia, s.v. "Queen's Guard" section "Gurkhas, Royal Marines and the RAF Regiment."

9. Farwell, *Gurkhas*, pp. 284–92.

10. Ibid.

11. "Old Soldiers Fade Away," *Economist*, 1 August 2009.

12. Ibid.

13. Wikipedia, s.v. "Royal Netherlands East Indies Army," http://en.wikipedia.org/wiki/Royal_Dutch_East_Indies_Army.

14. Wikipedia, s.v. "Irish and German Mercenary Soldiers' Revolt," http://en.wikipedia.org/wiki/Irish_and_German_Mercenary_Soldiers%27_Revolt.

15. Ibid.

16. Wikipedia, s.v. "mercenary," p. 1, http://en.wikipedia.org/wiki/Mercenary.

17. Wikipedia, s.v. "Swiss Guard," http://en.wikipedia.org/wiki/Swiss_Guard.

18. Ibid.

19. Ibid.

20. Wikipedia, s.v. "Giuseppe Garibaldi," section "Campaign of 1860," p. 5; "International Legion," p. 1, and "Swiss Guard," p. 3; and *Encyclopaedia Britannica*, vol. 4, 1974, pp. 418–19.

21. Frank E. Roberts, *The American Foreign Legion: Black Soldiers of the 93rd in World War I* (Annapolis, MD: The Naval Institute Press, 2004), cover leaf.

22. *Encyclopaedia Britannica*, vol. 9, 1974, s.v. "History of Italy and Sicily," pp. 1160–61.

23. Chaim Herzog, *The Arab–Israeli Wars: War and Peace in the Middle East* (New York: Vintage Books, 1984), p. 112.

24. *Encyclopaedia Britannica*, 1974, s.v. "Glubb, Sir John Bagot," pp. 581–82.

25. Ibid.

26. Major General Gustav Svoboda, *Czechoslovakian War Graves Abroad*, Association of Czechoslovak Legionnaires, February 1996, pp. 7–19.

27. Ibid.

28. John H. Galey, "Bridegroom of Death; A Profile Study of the Spanish Foreign Legion," *Journal of Contemporary History* 4, no. 2 (April 1969): p. 58.

29. Wikipedia, s.v. "Abraham Lincoln Brigade," http://en.wikipedia.org/wiki/Abe_Lincoln_Brigade.

30. John Scurr, *Spanish Foreign Legion* (London: Osprey, 1985), p. 21.

31. Wikipedia, s.v. "Abraham Lincoln Brigade," http://en.wikipedia.org/wiki/Abe_Lincoln_Brigade; Hauptmann Hermann, *The Luftwaffe, Its Rise and Fall* (New York: G.P. Putnam's Sons, 1943), pp. 177–79; and William L. Langer, *An Encyclopedia of World History* (Boston: Houghton Mifflin, 1952), pp. 983–84.

32. Wikipedia, s.v. "Ernest Hemingway on Abe Lincoln Brigade," http://en.wikipedia.org/wiki/Ernest_Hemingway.

33. Simon Akam, "Spain's Thanks to an American Who Fought Franco: Citizenship," *New York Times*, 27 August 2009, p. 25.

34. Wikipedia, s.v. "Philippine Scouts," http://en.wikipedia.org/wiki/Philippine_Scouts.

35. Lieutenant General Julian Ewell and Major General Ira A. Hunt Jr., *Sharpening the Combat Edge: The Use of Analysis to Reinforce Military Judgement* (US Department of the Army, 1974), pp. 41–42.

36. Office of the United Nations High Commissioner for Human Rights, "Protocol Additional to the Geneva Conventions of 12 August 1949," http://www2.ohchr.org/english/law/protocol1.htm.

37. Wikipedia, s.v. "Blackwater Worldwide," http://en.wikipedia.org/wiki/Blackwater_Worldwide.

38. Triple Canopy Security Services website, http://www.triplecanopy.com.

39. James Risen and Mark Mazzetti, "30 False Fronts Won Contracts for Blackwater," *New York Times*, 4 September 2010, p. 1.

40. David Gray and Joseph Doty, "Contractors on the Battlefield and Our Professional Military Ethic," *ARMY* 59, no 7 (July 2009): 20–22

41. "Some US Troops Out of Iraq, More Mercenaries to Go In," http://www.commondreams.org/headline/2010/08/19.

CHAPTER 5

1. Rudyard Kipling, "Hymn #147," 22 June 1897, *The Hymnal of the Protestant Episcopal Church in USA, 1940*.

2. *Washington Post*, 12 October 2009, p. A7, and 21 January 2010, p. A26.

3. Jules Richard, *La Jeune Armee* (Paris: La Librarie Illustree, [1890]), p. 132. Cited in Douglas Porch, *The French Foreign Legion: A Complete History of the Legendary Fighting Force* (New York: HarperCollins, 1991), p. xxi.

4. Ibid., p. xxiii.

5. John Robert Young, *The French Foreign Legion: The Inside Story of the World-Famous Fighting Force* (London: Thames and Hudson, 1984), p. 72.

6. Howard R. Simpson, *The Paratroopers of the French Foreign Legion—From Vietnam to Bosnia* (Dulles, VA: Brassey's, 1997), p. 23.

7. Ibid.

8. Molly Moore, "Legendary Force Updates Its Image," *Washington Post*, 13 May 2007, p. 14.

9. Ibid.

10. Young, *French Foreign Legion*, p. 68.

11. Ibid.

12. "The French Foreign Legion Today," French Foreign Legion—Recruiting, http://www
.legion-recrute.com/en/?SM=0, 2011.

13. Simpson, *Paratroopers*, chapt. 6, pp. 79–92.

14. Ibid.

15. Young, *French Foreign Legion*, p. 144.

16. Ibid, p. 161.

17. "Be Part of the News That Makes the Headlines," French Foreign Legion—Recruiting, http://www.legion-recrute.com/en/, 2011.

18. Evan McGorman, *Life in the French Foreign Legion* (Ashland, OR: Hellgate Press, 2000), p. 34.

19. Lieutenant Colonel Philippe Chabot, French Liaison Officer, US Army Infantry Center, Fort Benning, Georgia.

CHAPTER 6

1. Bennett Ramberg, "The Precedents for Withdrawal: From Vietnam to Iraq," *Foreign Affairs*, March/April 2009, p. 3.

2. Ibid., p. 4. Also Helene Cooper, "Obama Says a Way Out of Afghanistan Is Needed," *New York Times*, 23 March 2009, p. A11.

3. Ramberg, "Precedents," p. 5.

4. Ibid.

5. Mark Bowden, *Black Hawk Down: A Story of Modern War* (New York: Atlantic Monthly Press, 1999), pp. 7–8.

6. Ramberg, "Precedents," p. 8.

7. Anthony Shadid, "Departing U.S. Envoy in Iraq Sees Risks Ahead," *Washington Post*, p. A10.

8. Anthony H. Cordesman, "The Afghan-Pakistan War: The Rising Threat; 2002–2008," *Center for Strategic and International Studies*, 11 February 2009, http://csis.org/files/media/csis/pubs/090211_afghanthreat.pdf, accessed June 2010.

9. Richard A. Oppel Jr., "Stolen Oil Profits Keep Iraq's Insurgency Running," *New York Times*, 16 March 2008, p. 1.

10. Two unidentified Washington analysts pointing out "troublesome factors, including hijacked shipments by bribed drivers and divided Muslim leadership." The analysts were not identified, but similar reports by Michael E. O'Hanlon and Kenneth M. Pollack reflected much the same information in the *New York Times* on 27 February 2009. See online opinion, "Preparing for Withdrawal: Iraq's Year of Living Dangerously."

11. Henry A. Kissinger, "A Strategy for Afghanistan," *Washington Post*, 26 February 2009, p. A49.

12. William Dalrymple, "Pakistan in Peril," *New York Review*, 12 February 2009, pp. 39–42.

13. Ibid., p. 40.

14. Richard A. Oppel Jr., "Taliban Hit Pakistan Town That Fought Back," *New York Times*, 29 December 2008, p. A6.

15. Dexter Filkins, "Across a Table, U.S. Faces a Test in Recruiting an Afghan Militia," *New York Times*, 15 April 2009.

16. Thomas P. M. Barnett, *The Pentagon's New Map* (New York: Berkley Books, 2004), p. 3.

17. Ibid.

18. Helene Cooper and Sheryl Gay Stolberg, "Obama Ponders Outreach to Elements of the Taliban," *New York Times*, 8 March 2009, p. A1; and Sandra Mackey, *The Iranians, Persia, Islam and the Soul of a Nation* (New York: PLUME Books, 1998), opinion no. 1.

19. Reuben Brigety, the Center for American Progress, quoted by Helene Cooper, "Talk with the Taliban, It May Be Necessary," *New York Times*, 8 March 2009, accessed 5 April 2011, http://www.nytimes.com/2009/03/08/world/americas/08iht-assess.4.20685898.html.

20. Mackey, *Iranians*.

21. Wikipedia, s.v. "Iranian American," pp. 1–4; and Truthout—Special Investigation, 30 November 2009, p. 1.

22. Roxana Tiron, "US Spending $3.6 Billion a Month in Afghanistan," The Hill's Blog Briefing Room, 14 October 2009, accessed 5 April 2011, http://thehill.com/blogs/blog-brief ing-room/news/63121-crs-calculates-cost-of-us-troop-presence-in-afghanistan.

23. Cooper, "Obama Says a Way Out of Afghanistan Is Needed."

24. Anthony H. Cordesman, "How to Lose in Afghanistan," *Washington Post*, 31 August 2009, http://www.washingtonpost.com/wp-dyn/content/article/2009/08/30/AR2009083002252 .html, accessed August 2009.

CHAPTER 7

1. Thomas P. M. Barnett, *The Pentagon's New Map: War and Peace in the Twenty-first Century* (New York: Berkley Books, 2004), p. 149.

2. Ibid, p. 150.

3. Ibid, p. 155.

4. FARC (Spanish: *Fuerzas Armadas Revolucionarias de Colombia*), or the Revolutionary Armed Forces of Colombia, is a self-proclaimed Marxist-Leninist revolutionary guerrilla organization.

5. "Slush and Garbage," *Economist*, 5 January 2008, p. 32.

6. Barnett, *Pentagon's New Map*, p. 305.

7. Simon Romero, "More Killings in Venezuela Than in Iraq," *New York Times*, 23 August 2010, p. A1.

8. The national kidnapping rate is 2 in 100,000.

9. Simon Romero, "A State in Grip of Kidnappers and the Family of Hugo Chavez," *New York Times*, 21 July 2009, p. A4.

10. "Venezuelan Leader Praises Putin's Tough U.S. Policy," *New York Times*, 10 September 2009, p. A13.

11. "Report Details Violence and Lost Freedoms in Venezuela," *Washington Post*, 1 March 2010.

12. "Crime in Venezuela—Shooting Gallery," *Economist*, 21 August 2010, p. 30.

13. Global Voices Online, "Border Crisis in South America 2008," p. 1, http://global voicesonline.org/specialcoverage/2008-special-coverage/border-crisis-in-south-america-2008/.

14. "Uribe Edges toward Autocracy," *Economist*, 16 May 2009, p. 43.

15. Jacqueline K Mueckenheim, ed., *Countries of the World and Their Leaders Yearbook 2008*, vol. 1 (Detroit, MI: Thomson Gale, 2007), p. 439.

16. Simon Romero, "Plan to Increase U.S. Presence in Colombia Worries Neighbors," *New York Times*, 23 July 2009, p. A14.

17. *Countries of the World and Their Leaders Yearbook 2008*, vol. 2, p. 607.

18. "From the Guerrilla's Mouth," *Economist*, 25 July 2009, pp. 35–36.

19. Simon Romero, "Inquiry on Bribe Accusations," *New York Times*, 3 September 2009, accessed 4 April 2011, http://query.nytimes.com/gst/fullpage.html?res=980DE7D8153FF930 A3575AC0A96F9C8B63.

20. Wikipedia, s.v. "Internal Conflict in Peru," pp. 1–3.

21. Wikipedia, s.v. "United States Invasion of Panama," pp. 1–2.

22. Ibid.

23. Wikipedia, s.v. "The Panama Deception," p. 1.

24. Mary Anastasia O'Grady, "Honduras Defends Its Democracy," *Wall Street Journal*, June 29, 2009, p. A11.

25. "Lousy President, Terrible Precedent," *Economist*, 4 July 2009, p. 10.

26. The Inter-American Defense College at Ft. McNair, Washington, DC, offers an eleven-month course on military and defense affairs to senior officers of all countries holding full membership in the Organization of American States (i.e., all except Cuba).

27. Ginger Thompson and Marc Lacey, "Both Sides in Honduras Reach Out to the U.S.," *New York Times*, 7 July 2009, p. A4.

28. Marc Lacey, "Honduras Is Rattled as Leader Tries to Return," *New York Times*, 6 July 2009, p. A4; and Ginger Thompson, "Ouster Honduran Leader Seeks Tougher U.S. Stance against Coup," *New York Times*, p. A12.

29. "The Best Hope for Honduras Is to Let Zelaya Return," editorial, *Washington Post*, 9 July 2009, p. A18.

CHAPTER 8

1. Associated Press, "Cuba Suspends Communist Party Congress and Lowers Projection for Economy," *New York Times*, 1 August 2009, p. A7.

2. Associated Press, "Cuba: U.S. Officials Visit to Discuss Mail Service," *New York Times*, 18 September 2009, p. A11.

3. Neil MacFarquhar, "U.S. Embargo on Cuba Again Finds Scant Support at U.N.," *New York Times*, 29 October 2009, p. A8.

4. Marc Lacey, "Cuban Government Vows to Release 52 Prisoners," *New York Times*, 8 July 2010, p. A12; Wikipedia, s.v. "Guillermo Fariñas," http://en.wikipedia.org/wiki/Guillermo_Fariñas.

5. Howard Scheider, "Congress Puts Havana on the Horizon," *Washington Post*, 7 July 2010, p. A9.

CHAPTER 9

1. John Reader, *Africa, A Biography of the Continent* (New York: Vintage Books, 1997), p. 377.

2. Martin Meredith, *The Face of Africa: From the Hopes of Freedom to the Heart of Despair* (New York: Public Affairs, 2005), p. 1.

3. Ibid., pp. 1 and 2.

4. Neil MacFarquhar, "Congo: Short Extension for U.N. Force," *New York Times*, 24 December 2009, p. A8.

5. Meredith, *Face of Africa*, pp. 3 and 4.

6. Wikipedia, s.v. "Republic of Djibouti," 19 July 2009, p. 2.

7. The MPLA succeeded in achieving power, and in 2008 would be reelected by a landslide. The *Economist* reported that the party achieved more than 80 percent of the vote (13 September 2008, p. 56).

8. Peter Kornbluh, ed., *Conflicting Missions: Secret Cuban Documents on the History of Africa Involvement*, National Security Archive online, 1 April 2002, http://www.gwu.edu/~nsarchiv/NSAEBB/NSAEBB67/.

9. Wikipedia, s.v. "Liberia," 16 May 2009.

10. Gregory Copley, "Somaliland and the Kosovo Syndrome," Defense Foreign Affairs and Strategic Policy, 1 August 2009, p. 14.

11. Wikipedia, s.v. "Battle of Mogadishu (1993)."

12. Ibid. p. 5.

13. "Goma and Kigali, Jungle Alliance That May Just Endure," *Economist*, 7–13 March 2009, p. 56.

14. Wikipedia, s.v., "Polisario Front." Also "Report of the Secretary-General on the Situation concerning Western Sahara (2007-04-13)," United Nations Security Council, 19 October 2007, http://daccess-dds-ny.un.org/doc/UNDOC/GEN/N07/547/23/PDF/N0754723 .pdf?OpenElement. See also "Polisario Front: Credible Negotiations Partner or After-Effect of the Cold War Obstacle to a Political Solution in Western Sahara?" European Strategic Intelligence and Security Center, November 2005, website: Moroccan American Center for Policy, http://www.moroccanamericanpolicy.org/upload/documents/12_20061221083157.pdf.

15. Mohamed Ibrahim, "Fighting Islamists, Pleas for Aid," *New York Times*, 21 June 2009, p. A10.

16. Mary Beth Sheridan, "Leader Says Somalia's Plight Is Urgent," *Washington Post*, 3 October 2009, p. A3.

17. Nicholas D. Kristof, "The Grotesque Vocabulary in Congo," *New York Times*, 11 February 2010, p. A33.

18. "President Fires Head of Troubled Police," *Washington Post*, 9 September 2009, p. A8.

19. Jeffrey Gettleman, "Kenya's Bill for Bloodshed Nears Payment," *New York Times*, 16 July 2009, p. A13.

20. Jeffrey Gettleman, "UN Told Not to Join Congo in Operation," *New York Times*, 10 December 2009, p. A6.

21. Sarah Raine, *China's African Challenges* (New York: Routledge for the International Institute of Strategic Studies, 2009), p. 184.

22. Stephanie McCrummen, "In Kenya, Ethnic Distrust Is as Deep as the Machete Scars," *Washington Post*, 22 December 2009, p. A10.

23. Ahmedou Ould-Abdallah, "The International Community Faces a Test in Somalia," *Washington Post*, 20 June 2009.

24. Mohamed Ibrahim and Jeffrey Gettleman, "Several Dead in Somali Clashes, Possibly Including U.S. Jihadist," *New York Times*, 6 September 2009, p. 12.

25. Jeffrey Gettleman and Mohamed Ibrahim, "Somali Pirates Move Couple onto Land," *New York Times*, 1 November 2009, p. 14.

26. Jeffrey Gettleman, "Report Cites Vast Civilian Killings in East Congo," *New York Times*, 13 December 2009, p. A12.

27. Stephanie McCrummen, "Human Rights Watch Urges U.N. to Cease Aid to Congo Regime Accused of Brutal Acts," *Washington Post*, 15 December 2009.

28. Celia W. Dugger and Caiphete, "Rift in Zimbabwe's Government Widens," *New York Times*, 17 October 2009, p. A4, and "Tsvangiari Boycotts Governing Coalition," *Washington Post*, 17 October 2009, p. A6. See also Sebastian Berger, "Robert Mugabe's Regime Collapsing," *Daily Telegraph*, 15 January 2009, http://www.telegraph.co.uk/news/worldnews/africaandindian ocean/zimbabwe/4247103/Robert-Mugabes-regime-collapsing.html.

29. "Ranking Africa's Governments," *TIME*, 19 October 2009, p. 13.

30. "The World's 10 Worst Dictators," *Washington Post Parade*, 22 March 2009, p. 4.

31. "UN Chief Outlines Steps to Turn 'Responsibility to Protect' into Practice," UN News Service, 21 July 2009, http://www.un.org/apps/news/story.asp?NewsID=31533&Cr=protection +of+civilians&rl.

32. East African Community (EAC) portal, http://www.eac.int/about-eac.html.

33. Jeffrey Gettleman, "Fleeing Rebels Kill Hundreds of Congolese," *New York Times*, 28 March 2010, p. 1.

34. General William B. Garrett, "U.S. Army Africa—A Team Like No Other," U.S. Army Africa website, http://www.usaraf.army.mil/documents_pdf/READING_ROOM/US-ARMY -AFRICA-A-TEAM-LIKE-NO-OTHER-AUSA.pdf.

35. Great Lakes District: Eastern Congo, Uganda, Rwanda, Tanzania, Burundi, Kenya, and Zambia, *The Odyssey World Atlas*, Universal Edition (New York: Golden Press, 1966), p. 164.

36. "DR Congo: UN Mission Calls on Illegal Fighters to Lay Down Their Arms," UN News Center, 4 December 2007, http://www.un.org/apps/news/story.asp?NewsID=24905&Cr= democratic&Cr1=congo.

37. "UN Extends Mandate for Congo Peacekeeping Force," Reuters, 23 December 2009.

38. Wikipedia, s.v. "Technical (vehicle)."

39. "Qatar, Arab League Reject ICC Cooperation Request on Bashir Arrest: Report—Sudan Tribune: Plural News and Views on Sudan," *Sudan Tribune,* http://www.sudantribune.com/ spip.php?article30536, accessed 24 March 2010. As referenced by Wikipedia, s.v. "War in Darfur 2003–2009."

40. Samantha Power, "Bystanders to Genocide," *The Atlantic,* 2 October 2010.

41. "Piracy in the Gulf of Guinea: A Clear and Present Danger," *Economist,* 18 April 2009, p. 52. See also Clark Canfield, "Attacks by Pirates Spur New Training for Seamen," *Washington Post,* 8 February 2009, p. A7.

42. "Middle East and Africa," *Economist,* 18 April 2009, p. 51.

43. Associated Press, "Coup Leader Wins Election amid Outcry in Mauritania," *New York Times,* 19 July 2009, p. A6.

44. Eric Schmitt and Souad Mekhennet, "Qaeda Branch Steps Up Raids in North Africa," *New York Times,* 10 July 2009, pp. A1 and A10.

45. Adam Nossiter, "Guinea's Capital Fades into a Ghost Town after Soldiers' Rampage," *New York Times,* 30 September 2009, p. A5.

46. Will Conners, "Guinea's Ruler Flown to Doctors In Morocco," *Wall Street Journal,* 3 December 2009, p. A17.

47. Ian Urbina, "Taint of Corruption Is No Barrier to US Visa," *New York Times,* 17 November 2009, p. A1.

48. Wikipedia, s.v. "Nigeria." See also Owobi Angrew, "Tiptoeing through a Constitutional Minefield: The Great Sharia Controversy in Nigeria," *Journal of African Law* 48, no 2 (2002).

49. "Niger Oil 'Total War' Warning," *BBC News,* 17 February 2006.

50. "Boko Haram," *Language Log* (online), 29 July 2009; Joe Boyle, "Nigeria's 'Taliban' Enigma," *BBC News,* 30 July 2009.

51. Jeffrey Gettleman, "Two Sides of Nigeria Addressed by Clinton," *New York Times,* 12 August 2009, p. A8.

52. Wikipedia, s.v. "List of Countries by Infant Mortality Rate," updated 18 December 2010. (Nigeria no longer is the worst as of this writing.)

53. Rachel Donadio, "Repent or Resign, Bishops Tell African Politicians," *New York Times,* 24 October 2009, p. A4.

54. Interview with Chinua Achebe by Deborah Solomon, "Out of Africa," *New York Times,* 26 March 2010, p. MM12.

55. Robyn Dixon, "African Catholics Seek a Voice to Match Their Growing Strength," *LA Times,* 16 April 2005, http://www.latimes.com/news/printedition/la-fg-africa16apr16,0,6335364 .story?page=2.

56. "Ghana US Naval Partnering—Hosting US Sea Base?" Crossed Crocodiles website, 28 March 2010, http://crossedcrocodiles.wordpress.com/2010/03/28/ghana-us-naval-partnering -hosting-a-us-sea-base/.

57. Wikipedia and *CIA World Fact Book,* s.v. "Equatorial Guinea," 29 September 2010.

58. "Somalia's Dangerous Waters," *BBC News,* 26 September 2005, http://news.bbc .co.uk/2/hi/africa/4283396.stm.

59. "Getting Desperate, Will the Government's Latest Effort to Quash the Militants Lead to More Oil Flow?" *Economist,* 28 May 2009, http://www.economist.com/node/13745871?story_ id=13745871. Wikipedia and *CIA World Fact Book,* s.v. "Equatorial Guinea," 29 September 2010. See also Equatorial Guinea Travel Guide / Risks on the Direct Travel website, http:// www.direct-travel.co.uk/equatorial-guinea/risks.aspx.

CHAPTER 10

1. "The Slippery Slope in Bosnia," Opinion, *New York Times*, 1 June 1995.

2. Wesley K. Clark, *Waging Modern War* (New York: Public Affairs, 2001), p. 434.

3. *The New Encyclopaedia Britannica*, vol. 19 (William Berton, 1943–1973), Macropaedia, p. 1099.

4. Edward B. Atkeson, "Who Will Sweep the Augean Stables?" *ARMY*, May 1993.

5. Clark, *Waging Modern War*, p. 245–46.

6. Craig Whitlock, "Serbian Officials Say Mladic Is 'Within Reach,'" *Washington Post*, 30 July 2009, p. A10; Marlise Simons, "Videos on Bosnian TV Show War Crime Suspect in Serbia," *New York Times*, 11 June 2009.

7. For example, Agim Çeku, chief of staff of the Kosovo Liberation Army, arrested for war crimes, 22 June 1999, released; detained by Hungarian police, 29 February 2004, released; arrested in Bulgaria, 9 June 2009, released. Wikipedia, s.v. "Agim Çeku," http://en.wikipedia.org/wiki/Agim_Çeku.

CHAPTER 11

1. Lee Smith, *The Strong Horse: Power, Politics and the Clash of Arab Civilizations* (New York: Doubleday, 2009), p. 2.

2. Herman Kinder and Werner Higemann, *The Anchor Atlas of World History from the Stone Age to the Eve of the French Revolution*, vol. 1 (Garden City, NY: Anchor Books/Doubleday, 1974), pp. 15–17.

3. Smith, *Strong Horse*, p. 5.

4. Ibid.

5. R. Earnest and Trevor N. Dupuy, *The Encyclopedia of Military History from 3500 BC to the Present*, 2nd rev. ed. (New York: Harper and Row Publishers, 1986), p. 805.

6. T. Christian Miller, Mark Hosenball, and Ron Moreau, "The Gang That Couldn't Shoot Straight," *Newsweek*, 29 March 2010, pp. 26–31.

7. Smith, *Strong Horse*, 100.

8. Miller, Hosenball, and Moreau, "The Gang That Couldn't Shoot Straight."

9. Wendell Steavenson, "The Enemy Within," *New York Times Sunday Book Review*, 21 February 2010, p. 22.

10. Miller, Hosenball, and Moreau, "The Gang That Couldn't Shoot Straight."

11. Henry Allen, "Death of the American Century," *Washington Post*, 20 April 2010, p. A15.

12. Smith, *Strong Horse*, pp. 99–100.

13. Shlomo Gazil, Zeev Eytan, and Shlomo Gazit, *The Middle East Military Balance, 1992–1993*, 9th ed. (Boulder, CO: Westview Press, 1994), pp. 222–28.

14. Gazil et al., *Military Balance, 1992–1993*, p. 104.

CHAPTER 12

1. Known as "the country where good things happen to bad people," *Economist*, 7 August 2010, p. 42.

2. *Encyclopaedia Britannica, Ready Reference and Index*, s.v. "Burma, History of," vol. 2, 1947, p. 386.

3. Myint-U Thant, "Let's Talk to Burma, China Sure Is," 16 August 2009, *Washington Post*, Outlook, p. B3.

4. Ibid., p. 13.

5. Wikipedia, s.v. "Burma," http://en.wikipedia.org/wiki/Burma.

6. Ibid.

7. Andrew Chang, "Should Burma Be Part of the Axis of Evil?" *ABC News*, 22 October 2010, http://abcnews.go.com/International/story?id=79822&page=1. See also Mark Lander and David E. Sanger, "Clinton Speaks of Mideast from Iran," 22 July 2009. She expressed suspicion that North Korea might be transferring nuclear technology to Myanmar (*New York Times* and *International Herald Tribune*).

8. James T. Hackett and International Institute of Strategic Studies, *The Military Balance, 2008* (Oxfordshire: Routledge, 2008), p. 396.

9. Online posting by Funz, senior member, captain, "A Military Action in Burma," posted on Military Strategic and Tactics Defense Talks Online, http://www.defencetalk.com/forums/military-strategy-tactics/military-action-burma-6875/; Alex Chadwick, "U.S. Ships Stand By to Offer Myanmar Aid," *National Public Radio*, 24 September 2009, p. 1; "US Navy Ships Leave Burma, Still Carrying Aid," ABC News (Australian Broadcasting Corp.).

10. Chris Beyrer and Richard Sollom, "Burma's Rising Toll," *Washington Post*, 3 March 2009, http://www.washingtonpost.com/wp-dyn/content/article/2009/09/02/AR2009090203023 .html.

11. Wikipedia, "Daw Aung San Suu Kyi."

12. Jay Solomon and James Hookway, "Clinton's Defense Umbrella Stirs Tensions," *Wall Street Journal*, 23 July 2009, p. A7.

13. "Beijing Plans to Proceed with Pipeline through Myanmar," *Top News*, Beijing, 21 November 2008, http://topnews.us/content/2157-china-build-pipeline-through-myanmar. See also Poon Kim Shee, "The Political Economy of China-Myanmar Relations: Strategic and Economic Dimensions," *Ritsumeikan Annual Review of International Studies*, Vol. 1 (2002), 33–53; and Morentalisa Hutapea, "Myanmar-China Brotherhood: Securing the Energy for China," Institute for Essential Services Reform, 28 June 2010, http://en.iesr-indonesia.org/2010/06/myanmar-china-brotherhood-securing-the-energy-for-china/.

14. "Myanmar Fighters Cross into China," *Al Jazeera English*, 30 July 2009, http://english .aljazeera.net/news/asia-pacific/2009/08/20098306161918344.html.

15. Thomas Fuller, "U.S. Diplomat Meets Myanmar's Top Dissident and Urges Junta to Work With Her," *New York Times*, 5 November 2009, p. A6.

16. Saw Yan Naing, "Constitutional Crisis over the Border Guard Force," *Irrawaddy*, 16 June 2009, www.irrawaddy.org/article.php?art_id=16342.

17. Fuller, "U.S. Diplomat Meets Myanmar's Top Dissident," p. A5.

18. "The Battle for Thailand," *Foreign Affairs*, July/August 2009.

19. Amnesty International Public Statement (ASA 26/004/2009, 7 December 2009), "Laos: Peaceful Protesters Must Be Released Immediately."

20. John Pomfret, "Thailand Appears Set to Ignore U.S., Send Hmong Back to Laos," *Washington Post*, 25 December 2009, p. A15. See also "Laotian Hmong Refugees in Thailand— Shown the Door," *Economist*, 2 January 2010, p. 32.

21. Tim Johnston, "Thailand Begins Deportation of Hmong," *Washington Post*, 29 December 2009, p. A9.

22. Seth Mydans, "Thai Official Broaches Taboo Topic: The Role of the Monarchy," *New York Times*, 15 April 2010, p. A10.

23. Seth Mydans, "Ousted Leader Emits Heat as He's Orbiting Thailand," *New York Times*, 21 April 2010, p. A10; and Andrew Higgins, "Out of Poverty, But in Dissent," *Washington Post*, 9 June 2010, p. A10.

24. Andrew Burke and Justine Vaisutis, *Lonely Planet: Laos* (London: Lonely Planet, 2007), p. 27.

25. Ibid.

26. Ibid, p. 44.

27. Thomas Fuller, "In Hard-to-Define Laos, Communism and Capitalism Are Now Mixing," *New York Times*, 19 September 2009, p. A4.

28. Wikipedia, s.v. "Cambodia," http://en.wikipedia.org/wiki/Cambodia.

29. Edward B. Atkeson, "Vietnam Examination Is Not a Closed Book," *ARMY*, August 1995, pp. 11–16.

30. "A Special Report on Indonesia," *Economist*, 12 September 2009, p. 3. All historical notes are taken from *The Rough Guide to Indonesia*, researched and written by Stephen Backshall, David Leffman, Lesley Reader, and Henry Stedman, April 2003.

31. "U.S. Steering Away from Indonesia's 'Theological Struggles,'" *Washington Post*, 25 October 2009, p. 15A; and *Pocket World in Figures*, 2010 ed. (London: Economists, 2010), p. 16.

32. "Indonesia's Army Going Out of Business," *Economist*, 4 October 2008, p. 42.

33. Ibid.

34. Ibid.

35. "Banyan, The Books of Slaughter and Forgetting," *Economist*, 23 January 2010, p. 43.

36. "A Special Report on Indonesia," *Economist*, 12 September 2009, p. 3.

37. CIA Factbook, reported in the *Washington Post*, July 2000 census.

38. Thomas Fuller, "Southern Thailand's Turmoil Grows as Security Forces Try to Quell an Insurgency," *New York Times*, 5 September 2000, p. A4.

39. Teresa Cerojano, "Witness Links Clan to Philippine Massacre," Associated Press Manila News, 27 January 2010.

40. Carlos H. Conde, "Court Is Told Mayor Aided in Massacre of Filipinos," *New York Times*, 14 January 2010, p. A4.

41. Carlos H. Conde, "2nd Philippine Broadcaster Killed," *New York Times*, 17 June 2010, p. A8.

42. "Private Armies in the Philippines: Guns and Goons," *Economist*, 9 January 2010, p. 45.

43. Trefor Moss, "Philippine Troops Fight Abu Sayyaf Group on Basilan," *Jane's Defense Weekly*, 19 August 2009, p. 14.

44. Reuters, "The Philippines: Captive Is Beheaded," *New York Times*, 10 November 2009, p. A13.

45. Norimitsu Onishi, "Filipino Political Scion, Set to Assume the Mantle," *New York Times*, 26 March 2010.

CHAPTER 13

1. Thom Shanker, "U.S. Weighs Options, by Air and Sea," *New York Times*, 7 March 2011, p. A8.

2. Ibid.

3. "Text of Colonel Reese's Memo," *New York Times*, 30 July 2009.

4. Thom Shanker, "Gates Warns against Wars Like Iraq," *New York Times*, 26 February 2011, p. A7.

Index

About the Author

During his thirty-three years of active military service, Major General **Edward B. Atkeson**, a veteran of the Vietnam War, was appointed deputy chief of staff intelligence, US Army Europe, and, subsequently, national intelligence officer under the director of central intelligence. He also served with the Bureau of Political-Military Affairs, Department of State. General Atkeson holds a BS degree from the US Military Academy, an MBA from Syracuse University, and a PhD from the University of Luton, England. He is a graduate of the US Army Command and General Staff College and has been designated a "distinguished graduate" of the US Army War College at Carlisle Barracks, Pennsylvania. He is also a graduate of the Advanced Management Program, Harvard Business School, and was a fellow at the Center for International Affairs, Harvard University, from 1973 to 1974. He is a recipient of the Distinguished Service Medals of both the US Army and the CIA.

General Atkeson is a frequent writer and speaker on military affairs, having contributed more than one hundred articles to military journals and other publications. He is the author of four other books: *A Military Assessment of the Middle East 1991–1996* (1992); *The Powder Keg: An Intelligence Officer's Guide to Military Forces in the Middle East 1996–2000* (1996); a historical novel of the Vietnam conflict, *A Tale of Three Wars* (1997); and *The Final Argument of Kings: Reflections on the Art of War* (1998).